THE ULTIMATE ADVANTAGE

THE ULTIMATE ADVANTAGE

Creating the
High-
Involvement
Organization

EDWARD E. LAWLER III

Jossey-Bass Publishers · San Francisco

For sales outside the United States contact Maxwell Macmillan International Publishing Group, 866 Third Avenue, New York, New York 10022

Printed on acid-free paper and manufactured in the United States of America

The paper used in this book meets the State of California requirements for recycled paper (50 percent recycled waste, including 10 percent post-consumer waste), which are the strictest guidelines for recycled paper currently in use in the United States.

Library of Congress Cataloging-in-Publication Data

Lawler, Edward E.
   The ultimate advantage : creating the high-involvement organization / by Edward E. Lawler III. — 1st ed.
     p. cm. — (A Joint publication in the Jossey-Bass management series and the Jossey-Bass social and behavioral science series)
   Includes bibliographical references and index.
   ISBN 1-55542-414-7 (acid-free paper)
   1. Management—Employee participation. 2. Quality of work life. 3. Organizational effectiveness. I. Title. II. Series: Jossey-Bass management series. III. Series: Jossey-Bass social and behavioral science series.
HD5650.L354 1992
658.3'152—dc20   91-41095
                                         CIP

FIRST EDITION
HB Printing   10 9 8 7 6 5 4   *Code 9221*

A joint publication in

The Jossey-Bass Management Series

and

The Jossey-Bass Social
and Behavioral Science Series

Contents

Preface

Effective organizations are critical to the well-being of any organized society. Those societies that create the most effective organizations can provide their citizens with the highest standard of living. Thus, it is central to the vitality of a society that its organizations constantly look for better ways to organize and manage work.

Unfortunately, there is no simple answer to the question of what constitutes the best way to organize and manage work. The solution differs according to the particular products and services that an organization wishes to offer and depends on the kind of society in which the organization operates. Nevertheless, a substantial body of evidence shows that many organizations can obtain a competitive advantage through adopting a management style that involves employees in the business of their organization.

In 1986, I published a book, *High-Involvement Management*, which reviewed the research evidence on a number of specific employee involvement practices. I looked in some detail at quality circles, gainsharing plans, job enrichment, self-managed work teams, and a host of other practices. Overwhelmingly, the evidence that I reviewed supported the idea of giving individuals at the lowest levels in organizations more information, knowledge, power, and rewards.

Since 1986, many companies have launched large-scale

efforts to move toward an involvement-oriented approach to management. The reasons for this change are many, but they can perhaps best be highlighted with the term *competitive advantage*. Organizations are increasingly realizing that if they are going to compete in today's global economy, they need to use the latest and best approaches to organizing and managing. Therefore, many organizations have changed their management practices and committed extensive resources to programs of total quality management and employee involvement.

Because of these changes, much more is known today about how to design and manage high-involvement organizations than was known in 1986, when I published my book on employee involvement. At that point, it was difficult to talk about a total organizational approach to employee involvement. Few large organizations had systematically tried to restructure themselves around employee involvement, and the role of many of the total quality management techniques was still evolving. Today, knowledge about employee involvement is still developing, and a great deal more needs to be learned; but it is possible to describe with considerable specificity what an organization should do to create a high-involvement approach to management.

Even though we are still learning how to implement the high-involvement approach and how to make it operate effectively, the results of the approach are sufficiently encouraging to convince me of its worth. I believe that, for many organizations, the high-involvement approach to organizing and managing work can provide a competitive advantage beyond that which is available through total quality management or any other well-articulated approach. Total quality programs represent a step toward involvement but do not generally lead to a sufficiently radical restructuring of the entire organization to produce all the competitive advantages that result when employees have more information, knowledge, power, and rewards.

Indeed, it may well be that employee involvement is the ultimate competitive advantage for organizations in the United States and Europe. Without a doubt, Japanese companies have achieved an excellent fit between their management approaches and the Japanese culture. One approach to improving performance in other parts of the world is simply to emulate and copy what the Japanese have done. But it is hard to get better at an approach to management than the originator is. Furthermore, what is done in Japan may work there because it fits the culture and society particularly well.

I firmly believe that we need an alternative to the total quality management approach that builds on many of its key elements but goes beyond it to provide a competitive advantage for organizations in societies that are characterized by diversity, democracy, entrepreneurial behavior, and respect for the individual. High-involvement management, with its emphasis on few levels in the hierarchy, seamless organizations, quick adaptation and change, lateral work relationships, and the responsibility of organizations to create meaningful and satisfying work, is just such an approach. It is particularly suited to market-oriented economies, in which the market, rather than cumbersome and expensive traditional bureaucracies, is the controlling factor.

Overview of the Contents

In *The Ultimate Advantage: Creating the High-Involvement Organization*, I systematically review the major structural features that organizations need to put in place to achieve high employee involvement and gain the competitive advantages that the approach offers. The book begins with a review of the competitive environment that organizations face today. Chapter One stresses that today's organizations need to perform in ways that were never necessary when the traditional bureaucratic approach to management was conceived and developed. Therefore, the traditional approach often falls short of achieving the performance levels that are necessary in today's competitive environment. In particular, traditional management has trouble producing both the kind of continuous improvement that is required for an organization to remain competitive and the high-quality, low cost, quick responses to technology and customers that are increasingly important.

Chapter Two discusses the situations in which employee involvement works well. Clearly, it is not necessarily the right management approach for all environments and all societies. Indeed, it is a competitive advantage that is available only to certain organizations and societies.

Chapter Three discusses the organizational structures that are needed for employee involvement to work. This discussion leads directly to a consideration of work design in Chapters Four and Five. Choosing the correct work design is fundamental to any approach to employee involvement. A high-involvement organization must emphasize job enrichment or self-managing teams that give individuals considerable autonomy to control and manage their own work—or both. Work design is essential to fostering employee self-management and to eliminating the expensive external control process and the layers of bureaucracy that prevail in traditionally managed organizations.

Chapter Six reviews the use of problem-solving groups and organizational improvement groups. Such groups can be a particularly useful transition strategy as organizations move toward greater involvement, but their role needs to diminish in mature high-involvement organizations.

Chapters Seven and Eight focus on the reward systems that are necessary in high-involvement organizations—systems that emphasize rewarding individuals for skill development and for organizational performance. Generally, high-involvement organizations operate best with skill-based pay and pay-for-performance approaches that emphasize teamwork and collective responsibility for performance.

Chapter Nine highlights the important role that information and information systems play in successful high-involvement organizations. An information system that provides employees with ongoing business information and a sense of the organization's long-term direction is critical to employees' exercising greater self-management and coordinating their work laterally with other employees.

Chapter Ten considers the personnel and human resources practices that are needed to help employees become more knowledgeable about the business and be more involved in it. I point out that extensive training programs, as well as a host of other flexible human resources practices, are needed if the organization is to be managed in a way that is congruent with employee involvement.

Chapter Eleven focuses on the behavior of managers and what they need to do to make a high-involvement organization operate effectively. Managers are a critical support mechanism not only in the movement toward employee involvement but also in the continuing success of high-involvement organizations. They need to provide the leadership that replaces the bureaucratic controls and structures of a traditional organization.

Chapter Twelve looks at the role of unions in high-involvement organizations. I suggest that unions have a critical role in these organizations but one dramatically different from the role they exercise in traditional workplaces. Unions must be partners in the business, and work with management to ensure that employee involvement and commitment are an integral part of the way the business operates.

Chapters Thirteen and Fourteen synthesize what is presented in the earlier chapters. They provide an overall view of how business units should look if they adopt a high-involvement approach. They also talk about the issues involved in changing from a traditional to a high-involvement organization. Change strategies are discussed, as is the fit between high-involvement management and societal values such as democracy, entrepreneurial behavior, and team performance. Managers, employees, and union leaders all need to change in order to create effective high-involvement organizations.

Acknowledgments

The concepts in this book were heavily influenced by research done at the Center for Effective Organizations at the University of Southern California. During my time as director of the center, I have had the good fortune to be associated with an exceptional group of researchers. They have all contributed ideas that have found their way into this book. I am grateful to my colleagues for their input and would like to acknowledge that, in many respects, *The Ultimate Advantage* is the product of their efforts, rather than those of any one person. Jay Galbraith has shared with me his reflections on the issue of organizational design. Susan Cohen, Gerald Ledford, Allan Mohrman, and Susan Mohrman have all contributed to my thinking on work teams, employee involvement, and managerial behavior. Finally, Morgan McCall has influenced my thoughts on management development and the role of managers.

Los Angeles, California   Edward E. Lawler III
January 1992

The Author

Edward E. Lawler III is research professor and professor of management and organization in the Graduate School of Business Administration at the University of Southern California. He joined the university in 1978 and during 1979 founded and became director of the university's Center for Effective Organizations.

After receiving his B.A. degree (1960) from Brown University and his Ph.D. degree (1964) from the University of California, Berkeley, both in psychology, Lawler joined the faculty of Yale University. He moved to the University of Michigan in 1972 as professor of psychology and program director in the Survey Research Center at the Institute for Social Research.

Lawler has been honored by many professional associations for his research work. He has served as consultant to more than one hundred organizations on employee involvement, organizational change, and compensation and is the author or coauthor of more than two hundred articles and twenty books. His most recent books include *Doing Research That Is Useful for Theory and Practice* (1985), *High-Involvement Management* (1986), *Designing Performance Appraisal Systems* (1989, with others), *Employee Involvement in America* (1989), *Strategic Pay* (1990), and *Employee Involvement and Total Quality Management* (1992).

THE ULTIMATE ADVANTAGE

PART ONE

Searching

for

Competitive

Advantage

Chapter One

Make Management
an Advantage

Creating an organization in which members feel responsible for and involved in the success of the organization is an attractive and effective approach to management. Managers can achieve this approach by correctly structuring work, providing good leadership, and putting appropriate management practices in place. In reality, however, most organizations are not managed in a way that involves most individuals, that uses even part of the potential of most human beings, or that leads individuals to be committed to the success of the organization. Why does this enormous gap exist between what seems so right and so logical and the reality of how most organizations are managed?

Not surprisingly, this question has no simple answer. How organizations are managed is determined by a wide variety of societal, economic, and technological pressures and realities. Even though most Western countries practice democracy in the political arena, their business leaders have assumed that the highest level of organizational effectiveness can only be obtained by practicing a form of management that is at best described as control oriented and bureaucratic and at worst as arbitrary and autocratic. Many European countries have passed legislation to force companies to move away from a traditional autocratic management style to a more participative style. The United States has chosen not to do this. Instead, it has allowed —

3

in some cases even perhaps encouraged — organizations to practice traditional top-down management.

Clearly, the risks associated with an uninformed, ill-conceived abandonment of traditional management practices are substantial. Because organizational design and management style are integral to the success of any organization, poor choices in these areas can cause an organization to fail and, indeed, a whole society to lose its economic competitiveness. Thus, comfort often causes organizations to stay with what has worked. However, a number of forces can push organizations toward change, including the attractiveness of having a democratic workplace, helping individuals develop their skills and abilities, and respecting the dignity and worth of each individual. These values, along with a host of others that are associated with the concept of *employee involvement*, are core to the principles of most democratic countries. But any management practice ultimately needs to meet a financial test; it has to be at least as effective as any competing approach. Indeed, if a practice is to displace an existing approach, it probably has to be more effective than the current approach.

Work on employee involvement and organizational effectiveness over the last decades has provided a great deal of research information on and practical experience in how organizations need to be designed in order to effectively operate as "high-involvement" organizations. I believe it is possible today to design an organization that involves individuals throughout the organization in the business of the organization. They can receive ongoing information about it, make decisions that influence the organization's success, and be rewarded based on how effectively the organization operates. This approach to organizing, which I call the *high-involvement approach*, is not right for all organizations. However, it is the right approach for many businesses that are trying to compete globally and need to make substantial gains in their effectiveness.

Employee involvement, and most of the management practices that are part of it, has been shown to have significant positive effects on organizational effectiveness. Despite this, organizations have been relatively slow to implement employee involvement for a number of reasons. One of the most important reasons is the integrated and interdependent nature of most complex organizations. Effective organizations are like finely functioning watches (the windup kind). All the pieces need to fit together and operate in concert with each other. Much of the work on participative management and employee involvement has focused on looking separately at such issues as leadership style, job design, and pay systems (Lawler, 1986). Each of these areas clearly is critical to employee involvement, but simply changing leadership style (or job design for that matter) is a small step toward creating a high-involvement organization.

Creating a high-involvement organization involves making choices about organizational design that create a world in which individuals know more, do more, and contribute more. Such an organization is not the result of a change in job design or pay systems; it is the result of a change in the entire design of the organization.

Everyone who has worked has seen the potential that can be tapped and developed when individuals care about the business of their organization. Most small organizations, in fact, succeed because of this caring. The owners of the neighborhood store and the child with the lemonade stand are highly motivated because they own and control a business. Large organizations are structured on the basis of a different model of organizing, and all too often much of the enthusiasm and many of the contributions that their employees could make are lost. It is not simple to capture these contributions and this enthusiasm in large organizations, but it can be done if the organizations are structured and managed properly.

Structuring organizations for employee involvement requires that a number of critical choices about information, power, knowledge, and rewards be made correctly. In many respects, these choices seem deceptively simple: it would seem that managers need only to give individuals control of a business and hold them accountable for its success. The challenge is to install an approach that involves employees, and at the same time takes advantage of the economies of scale and size that are necessary for an organization to compete in many global businesses. In short, the critical issue is how to "act small" when involving employees and "act big" when competing in the marketplace.

Before we look in detail at the specific choices that are involved in designing a high-involvement organization, we need to consider the relationship between organizational design and global competitiveness. Once we have done this, we can consider the choices and key decisions that are involved in creating a high-involvement organization.

Sources of Competitive Advantage

All organizations face competition. Businesses compete with other businesses, universities compete with other universities and at times with businesses, governments compete with other governments and at times with businesses. In a competitive world, an organization can achieve success only by having a competitive advantage. Thus, the search for competitive advantage is as natural to organizations as is the search for food and water by humans and animals.

There are a number of sources of competitive advantage, some that are under the control of an organization and some that are not (Porter, 1985). Sources of competitive advantage also differ in how sustainable they are, how difficult they are to obtain, and how available they are. The ideal situation for an organization is one in which it has important competitive advantages that are sustainable over time.

Historical Advantages

Many organizations in the United States found themselves in very favorable situations for several decades after the end of World War II (Dertouzos, Lester, and Solow, 1989). They were located in the wealthiest country in the world, which had an enormous domestic market (eight times larger than the next largest market) that was growing rapidly and was hungry for new goods and services. The United States also had a technological advantage over other countries. It was and still is rich with universities that lead the world in basic scientific research (Porter, 1990). Many companies such as AT&T and IBM were and still are leaders in technology in their fields.

Following World War II, many Americans returned to school, and the education level in the United States increased dramatically. At the same time, the country made a massive commitment to public education and developed what many considered to be the world's greatest public education system. Thus American companies had ready access to a growing and increasingly well-educated work force. The high level of wealth in the United States also meant that capital was relatively available. Either by going to the stock market or by borrowing, organizations could obtain financing for expansion and growth fairly easily.

The United States also developed an excellent infrastructure, with an impressive telephone and electronic communication system. The development of the interstate highway system, along with the rapid growth of the airline industry, made it easy for organizations to manufacture and market products nationally. Coordination and communication among geographically diverse parts of an organization were also easy. Therefore, large-scale organizations could flourish and orient themselves toward national, and in some cases, international markets. The United States was largely undamaged by World War II, but much of Asia and Europe was in ruins. Japan and Germany were left with little manufacturing capability, and many of their skilled workers and managers were killed in the war. As a result, they were unable to compete in world markets for several decades.

The U.S. government was generally favorable to private enterprise. Certainly, regulations and "government interference" in private enterprise existed, but the government basically supported private enterprise and never questioned its right to exist, flourish, and make a profit.

American managers were among the best educated in the world (Servan-Schreiber, 1968). Many had college degrees or got them soon after the war. They, like the work force in general, were beneficiaries of the strong public commitment to education at all levels of the society.

At least partially because of the competitive advantages that being located in the United States offered, many U.S. companies were highly successful in producing products for the domestic market, a market in which there was virtually no competition from foreign companies. Some U.S. companies also were successful overseas, particularly in Western Europe. The United States became the leading producer of consumer electronics, steel, automobiles, machine tools, paper products, and a host of other consumer and industrial products (Dertouzos, Lester, and Solow, 1989).

The success of many U.S. companies led their managers and others to conclude that they were effective, well-managed organizations (Servan-Schreiber, 1968). Research shows that people tend to take credit for their successes but to blame the environment, luck, or others for their failures (Weiner, 1986). The fallacy of the assumption that U.S. companies were successful because they were effectively managed became all too clear during the 1980s.

Many of the competitive advantages that an organization had by being based in the United States disappeared during the 1970s and early 1980s. Markets became increasingly global, and other countries began to develop their own markets and wealth and borrow or buy U.S. technology. Many American companies began performing poorly (Grayson and O'Dell, 1988; Kanter, 1989b). They were now forced to compete without having a competitive advantage simply because they were based in the United States. In fact, in some situations being based in the United States became a major disadvantage. Organizations based in the United States often faced higher labor costs, more government restrictions, and a different capital structure than their competitors in other nations (Grayson and O'Dell, 1988). Thailand and China, for example, clearly offered and continue to offer lower labor costs than the United States. Japan had and still has better-protected home markets and a more supportive government.

In the decades since World War II, some companies have gained a competitive advantage because their host countries have provided inherent competitive advantages. Other companies have lost their competitive advantage because their host countries no longer provide the advantages that they used to provide (Porter, 1990). Clearly, organizations based in the United States have lost many of the advantages that they used to have, while those based in some parts of Asia and Europe have increasingly gained competitive advantages because of developments in their countries.

Future Advantages

How can organizations gain competitive advantage in the future? We are increasingly headed toward a global marketplace based upon enormously large regional markets in Asia, Europe, and the Americas. Thus it seems unlikely that in the future companies will gain a great deal of competitive advantage by being located in a particular country. Indeed, many large global companies will not even be predominantly located in a particular country (Reich, 1991). This is already true for a number of large corporations such as Shell Oil Company, IBM, 3M, and the somewhat misnamed British Petroleum. Their operations span the world.

A high-quality work force, available capital, and access to markets and technology still are likely to be significant sources of competitive advantage, even in a global economy (Porter, 1985; Johnston, 1991). But how sustainable are these sources going to be in the future? Because of the increased globalization of business, none of these sources will be capable of providing a sustainable competitive advantage in most industries. Leadership in technology illustrates this point.

By training and developing their own scientists and engineers, countries such as Singapore, Taiwan, and Japan have been very successful in importing and developing technology. Sun Microsystems and Dell, two successful computer manufacturers, are good examples of what companies can do. In very short periods of time, they have successfully developed or acquired technological competencies that have given them favorable competitive positions in respect to such technological giants as IBM, Digital Equipment, Xerox, and Hewlett-Packard. In one sense, leadership in technology walks out the door of every organization every evening because it rests in the skills, abilities, and knowledge of an organization's employees.

A skilled work force is clearly a competitive advantage in many businesses. But unlike capital assets, the knowledge and skills of workers are not owned by organizations. They can be hired away by organizations who wish to utilize them. National boundaries are no obstacle to acquiring the human resources that are needed to be competitive. Historically, it may have been true that because a particular kind of technology was developed in one country, organizations in other countries could do little to acquire it. Individuals who knew that technology were "unemployable" by companies in other countries because they were usually unwilling to move. Today, organizations can go to a country in which the human assets are located and utilize them (Reich, 1991). For example, software programmers can be and are employed by American companies in India, Taiwan, and around the world. Olivetti, an Italian company, designs its computers in California because that is where the talented computer designers are located. Japanese auto companies rely on California design studios for the look of their cars.

Capital, like technology, increasingly moves easily across national boundaries. Many of the largest banking institutions in the world now operate globally. They make loans to American companies, European companies, and Japanese companies. Thus, few organizations are able to reliably and consistently get access to cheaper capital because of national conditions. Similarly, so many financing options are available today that established companies cannot count on their existing financial assets as a guarantee that competitors will not develop to challenge them. For example, in the 1970s many U.S. airlines assumed that the price of entry into the industry was so high that new competitors would be unlikely to enter the market, but over a hundred new airlines appeared when the U.S. government deregulated the industry. Not only could these new airlines sell stock, they were able to lease airplanes, terminals, employees, and whatever else it took to get started.

In the computer industry, IBM was once seen as an unchallengeable leader because of its tremendous financial assets and its advanced technology. Although it is often forgotten, IBM was the subject of a major antitrust suit because of its monopoly position in the industry. In the 1980s, however, Digital, Sun Microsystems, and Compaq Computer competed quite success-fully with IBM in a number of market areas. During the 1990s, Dell and AST joined the list of successful competitors.

There is no question that special access to markets can help establish a predominant market position in consumer goods and services and industrial goods. Historically, special access has provided a number of organizations with a sustain-able competitive advantage as well. This may not continue to be the case and may not even be the case today in many markets. Substantial evidence suggests that the world is moving toward dramatic reductions in the political barriers that often give companies an overwhelming competitive advantage. The eco-nomic integration of Western Europe during the early 1990s provides a clear example of how special access to a domestic market can disappear overnight. The transportation and logis-tical advantages of being located in any specific country have been decreasing for decades. Modern air transportation has contributed to this change as has the development of global distribution companies (such as DHL, Federal Express, and United Parcel Service [UPS]).

Management Approach as a Source of Competitive Advantage

Management is sometimes listed as a potential source of com-petitive advantage. Financial analysts often say that the quality of the management is an important consideration in determin-ing the value of a company. Indeed, the stock market's evalua-tions of companies often change when the companies lose or gain key executives. Popular magazines such as *Fortune* rate companies in terms of how well they are managed.

Historically, the term *well managed* has been applied to organizations that have strong leadership at the top and that execute the traditional control model of management better than other companies do. Organizational effectiveness has meant holding individuals accountable for their performance, clearly structuring jobs and responsibilities, training and developing people to fit the jobs to which they are assigned, and organizing and dividing the work in ways that fit technology and markets. In one respect, it is hard to argue with the view that those organizations that are better at traditional bureaucratic management will have a competitive advantage. As long as everyone is basically adopting the same management approach, those organizations that execute it better must have a competitive advantage. In addition, if it is difficult to learn and execute a new management approach, performing the traditional approach well may prove to be a sustainable competitive advantage (Ulrich and Lake, 1990).

Approaches to management are hard to copy and transport from organization to organization. Simply hiring a few individuals away from an organization does not allow a competitor to gain access to the organization's management approach in the same way that it may allow it to gain access to the organization's technology. Similarly, although managers can learn about new management approaches through books and conferences, it is often difficult for them to go from these explanations to operating management systems. The learning curve in adopting a new management approach may be years long. Thus, those companies that start learning new approaches early often have a competitive advantage that can last them as long as they are still moving up the learning curve — perhaps for decades.

I need to stress at this point that an effective management system is more than just the sum of the parts; it is a set of integrated policies, practices, and behaviors. Sometimes having a good management system is confused with having high-quality employees. This is a mistake — the two are quite different in some important ways. Having high-quality employees does not assure an organization of having a sustainable competitive advantage or even a short-term advantage. If the employees are poorly motivated or if the correct organizational systems are not in place, the employees' talent may be wasted. And high-quality employees can go to work for a competitor, which limits the sustainability of this advantage.

Traditional thinking about what kind of management approach can provide a competitive advantage was significantly shaken by several books that appeared in bookstores and on the coffee tables of executives during the 1980s, including *Theory Z* (Ouchi, 1981), *In Search of Excellence* (Peters and Waterman, 1982), *Vanguard Management* (O'Toole, 1985), and *Change Masters* (Kanter, 1985). These books argued that competitive advantage can best be achieved not by doing the old management better but by adopting new and innovative management approaches that are more effective at organizing and managing people. They varied substantially in the new practices they recommended, but they all stated that organizations had to move away from the top-down model that was mechanistic and bureaucratic and that most large companies had long assumed was the best approach.

These books pointed out that those organizations that were better at changing their management approach would have a competitive advantage. They added that this might prove to be a more sustainable competitive advantage than could be gained from being the best at traditional management. Companies that adopted new approaches before the approaches became popular would be ahead on the long learning curve that is involved in developing and utilizing new management approaches (Barney, 1986). This is a compelling argument. It leads to the important conclusion that the management style and the approach to organizing that an organization uses may be the ultimate competitive advantage in the future. It is a competitive advantage that is capable of providing significant gains and one that can provide early adopters with a sustainable advantage.

The idea that a nonhierarchical management style can be a source of competitive advantage is not new. In the late fifties and early sixties, for example, a number of authors were highly critical of the way most organizations were managed (such as Argyris, 1957; Likert, 1961; McGregor, 1960). They pointed out that even the best organizations were significantly underperforming because of the way they organized and treated people.

They went on to argue that much higher levels of performance were possible if organizations used participative management approaches.

Organizations were not ready to hear this message, however. As noted earlier, most senior managers assumed that their organizations were successful because of the way that they were managed and felt little need for change because U.S. organizations were dominant in many industries. A much more popular message than the one sent by the critics of traditional management approaches was the one sent by Servan-Schreiber (1968). He argued that U.S. companies were on their way to long-term dominance of world markets because they were better managed than companies in other countries. Not surprisingly, most successful companies in the United States took an "if it ain't broke, don't fix it" approach to management, while those who were not successful looked to the more successful companies to learn what approach to use.

In the 1970s, companies based in the United States fell behind foreign competitors in a number of industries. The most popular explanation for this change focused on the problems associated with doing business in the United States and with the unfair advantages some foreign companies had because of low wages and help from their governments. Managers argued that they were handicapped by too many governmental regulations, antitrust restrictions, the dumping of products from Asia, and so on. Thus, they felt the solution was for the government to behave differently and for it to help business more by getting out of the way and working to open foreign markets. This view gained wide acceptance and led to a number of governmental initiatives during the Reagan presidency.

In the 1980s, managers began to be receptive to the message that they needed to change their management approaches. Many of even the most successful U.S. companies were losing out to offshore competitors. But, perhaps more important, some were losing out to onshore competitors who were owned and managed by Japanese firms, thus "proving" that automobiles, televisions, and a variety of products could be successfully manufactured in the United States if the management approach was right. It gradually became obvious that simply doing the old things better might not be good enough. Most of the competitive advantages that U.S. companies had enjoyed were gone and so was the superior performance of these companies. The U.S. approach to managing was revealed to be a weakness, not a strength. For decades, this management style was credited with providing a competitive advantage that most likely resulted from a host of other factors, primarily the many advantages associated with being based in the United States.

The automobile industry provides a dramatic example of how organization and management can provide a sustainable competitive advantage. Everyone knows the story of the successful Japanese attack on the dominance of U.S. automobile manufacturers. The major Japanese companies have substantially cut into the market share of U.S. automakers (Womack, Jones, and Roos, 1990). During the early stages of the success of these companies, a number of explanations were offered for their competitive advantage, including the low wages they paid their work force, the support of their government, their willingness to dump products in the United States, and their more advanced manufacturing technologies. These all sounded like good explanations, and they probably did contribute something to the early success of the Japanese companies.

But now, clear evidence suggests that the ultimate and perhaps most important competitive advantage of the Japanese automakers is their ability to organize and manage work (Womack, Jones, and Roos, 1990). The most dramatic evidence for this conclusion is the ability of Japanese companies to successfully design and build cars in the United States. The major Japanese automakers (Honda, Nissan, Toyota) successfully build cars in the United States using American workers and, to a degree, American managers. Nissan also successfully builds cars in England with English workers and Japanese managers. Surveys by the J. D. Power Company, an independent research organization, clearly show that the best-quality cars built in the United States are coming out of the Japanese "transplant" manufacturing facilities.

Based on my visits to the U.S. manufacturing plants of Japanese automakers and on what I have read, I do not believe that these plants are using superior manufacturing technology. Their wages and work forces are no different than those of the U.S. automobile manufacturers. Despite the similarities in location, technology, wages, and work force, the Japanese plants are building better cars and are more productive than the plants of U.S. automakers. The reasons for this superiority are clearly rooted in the approach to management that is used in these plants (Womack, Jones, and Roos, 1990).

In the early eighties, U.S. automobile companies began to adopt some of the Japanese management practices, but so far these companies have not been able to match the performance of the Japanese companies. They have improved, but so have the Japanese companies. This is a predictable result, given what was said earlier about long learning curves and sustainable competitive advantage. It raises a series of important questions: What approach can provide U.S. companies with a competitive advantage? Should they just copy the Japanese? What about the cultural differences between the United States and Japan?

Demands of Organizational Performance

Before we can talk in detail about those approaches to management that are likely to provide a competitive advantage in the future, we need to focus on what types of behavior organizations need if they are to compete successfully. The choice of a management approach must be strongly influenced by the kind of performance an organization needs in order to be successful in its marketplace. Different kinds of performance call for different approaches to organizing. In fact, given the need to produce a high volume of low-cost products, the management approaches used by many companies during and after World War II may have been appropriate. The competitive environment has changed dramatically, however, and as a result different kinds of performance are needed.

The four types of performance that organizations must demonstrate to gain a competitive advantage—cost competitiveness, high-quality products and services, innovation, and speed—are not substitutable for each other in most markets. Simply being good in one, two, or three areas is not enough. For example, having outdated, high-quality, cost competitive products does not lead to success any more than does having innovative, poor-quality products. The management approach that an organization takes must be able to bring innovative, high-quality, cost-competitive products to market quickly.

Cost Competitiveness

Saying that an organization needs to be cost competitive is, in most respects, another way of saying that it needs to be productive in the use of all of its resources. Having a competitive cost structure does not by itself guarantee the success of an organization, but it is a necessary condition for success.

Overall cost effectiveness is the result of managing a number of costs. The cost of labor is one obvious and frequently discussed cost. Because more and more low-wage countries are entering work markets (Grayson and O'Dell, 1988) and because of a host of other factors, the competitive standard in the area of labor costs is constantly more difficult to meet. Many countries offer inexpensive unskilled labor, and a small but increasing number of countries such as Ireland, Singapore, and India offer inexpensive skilled labor. Most organizations simply cannot continue to exist unless their labor costs are competitive. However, this does not always mean that low costs per hour are necessary; when the total labor force is considered, an organization has to have labor costs that are favorable given the quality and rate of output the employees achieve. An organization can achieve favorable costs through a low-wage strategy or through a value-added strategy in which well-paid employees add more value to the product than do the poorly paid employees of competitors.

Employees influence many costs, not just labor costs. They make decisions and engage in activities that influence most of the costs that an organization incurs. For example, they often determine yield from raw materials, and they make decisions that influence the amount of capital needed. Indeed, in some companies (such as chemical and energy companies), labor costs are a very small part of an organization's cost of doing business, but employees are still crucial in determining the cost structure of these organizations. It is impossible to overstate the impact that employee behavior has on the cost of producing most products and services. How effective employees are at continuously reducing costs is one of the critical determinants of whether an organization can survive in most global and nonglobal businesses.

High-Quality Products and Services

Like cost competitiveness, high-quality products and services are necessary for most companies to survive in a global marketplace. They allow organizations to play the game but do not assure success. The standards of acceptable quality for products and services continue to increase (Dertouzos, Lester, and Solow, 1989; Bowen, Chase, Cummings, and Associates, 1990; Schlesinger and Heskett, 1991a; 1991b). To survive, most organizations cannot stand still; they have to improve the quality of their products and services. In many respects, competing on the basis of quality is not new, but it certainly has become much more important.

The emphasis on quality has had a profound effect on customer service; customer satisfaction has become a major basis of competition (Bowen, Chase, Cummings, and Associates, 1990). Nordstrom, Xerox, and SAS airlines have adopted satisfying the customer as their major objective in the delivery of services. Lexus and Saturn have gone to extraordinary measures to correct manufacturing defects in their cars.

The influx of Japanese products into global markets has unquestionably brought about this emphasis on quality. During the 1980s, Japanese products raised the standard for product quality enormously, and by every indication, quality will continue to be a critical basis of competition (Deming, 1986). Certainly, the quality of many products and services will continue to improve, and this trend has profound implications for management.

Perhaps more than any other single feature of an organization's performance, the quality of the products and services a company produces is under its control. The quality of products and services is strongly influenced by the way a company is organized and managed. It is often said that quality is built into products, not added to them or achieved through inspections (Deming, 1986). This statement is one way of stressing that the behavior of employees throughout an organization is the critical determinant of quality. In service organizations, quality is directly visible in the interaction between the employee and the customer (Bowen, Chase, Cummings, and Associates, 1990; Carlzon, 1987). The quality of products is visible in the presence or absence of the many assembly and design errors that can undermine the marketability of a product.

Because of their high-quality products, Japanese automakers have been able to gain a significant share of the U.S. market, and they have shown consumers that cars can be virtually fault free. In fact, Japanese automakers have moved beyond producing fault-free cars to focus on experienced quality—whether the product looks and feels like a quality product.

Despite the dramatic improvements in quality made by U.S. automakers, they still lag behind the Japanese in overall product quality, both in number of defects and experienced quality. American automakers seem to lag about four or five years behind the Japanese, a common problem when an organization tries to copy and learn someone else's systems. Since the quality-improvement curve is flattening, the absolute distance between the quality of U.S. and Japanese automobiles has narrowed substantially, but the Japanese still lead in quality and probably will continue to lead as long as they can continue to improve their own quality and other countries are simply copying their methods.

Innovation

Increasingly, companies are competing on the basis of the rapid introduction of innovative products and new services (Bower and Hout, 1988). Thus, organizations must be able to develop and market new products and services and adapt to changes in the environment. Not only has the life expectancy of many products been shortened dramatically because of rapidly advancing technology and consumer demands, the life cycle of many assumptions about the marketplace is also shortening (Handy, 1989).

Perhaps the best example of the increasing rate of the introduction of new products is in high-technology areas such as computers and home electronics. Technology is changing so quickly in these areas that the life cycles of products have been cut in half. New personal computers, for example, seem to have a life expectancy of no more than two years and often less, as do new copying machines and televisions. The time needed to design new automobiles has shrunk from five or more years to the new world standard of about three years from conceptualization to market. Hewlett-Packard, for instance, stresses speed by measuring the time it takes to break even on a product.

Entire new industries can develop very quickly. For instance, not too long ago, there were no videocassette recorders or personal computers. In today's environment, companies must be able to frequently introduce new products and new technology to be competitive.

Marketplaces also change rapidly because of rapid political and social changes (Handy, 1989). Mass communication, new communication technologies, and a host of other social changes constantly open new markets and change others. Markets can also be altered as companies reposition themselves in the marketplace and as local market preferences change. Thus, a critical success factor for an organization has become its ability to innovate in order to adjust to market conditions.

Speed

The speed with which an organization can respond to the market has become an important competitive dimension in many markets (Stalk and Hout, 1990). Organizations increasingly compete in how fast they can get a product or service to market and how fast they can respond to customer requests.

Getting a product or service to a customer just a few days or even minutes earlier can make an enormous difference in the success of a product, particularly when the total life expectancy of the product is very short and the window of opportunity for meeting a customer's needs for a service is very small. Giving a customer an immediate answer to a question has a major influence on customer satisfaction (Bowen, Chase, Cummings, and Associates, 1990). Customers want quick answers to their requests for loans, credit cards, and home repairs just as they want their fast food served quickly!

Motorola can now manufacture a custom paging device (such as a beeper indicating a message) within two hours after the order has been placed. General Electric (GE) has reduced its time to produce a custom circuit breaker box from three weeks to three days. These examples of "custom mass production" show the degree to which competition demands that organizations be innovative and at the same time fast to market.

Demands of Context and Environment

An organization's approach to management has to be sensitive to a number of contextual and environmental issues. Specifically, a management approach must be able to attract and retain the kind of employees that the organization needs, and fit the national culture, government regulations, and legal structure of the country in which the organization operates.

Labor Force

To be competitive, organizations in many industries must have highly skilled, knowledgeable workers. They must also have a relatively stable labor force since employee turnover works directly against obtaining the kind of coordination and organizational learning that leads to fast responses and high-quality products and services.

As was mentioned earlier, the United States has had a relative abundance of skilled labor, and as a result, U.S. organizations have not had to worry a great deal about whether their

management approach helped them attract and retain skilled
employees (Freeman, 1976). However, the work force is predicted to change during the 1990s and the twenty-first century
(Johnston, 1987, 1991). The U.S. educational system is likely to
produce fewer and fewer engineers, scientists, and other technically trained individuals, and organizations are going to need
large numbers of these individuals (Commission on the Skills of
the American Workforce, 1990).

One estimate suggests that by the year 2000, 70 percent of
all jobs in Western countries will require cerebral rather than
manual skills (Handy, 1989). Jobs requiring manual labor will
have been automated or sent to low-wage countries. Thus, organizations that are particularly good at attracting, retaining, and,
of course, motivating those individuals who are scarce in the
labor market should be able to perform better than those that
are not.

In order to be competitive, organizations need to do
more than just attract people to fill jobs; they need to engage the
full efforts and capabilities of their employees. Involving employees in this way has always been a challenge, but it seems to
be increasingly difficult to do. Nonwork activities are more and
more effective competitors for the time, efforts, and thoughts of
most individuals. Not only does the world of entertainment
(movies, books, television) continue to grow but also hardly a
day seems to pass without a new hobby or sport being created.
These activities are tough competition for organizations that
want their employees to care about the effectiveness of the
organization.

The U.S. work force is also predicted to become increasingly diverse ethnically and perhaps also in terms of individuals' values (Johnston, 1987). This diversity will present a
particular challenge for the managers of organizations because
they will not be able to count on high levels of agreement on
many issues involving values and personal preferences. They
will have to take into account large individual differences in life-
styles and preferences about work arrangements. Those organizations that are particularly effective at dealing with the diver-

sity of the work force can gain a competitive advantage because they will have superior talent with which to operate.

National Values

Nations differ substantially on how much importance their people place on individualism versus team effort and on discipline, respect for elders, the right of an individual to influence decisions that affect him or her, and a host of other values that affect behavior in organizations. Although there are great individual differences, people within the United States tend to value individual rights, innovation, competition, teamwork, democratic processes, individualism, and personal freedom. In addition, the United States still tends to be a center of entrepreneurial behavior because it has strong values concerning risk taking, innovation, and individual fulfillment. Even people who do not want the risk of starting their own business may want to "own" their workplace and put their fingerprint on it by influencing how it operates and looks.

The implications of this set of values for management are profound. Whatever management practices are adopted by U.S. organizations must—if these organizations are to operate comfortably and effectively in the society—take into account the emphasis on individualism, democracy, and ownership that are such strong values in this society. Working within these values presents a challenge because the very essence of an organization is the coordination of actions among individuals in order to make a product or deliver a service. Obtaining coordination often means getting individuals to give up some of their individual freedom. In addition, it may be that speed is best obtained by unilateral decision making rather than more democratic and participative decision making, which often is slow (Vroom and Yetton, 1973).

Indeed, traditional wisdom concerning what makes an organization effective is often cited to justify the popularity of top-down bureaucratic management approaches in the United States. For decades, people have recognized that many U.S.

organizations have operated in ways that restrict individual rights and decision making, but this restriction has been justified as the only way for organizations to be successful. The largely unchallenged assumption has been made that the gains in organizational effectiveness that come from autocratic management styles are worth the consequences of asking employees to check their values and society's values at the door to the workplace (Sashkin, 1984; U.S. Department of Health, Education, and Welfare, 1973).

Innovations are often produced by individuals who are entrepreneurially oriented and who value individualism. In many respects, the values of U.S. culture put U.S. organizations in a favorable position to compete in this dimension. The challenge for many organizations is to translate their innovations into marketable products and services.

The challenge for all organizations is to find a management style that helps them attract and retain the best and brightest employees and that fits the national cultural values of the country or countries in which they operate. Many Japanese organizations appear to have met this challenge. They have developed a management approach that emphasizes the core Japanese values of uniformity, discipline, group membership, conformity, continuous improvement, attention to detail, respect for age, individual dignity, obligations to others, and loyalty to large organizations and to country (Ouchi, 1981). It has helped them gain a competitive advantage. Although all these values are held to a degree by people in the United States and other Western countries, they are not the predominant values in these countries. Thus, what works best in Japan may not be the best approach in Western countries.

Chapter Two

Choose the Right Management Style

Two fundamentally different approaches dominate modern writings about management. These two approaches have their own advocates and history, and they call for significantly different management practices. In a sense, they can be viewed as competing paradigms or models of how organizations should be managed.

The oldest, best-established approach has been referred to as top-down, pyramidal, hierarchical, mechanistic, and bureaucratic, but perhaps it is best described as the *control-oriented approach*. The second approach, which is often called the *commitment* or *involvement-oriented approach*, is newer and much less well developed than the control-oriented approach. Evidence suggests, however, that it is gaining in popularity and may eventually become the dominant model (Lawler, Ledford, and Mohrman, 1989). We will briefly consider the evolution of the two models and then look at how they can be expected to perform in today's environment.

Control-Oriented Approach

In one respect, the control-oriented approach as is as old as organized human behavior. It is based on the assumption that hierarchy and vertical relationships are the best ways to assure that work gets done in a productive and high-quality manner. It has its modern roots in the work of Max Weber (1947), who helped develop the bureaucratic approach to management. The approach gained sophistication and early popularity in the United States as a result of the pioneering work of Frederick Winslow Taylor. He wrote about and implemented what was then called *scientific management* (Taylor, 1911, 1915). Scientific management is based on the principle that productivity is maximized when the work of low-level participants in an organization is specialized, standardized, and simplified. Low-level participants work on only a small part of a product or service. Their every action is subject to scientific study to determine the best way to perform their job, and they are told exactly how to do their job. Managers are the only ones who are expected to think, coordinate, and control.

During the early part of the twentieth century, scientific management gained increasing acceptance and sophistication. Assembly lines were used to be sure that the production rate was predictable and the work less physically demanding. For example, Henry Ford became famous for his development of the automobile assembly line. Organizations developed pay incentive plans to be sure that employees were motivated to perform the simplified, standardized jobs. They added staff groups to be sure that people with appropriate expertise were present to deal with the complex planning and scheduling issues that grew out of the high level of specialization. Layers of hierarchy were used to control and coordinate the workplace.

The early use of scientific management in Bethlehem Steel and other heavy manufacturing companies resulted in tremendous productivity gains, often because improvements in work methods were put in place and machine pacing led to higher rates of production. In many respects, Taylor's concepts were ready-made for an American work force that consisted of poorly educated immigrants. These concepts also fit the needs of the time because productivity was the most important outcome for an organization; the country was starved for manufactured goods. Furthermore, at the time Taylor developed scientific management, no competing management model for large-size manufacturing organizations existed. Thus, it won easy and rapid acceptance.

Although the term *scientific management* is not widely used today, most of the concepts that were inherent in Taylor's early work dominate current thinking about how to organize and manage corporations. The bureaucratic, or control-oriented, model that Taylor, along with other organizational theorists, initally developed has become a mature management approach. It has been widely adopted and studied, and the technology to support it is well-developed and readily available.

The control-oriented approach reached its greatest popularity in the 1960s, when, as was noted in Chapter One, many people assumed that it gave American industry a competitive advantage in the world. At that point, American companies were the technological leaders in installing the control-oriented approach to management. They produced sophisticated organizational charts, trained managers to direct and control employees, and developed elaborate information systems to support the control-oriented approach. Such specialties as writing job descriptions, designing production work flows, developing job evaluation systems, and selecting the "right" individuals for jobs flourished and were widely practiced.

During the 1960s, companies like AT&T, Exxon, Kodak, IBM, and General Motors seemed to have perfected the control-oriented approach to management. AT&T, for example, successfully ran a nationwide phone system with over one million employees. It was a strongly hierarchical company, with careful gradations of power, business knowledge, access to information, and rewards attached to each level in the hierarchy. Employees at the lowest level of the hierarchy were expected to behave in a similar manner in the same situation across the country. You could hear the same phrase being uttered by operators in Memphis, Tennessee; Los Angeles, California; and Pinkney, Michigan. The company instituted controls everywhere to ensure this consistency. Operators' conversations were recorded, scored, and timed, and supervisors were ever present.

AT&T, Kodak, IBM, General Motors, and other control-oriented companies flourished during the 1960s and the 1970s and were often identified as the best-managed companies in the world. In retrospect, it is not clear that their excellent performance was as much due to the way they were organized and managed as it was to the competitive advantages that they enjoyed because they were based in the United States. Nevertheless, these companies were perceived as well managed and probably were among the best at utilizing the control-oriented model. It is also possible that they were organized correctly given the competitive environment they faced.

Involvement-Oriented Approach

Like the control-oriented approach, the involvement-oriented approach has a long history. Writings about democratic supervision and participative management started appearing with some regularity in the 1930s (see Weisbord, 1987, for a review). From the beginning of modern civilization, societies have debated the advantages and disadvantages of democratic and autocratic forms of government. In many respects, decisions about how to manage a work organization are simply a special case of this larger issue.

The fundamental difference between the control-oriented approach and the involvement-oriented approach concerns how work is organized and managed at the lowest level in an organization. Companies using the control-oriented approach assume that work should be simplified, standardized, and specialized and that supervision and pay incentives should be used to motivate individuals to perform their tasks well. In essence, the thinking and controlling part of work is separated from the doing of the work. Employees are expected to perform well because they know what is expected of them, they are able to do it, and they are supervised closely to ensure that they perform as instructed.

The involvement-oriented approach relies much more on self-control and self-management. Typically, work is organized to be challenging, interesting, and motivating. Individuals at all levels in the organization are given power to influence decisions.

They are given information about the organization's operations and performance, and they are trained so that they can operate with a good understanding of the business. If the smoothly running assembly line is the best image for the control-oriented approach, then the small business unit that controls its own fate and involves everyone in the business is the best image for the involvement-oriented approach.

The key assumption in the involvement-oriented approach is that if individuals are given challenging work that gives them a customer to serve and a business to operate, they can and will control their own behavior (Manz and Sims, 1980; Manz, 1990). Although supervision will be needed initially to organize, train, and lead employees and, at times, to deal with coordination, conflict, and some customer interface issues, the involvement-oriented approach assumes that individuals can exercise considerable amounts of self-control. In addition, the approach assumes that all individuals can add value to a product by using their minds as well as their hands. Thus, employees are asked to make suggestions and in many cases to respond in nonprogrammed ways to events that occur in the process of making products and delivering services. While the control-oriented approach seeks to develop employees who are perfectly programmed robots and are 100 percent reliable, the involvement-oriented approach strives to develop employees who are responsive to change and in many respects self-programming.

The involvement-oriented approach has evolved and gained acceptance much more slowly than the control-oriented approach. In many ways, it is not yet a mature approach; it has not been as widely adopted as the control-oriented approach and, as a result, the practices and policies that are needed to support it have not been developed as completely.

Three writers were particularly influential in bringing the involvement-oriented approach to the attention of U.S. managers in the 1960s: Chris Argyris, Douglas McGregor, and Rensis Likert. All wrote influential books on *participative management*, as it was then called, that compared the involvement-oriented approach with the control-oriented approach. At the time,

McGregor's book *The Human Side of Enterprise* (1960) gained considerable visibility and was widely read, although its popularity pales in comparison to the popularity of Peters and Waterman's book *In Search of Excellence* (1982).

Rather than writing an elaborate textbook on how to operate an involvement-oriented organization, McGregor highlighted the assumptions about the nature of people that differentiate a control-oriented approach to management from an involvement-oriented approach. He introduced the well-known terms *Theory X Management* and *Theory Y Management* in this book. Theory X management rests on the assumption that people must be coerced and controlled in order to perform well. Theory Y management, on the other hand, assumes that individuals can be trusted and motivated to perform well if they are given interesting and challenging work; in essence, work is natural and people want to perform well.

In the years since McGregor's book was published, many other writers have contributed to the literature on how organizations can be managed in an involvement-oriented way. Fundamentally, these writings maintain that creating a distinction between employees who think and employees who do is counterproductive because it alienates and underutilizes many individuals and creates excessive overhead costs. According to the involvement-oriented approach, organizations should be structured so that individuals at the lowest level in the organization not only perform work but also are responsible for improving work methods and procedures, solving problems on the job, and coordinating their work with that of others. Employees also can and should be expected to operate without a controlling supervisor. Of course, it is one thing to say that this is the way an organization should be run and it is quite a different thing to specify how organizations can be designed and operated in this manner.

Much of the early writing on participative management focused on the importance of managerial behavior in creating effective organizations (Likert, 1961; Bass, 1981). These authors argued that managers should listen, care about their people, and ultimately be democratic and participative in their supervisory and decision-making processes. Companies instituted training programs to change management behavior to meet these goals and also gave some attention to ways to design work so that individuals would be motivated by a desire to perform it well. This work on job enrichment and work teams was very influential and will be discussed in some detail in Chapters Four and Five.

Only recently, however, have writers been concerned with the broader organizational design and systems issues that arise when an entire organization is managed with the involvement-oriented approach. Advocating participative supervision and advocating the creation of involvement-oriented organizations are significantly different. The former can potentially be accomplished "simply" by getting managers to behave in a participative way. The latter, as will be shown in this book, requires the creation of new work systems, policies, procedures, practices, and organizational designs—in effect, the creation of a new type of organization.

Comparison of the Approaches

Now that we have briefly described the control-oriented and involvement-oriented approaches, we can turn to an analysis of how they are likely to perform in terms of cost, quality, speed, and innovation. We can then look at how they relate to the labor force and national cultural values. Finally we can consider the evidence that exists on the effectiveness of the two approaches.

Cost and Productivity

The early adoptions of the control-oriented approach were primarily stimulated by its obvious contributions to productivity. There seemed to be little question that the approach improved the productivity of many manufacturing workers. Organizations could hire inexpensive labor and keep training costs to a minimum. In many situations, the approach also allowed organizations to use inexperienced, untrained labor and sometimes to save money by substituting capital for labor, such as through the use of the assembly line.

The control-oriented approach has significant costs associated with it. Because the approach does not motivate employees through the nature of their work or their commitment to the organization, it often takes an elaborate hierarchy of supervisors, measurement systems, reward systems, and discipline systems to be sure that employees perform their work well. Many supervisors are also needed to coordinate the employees doing the work because none of the employees has responsibility for or even an understanding of the complete task. In the 1970s, Bethlehem Steel, for example, had fourteen layers of management, thirty-four hundred wage incentive schemes, and four hundred industrial engineers timing jobs and setting rates. Despite this, only 70 percent of the company's production was of satisfactory quality, at a time when the world standard was 95 percent.

Although labor costs may start out low in the control-oriented approach, they often rise precisely because the work is not motivating or satisfying. In steel, automobile, chemical, and a host of other industries, employees have formed unions to bargain for better wages and working conditions. These are the major rewards they can receive when the control-oriented approach is used, and employees feel they deserve high levels of these rewards because of the boring work they do and the poor treatment they receive (Walker and Guest, 1952).

Significant overhead is also involved in designing the work flow systems that lend themselves to standardized, specialized, and simplified work. Sometimes significant capital costs are involved because automated equipment is required. Perhaps a good way to summarize the cost parameters of the control-oriented model is to say that the individuals actually doing the production work or delivering the service add little value to the product or service. For this model to be effective, labor costs must be low because individuals other than the production employees are needed to add value to the product or service. Supervisors are needed to coordinate the work of others, design the systems, and control the ongoing functioning of the organization.

The involvement-oriented approach tries to deal with

labor costs by having the employee who is performing the work add more value to the product or service than does the employee who is working under the control-oriented model. In the involvement-oriented approach, employees are expected to exercise more self-control and in many respects directly coordinate their work with the work of others. In addition, they are expected to solve problems and improve the work process, do their own quality inspection, and, where appropriate, make ongoing adjustments and changes as demanded by the work situation. Of course, for this system to work, employees need to be selected carefully, trained extensively, and paid good wages because individuals operating under the involvement-oriented approach need to have more ability and skills than workers operating under the control-oriented approach.

Whether the control- or the involvement-oriented approach is the most cost effective depends on the type of work being done and the wage structure of the location where the work is being done. If the work is relatively simple and there is little need for coordination and problem solving, then it is quite possible that the control-oriented approach will produce better results. It is hard for a company to operate in an involvement-oriented way if the work is simple because employees cannot be motivated to perform by the work itself and thus external control is needed. To a significant degree, self-control depends on individuals being intrinsically motivated to do the work well; it is hard to develop intrinsic motivation when the work is highly repetitive and provides no challenge (Lawler, 1973).

The control-oriented approach also works well if the type of work is highly stable so that it can be programmed to be done in the same way for a long period. This stability helps to spread the cost of the development and programming of control systems over a long period of time and over many products and services.

Low labor costs that are likely to remain low also favor the control-oriented approach. Even though it may take more labor to operate with this approach, if labor costs are relatively low, this disadvantage may be unimportant. Also, if the work force is poorly educated and unskilled, it may be too expensive for organizations to develop employees with the knowledge and skills they need to operate in an involvement-oriented approach, even if wages are low.

Where labor costs are high and the competition is global, the involvement-oriented approach seems to be the clear choice. It is the best way to utilize the ability of employees to add value to the product in a cost-competitive manner. If employees do not think, solve problems, and control themselves, they simply cannot add enough value to the product to compete with low-wage employees elsewhere in the world. If the organizational structures and management approaches of a company are control-oriented, the company will almost always have lower total production costs in a low-wage situation.

One implication of this argument is that simple work probably should not be done in locations with high labor costs. If the work is extremely simple and repetitive, employees may not have the opportunity to do a great deal of problem solving and to add value to the work. In these cases, it is hard to see how organizations in a high-wage country can compete effectively regardless of their management approach. Sometimes automation can help because it substitutes capital for labor and makes work more interesting, but it cannot be used in all situations.

Quality

The control-oriented approach tries to produce quality products and services by "inspecting in" quality. The involvement-oriented approach tries to produce quality products and services by motivating and training employees to build it into the product or service. For decades, the dominant thinking about quality was that it could be achieved through inspections, but this thinking has changed dramatically in recent years. The criteria for winning the Baldrige National Quality Award in the United States and the Deming Award in Japan present evidence of this change. To win these awards, companies must place an emphasis on employee development and involvement. The change in thinking is also evident in the popularity of the ideas of Juran (1989), Deming (1986), and others who have written about the advantages of self-inspection and using employee empowerment to improve quality.

Attitudes toward the control-oriented approach to quality have changed for a number of reasons, not the least of which is that in many cases it simply does not work. Inspectors miss defects partially because they do not care about their work performance and in some cases employees "outsmart" inspectors as part of games they play in order to make dull and uninteresting work somewhat challenging. Studies of the cost of quality have helped bring to the forefront the fact that inspecting quality in is a very costly approach to producing quality products and services (see, for example, Crosby, 1979; Juran, 1989). This approach to quality results in high material, supply, and labor costs. For customer service organizations, it often results in poor customer satisfaction and in lost customers who are very expensive to win back (Bowen, Chase, Cummings, and Associates, 1990).

The self-inspection, or do-it-right-the-first-time, approach to quality has a number of benefits. With this approach, few products need to be thrown away because of defects and the amount (and therefore cost) of inspection that is needed can be reduced tremendously. The involvement-oriented approach argues that employees can be trained and motivated to "do it right the first time" if they are given meaningful, challenging jobs and the training to perform them well.

The involvement-oriented approach also argues that employees often can add significant value to the quality of products and services by solving problems and responding correctly to unpredicted events. This point is often most obvious in service situations, where unpredictable events can occur with great regularity. Customers have a tendency to raise unexpected issues, and, of course, many factors such as the weather and what the competitors do are uncontrollable.

Instead of holding that employees should be programmed to respond correctly to problems, the involvement-oriented approach argues that employees should be given general missions and philosophies as guides for their behavior and then allowed to respond to the customer as they see fit (see

Carlzon, 1987). In essence, employees are told to satisfy the customer in the best way that they can, given corporate strategy and the particular situation. They also are expected to improve the work system as time goes on so that it will operate at a high level of quality. This is in contrast to the control-oriented approach, which tries to program employees with responses to all situations so that there is never any doubt about what they should do. During its years as a regulated monopoly, AT&T developed the control-oriented approach to a very high level and had volumes of policy and procedure manuals that covered just about every possible situation.

The involvement-oriented approach seems likely to produce high-quality products and services in most situations. However, if a sufficiently talented and motivated work force is not available and the work is simple and easy to do, a control-oriented model may operate effectively. The existence of a stable environment can also help make the control-oriented approach to quality viable. A stable environment allows organizations to study, plan, program, and deliberately execute many of their major moves. The control model may also be appropriate if labor is relatively cheap and materials and supplies are inexpensive so that high levels of defective products that are thrown away are not a major problem for the organization.

Speed

Organizations using the control-oriented approach are likely to respond quickly in stable production or service situations. By carefully programming and controlling the behavior of employees, it is possible for an organization to react very quickly to an expected or predicted event. If correct policies and procedures are in place, the organization can without "thinking" respond correctly to what is occurring. This quick response can be facilitated by the many managers and supervisors who are employed to facilitate the completion of work from beginning to end. Organizations using the control-oriented approach cannot respond as quickly when unexpected changes occur or when complex interdependencies are involved in producing a product or serving a customer. Let us look first at the issue of complex interdependencies.

Because work is often broken up into specialized and simplified pieces in the control-oriented approach, complicated products or services must often move from individual to individual or group to group in the organization. Two problems can occur with this type of hand-off process. First, work may sit until the next employee is ready to take it and, perhaps more important, awkwardness or lack of coordination in the hand-off process can cause errors and problems (Tichy and Charan, 1989). Thus, a task may be done slowly or incorrectly and may need to be redone.

The involvement-oriented approach deals with the hand-off process by emphasizing a horizontal organizational structure. It tries to incorporate key coordination activities within the responsibilities of an individual or a work team, which eliminates many of the hand-offs and the problems associated with them. The response time on everything from processing mortgage applications to producing custom products becomes faster if hand-offs are eliminated.

New or unusual situations are particularly problematic for the control-oriented organization. If no programmed or practiced response to a situation exists, a control-oriented organization can be very slow to respond. Typically, the issue has to be passed up the hierarchy to someone who is in a high enough position to make an overall decision about what should be done. Depending upon how hierarchical the organization is and where the appropriate knowledge rests, this process can take a considerable period of time. Control-oriented companies often are too slow in developing and marketing new products. IBM, Xerox, Ford, and other companies have found that they have to reduce the number of steps and controls in the product development process in order to reach world class speed standards for new product development (Stalk and Hout, 1990).

The involvement-oriented approach emphasizes dealing with new situations at a low level and empowering employees to solve problems as close as possible to where they occur. Product development teams are used to speed products to market. The team approach involves individuals from different areas and gives them great amounts of freedom to develop products. Customer service problems are solved quickly by creating a world in which employees effectively deal with any problem that a customer may raise. Production problems are solved quickly by allowing employees to make ongoing adjustments in the production process rather than requiring them to submit a suggestion or ask permission to make a change. This approach obviously can produce faster responses, although it raises the issue of the quality of the response. If the employee who is making these on-line decisions is not well trained and committed to the organization, the results can be disastrous. If he or she is well trained and committed, however, allowing the employee to make decisions can lead to much faster response times than is possible in a situation in which employees must seek answers by going up the hierarchy, getting approvals, consulting staff experts, and ultimately following a new policy or procedure to handle the problem.

Overall, organizations using the involvement-oriented approach to management can respond more quickly to problems than organizations using the control-oriented approach. The exception to this statement appears to be situations in which a highly programmed and relatively complex response to a predictable environmental demand is needed. The control-oriented approach may well provide quicker responses in these situations. On the other hand, when an organization finds itself operating in an unpredictable and uncontrollable environment, the involvement-oriented approach is likely to allow it to respond more quickly because the approach empowers people at low levels to directly and immediately respond to ongoing events.

Innovation

The control-oriented approach typically relies on staff experts and senior managers for solving problems and thinking of innovations. The involvement-oriented approach, on the other hand, tries to structure work in the organization so that individuals throughout the organization can do this type of work. It can be argued that organizations using the control-oriented approach can more quickly make strategic changes and make them better than other organizations because the approach centralizes decision making in the hands of a few knowledgeable individuals. Decisions are usually made more quickly if made by a few people; involving many people and developing a consensus takes time and costs money. It is often easier to get two or three people to agree that a major change is needed than to build a consensus in a large, diverse organization.

However, the problem with producing change and innovation in a large bureaucratic organization is not in getting the decision made but in implementing the change (Tichy, 1983). Even though the decision to change may be made quickly, implementation does not necessarily follow immediately (Tichy and Charan, 1989). Often, it takes extensive reprogramming of control-oriented organizations to implement large-scale changes and innovations. In many cases, people in such organizations resist changes because changes threaten their existing comfortable situations. Since most individuals in these organizations have had no input in determining the change, they have no commitment to implement it or to see that it operates effectively.

If a major change requires employee acceptance for the change to be implemented, an involvement-oriented approach to management probably is superior both in terms of the speed with which the change can be implemented and the quality of the implementation. But the reverse is probably true if the change is one that does not require broad-scale acceptance and commitment by employees in order to be effective. For example, if buying and selling new businesses and changing the financing of an organization do not require broad-scale acceptance in order to be effective, then the involvement-oriented approach may not be the preferred approach. However, if commitment is needed and individuals throughout the organization have expertise relevant to the change, then employee involvement is preferred.

A decision to change the way a service is offered or the way a major part of an organization is structured may in fact be much more effectively implemented with the involvement-oriented approach. This approach is more likely to develop a consensus among members of an organization that change is needed and is correct, and it also can assure that all relevant outcomes are considered—which should result in a better decision as well as less resistance to change and quicker, more effective implementation of changes.

There are a number of reasons for believing that the involvement-oriented approach will, in most cases, produce more and better changes. First, because the involvement-oriented approach encourages innovation, change, and problem-solving activity to take place throughout the organization, it simply involves more people in the process, thus creating more opportunity for innovations to be developed. Second, in many cases, the people who actually work with customers and products know more about the way the organization operates than individuals in staff and senior management roles and, therefore, are in a better position to make suggestions and develop innovations than others are (Avishai and Taylor, 1989). They may not be able to totally redesign products or come up with new organizational designs, but they certainly can make changes and provide suggestions about ongoing modifications to the production and service process. Third, research shows that innovation is most common when successful innovation is rewarded and good risk taking is not punished (Kanter, 1989b). It is high in organizations that give employees freedom to think and experiment and in organizations that value learning and growth (Mohrman and Cummings, 1989). All these organizational characteristics are more likely to be true of an organization practicing an involvement-oriented rather than a control-oriented approach.

Labor Force

Two critical labor force issues must be considered in choosing a management approach. The first is the availability of labor, particularly skilled labor, and the second is the type of skills that the labor force has. A key issue in the United States is the potential shortage of skilled labor (Fullerton, 1989; Kutscher, 1989; Johnston, 1991).

An organization using an involvement-oriented approach to management has advantages in facing the first of these critical labor issues. Considerable research indicates that involvement-oriented organizations have much less turnover because they are much more attractive places to work than control-oriented organizations (Lawler, 1973, 1986; Mobley, 1982; Mowday, Porter, and Steers, 1982). Simply stated, most employees prefer to work in an environment where they are involved in the decision-making process; have challenging, interesting work; and are expected to be more than a pair of hands. This is particularly true of professionals such as engineers and scientists, who have the kind of skills that are in short supply. If individuals with valued technical skills are scarce, the involvement-oriented approach would seem to be the preferred choice. Organizations using this approach are much more likely to attract and retain these individuals and, of course, to use their skills and abilities in ways that justify their cost to the organization than are control-oriented organizations.

It is worth noting that even when labor is readily available the costs of employee turnover can be quite high. Research has shown that because of the selection activities and training involved and the lost production time, turnover costs are often several times an employee's monthly salary even when the work is relatively simple (Mirvis and Lawler, 1977; Seashore, Lawler, Mirvis, and Cammann, 1983).

Organizations using an involvement-oriented approach to management may be at a disadvantage, however, when facing the second critical labor issue: whether the population contains enough people with the right kind of skills for the approach to work. In a sense, this is not a problem for the control-oriented approach because, as was mentioned earlier, it requires relatively low skills on the part of much of the organization's work force. An organization only needs individuals who are willing to operate within a control-oriented environment and who can learn basic work skills.

The situation is quite different for organizations using the involvement-oriented approach: employees are expected to add value to the product or service in a number of respects and, to a substantial degree, manage themselves. The approach requires a supply of individuals who are capable of and interested in developing themselves and being responsible for their own performance. It is beyond the scope of this book to go into all the arguments about the problems of the U.S. educational system (see, for example, Business–Higher Education Forum, 1983; Johnston, 1987; Secretary's Commission on Achieving Necessary Skills, 1991). However, I can point out that if the educational system does not produce large numbers of individuals with the critical basic skills, the widespread adoption of the involvement-oriented approach will be hindered. At the present time, this is not a problem. So far in my work with firms, I have found that there is an adequate supply of employees who are able to work in involvement-oriented organizations, but this may change as more organizations change their management approach.

To be involved in an organization, employees need basic problem-solving, communication, and quantitative skills and must be willing to make a commitment to learning, developing, and being a responsible and productive member of an organization. If the schools, families, and communities do not produce individuals who have these characteristics, it may be at best excessively costly and at worst futile for many organizations to try to manage with an involvement-oriented approach. They can, of course, train employees in order to make up for the failings of the educational system, but this training can be expensive and, given the wage cost in the United States, hard to justify. The United States is paying wages that are equivalent to those paid in Japan and much of Europe, but in these countries organizations can expect to get a worker with good basic skills for those wages (Kutscher, 1989; Reich, 1991). Most organizations cannot afford to operate in any country in which they have to pay to develop skills that can be obtained for free elsewhere.

National Values

Most of the institutions in the United States and Europe are committed to democratic decision making, due process, freedom of speech, individual rights, and personal growth. The control-oriented model is based on an opposite set of principles. Freedom of speech and due process are rarely available in a control-oriented organization, and decision making is top down rather than democratic. Organizations in the United States and most of Europe have been allowed to use control methods for decades because the belief has been that these methods are the most efficient way to operate a large business organization (U.S. Department of Health, Education, and Welfare, 1973; Ewing, 1977, 1983; Slater and Bennis, 1964).

Many people have accepted the argument that democracy is inefficient and, therefore, cannot be trusted in business organizations that compete on a global basis. Obviously, this argument has lost much of its credibility since many control-oriented organizations have ceased to compete effectively in global markets. The exemption of corporations from the general values and principles of U.S. society seems to have or is about to run out. Companies simply no longer are delivering what they need to deliver to justify their countersocial ways of operating.

The involvement-oriented approach is highly congruent with democratic values about decision making and respect for individual rights. Those organizations that adopt it clearly find themselves in alignment with the values that dominate not just the United States and Europe but, increasingly, the entire world. In this respect, the involvement-oriented approach has a definite competitive advantage (perhaps the single most important advantage) over the control-oriented approach. Indeed, even if it is less efficient in some situations, it may be that because of national values, individuals and societies will feel that it is the right approach and, therefore, that it should be used. In a number of European countries, companies are mandated to practice involvement-oriented management.

The involvement-oriented approach is also directly

aligned with the strong entrepreneurial bent in the American culture. Fully implemented, the involvement-oriented approach should provide the opportunity for individuals to have a business-related entrepreneurial experience within the context of a large organization. The control-oriented approach, on the other hand, with its emphasis on top-down control, creates this experience only for a few relatively highly positioned senior managers. Thus, most individuals feel as though they are more of a cog in a large bureaucratic machine than as though they are part of a competitive venture that is winning or losing in the marketplace.

I need to make one final point about the advantage of using a management style that is congruent with the dominant societal values: it should lead to a reduction in two additional costs. First, because the approach is congruent with common values, new employees do not need to be socialized to a different value system. Second, the approach should reduce the number of confrontations that occur between business organizations and the laws and norms of the society. Autocratic organizations in democratic societies can find themselves spending considerable time in court defending themselves, for example, against charges of wrongful discharge, work-related stress, and discrimination, to mention some of the most prominent disputes that occur in the United States.

Effectiveness of the Involvement-Oriented Approach

So far we have compared the involvement-oriented and the control-oriented approaches in terms of their expected ability to deliver the kind of performance that is required in today's competitive business environment and in terms of how they fit the work force and the society. I have argued that, in general, the involvement-oriented approach should produce superior results. The exceptions to this argument are largely situations in which an organization produces relatively simple products or services and faces a relatively stable environment. In these cases, the control-oriented approach may have a competitive advantage if wage costs can be controlled and the right people can be found to work in the environment.

The argument that the involvement-oriented approach is superior in most situations is supported by some research evidence. However, relatively few studies have systematically compared the two approaches. One reason for the lack of comparative studies is that only a few large organizations have even tried to implement the involvement-oriented approach to management on an organizationwide basis. Motorola and Xerox, for example, have tried to implement it on a companywide basis. The approach has been much more popular in smaller companies—W. L. Gore, Donnelly Corporation, Herman Miller, Nucor Steel, and a host of other successful small and medium-sized companies serve as examples. In addition, even those organizations that have moved in this direction are still learning how to use the approach. Thus, when one compares involvement-oriented organizations with control-oriented organizations, the comparison is often between organizations that are at a mature place on the learning curve with respect to their management approach and those that are just at the beginning stages of learning how to implement their management approach. With this qualification in mind, let us turn to a consideration of the research evidence.

Most of the research (literally thousands of studies) has looked at the effectiveness of the many practices that are commonly part of an organizationwide installation of the involvement-oriented approach. Most of these studies have found positive results and support the argument that the approach is likely to produce better results than the control-oriented approach. For example, a great deal of research shows the effectiveness of gainsharing, work teams, job enrichment, and participative supervision (Cummings and Molloy, 1977; Lawler, 1986). Since these topics will be discussed in later chapters, the research on them will not be considered here. It is important to keep in mind, however, that just changing the way work is designed or changing only a few features of an organization is not the same as changing all the features of an organization to be consistent with the involvement-oriented approach.

Thus, the few studies that have looked at the overall operating effectiveness of organizations and compared this to the degree of employee involvement in the organizations are particularly interesting.

A major study by Denison (1984; 1990) looked at the economic performance of 40 companies. In general, Denison found that organizations that operated with the involvement-oriented model obtained superior economic performance. Another large-scale study by Mitchell, Lewin, and Lawler (1990) also found evidence that supports the view that involvement-oriented organizations perform better economically than control-oriented organizations. Kravetz (1988) studied the performance of 150 companies and scored them on the degree to which they adopted involvement-oriented management practices. Included in the scoring were measures of flattened hierarchies, management development, training, and participative management behavior. The results showed that the involvement-oriented firms performed much better than the rest on a wide variety of financial measures, including profitability, growth, and profit margin.

The U.S. General Accounting Office (1991) studied 20 companies that adopted total quality management programs (these programs will be discussed later in the book). Most of the policies these companies adopted as part of their programs increased employee involvement. The results must be interpreted with caution because rigorous statistical analyses were not possible; nevertheless, it is worth noting that the firms showed improvements in employee relations, customer satisfaction, productivity, and profitability.

Levine and Tyson (1990) did an extensive review of the studies that focus on economic performance and participation. Their review showed that high levels of participation are associated with better productivity and better economic performance. Their carefully worded conclusion is that "the empirical literature from economics, industrial relations, organizational behavior and other social sciences indicates that participation usually leads to small, short run improvements and performance and sometimes leads to significant long-lasting improvements in performance" (p. 203). They go on to note that participation is more likely to produce a significant, long-lasting increase in productivity when it involves decision-making processes of substantial influence rather than consultative arrangements. In other words, the more committed an organization is to employee involvement, the more it seems likely to obtain significant improvements in performance.

The empirical research on the involvement-oriented approach is both tantalizing and positive. What little research there is suggests that significant gains can be realized if employee involvement is effectively implemented and developed, but it does not provide definitive evidence that the involvement-oriented approach always produces superior results. For one thing, the studies are all correlational, and thus causation cannot be proven. There is reason to believe, however, that the causal link is from management style to performance. For example, some of the most successful involvement-oriented companies have always been managed with this approach (such as Tandem Computers and Sun Microsystems), while other companies have improved after they have changed to the involvement-oriented approach (such as Xerox and Motorola).

Given the arguments that I have presented here so far, it is unlikely that the involvement-oriented approach will always produce superior results, but, where it fits, it shows promise of being a superior approach to management. What is needed to finally prove the case and to produce widespread adoption of the approach is further development and further successful implementation of it.

The stage seems to be set for widespread implementation of employee involvement in many major corporations. A substantial amount of data is accumulating that argues that American companies and Western European companies are moving toward a more involvement-oriented approach to management (Lawler, Ledford, and Mohrman, 1989; Lawler, Mohrman, and Ledford, 1992). Survey after survey shows that people now perceive the approach as the most competitively effective management style and believe that adoption of it is an important way to gain a competitive advantage in the marketplace. For example, a recent study of industrial engineers found that they feel the greatest gains in productivity can now be realized by improved motivation and employee involvement (Institute of Industrial Engineers, 1990). Apparently, the great amount of writing that argues that management style can be a competitive advantage is making a difference.

Developing an involvement-oriented approach that can provide U.S. organizations with a competitive advantage is not simple. The approach needs to draw energy from the entrepreneurial spirit and desire for democratic decision making and individualism that is so strong in the U.S. culture, but also needs to allow for the substantial diversity and individual differences that exist in the United States. At the same time, it must allow for both innovation and relatively fast decision making and implementation. Obviously, no management approach can hope to be optimal on all these dimensions, but there is reason to believe that an approach that emphasizes high levels of employee involvement will produce the best overall results.

In the chapters that follow, the focus will be on the development of a high involvement-oriented approach to management. We will look at the major features of an organization and consider how they should be designed in order to fit with this approach.

PART TWO

Designing

Organizations,

Work,

and Rewards

Chapter Three

Create
a High-Involvement
Structure

To design an effective organization, managers must begin by considering the business strategy of the organization (Galbraith and Kazanjian, 1986). Depending upon the choices about strategy that organizations make, different organizational designs and structures are appropriate, for one simple reason: different designs produce different behaviors and different outcomes. As has already been indicated, the involvement-oriented design does not fit all business strategies and all situations. In particular, it fits strategies that emphasize high-quality products and services, speed of response, and innovation and that require at least competitive if not lower than competitive costs.

Any organization's design must be guided by much more detailed specifications of the type of behaviors needed than simply to say high quality, low cost, and speed are required. An organization must specify exactly what is meant by quality, what kind of costs are acceptable, and just how fast the organization needs to get products and services to market. Beyond this, it needs to look more specifically at which kinds of behaviors are likely to produce high quality, low cost, and speed given the type of product or service that the organization wants to deliver.

The challenge in designing a high-involvement organization is to develop a good understanding of what it takes to compete and then to convert that strategy into specific policies

51

and structures that will yield the correct kind of performance. Because organizations must be custom designed, it is impossible to specify in detail what the structure of a high-involvement organization should look like. It is possible, however, to indicate some of the general principles that should be considered in designing the structures of high-involvement organizations.

The Concept of Fit

The concept of *fit* is perhaps the most important concept in the organizational design literature. It first appeared as early as 1950 and has increasingly gained prominence and popularity (Leavitt, 1965). In many respects, it is a simple concept, and perhaps that is why it is so useful in the area of organizational design and effectiveness. A number of fit models are portrayed in the literature (see, for example, Galbraith, 1973, 1977; Nadler and Tushman, 1988). They all specify core parts or systems of an organization (from as few as three to as many as seven or more) and argue that an organization's effectiveness is strongly influenced by how well these parts fit together.

The current thinking about organizations argues that no one part of an organization can be evaluated without knowing its role in the whole system. Organization design is like the design of a car or any complex piece of machinery; it is impossible to specify whether a car will be effective without knowing how the engine, transmission, body, and so on fit together and complement each other. And it is impossible to evaluate whether the car is effective without specifying the kind of performance that will meet the needs of the customer. Specifying needed performance involves strategy and is the starting point for fit. An organization should first specify what business it is involved in, who its customers are, and how it intends to perform in order to gain competitive advantage (Porter, 1985).

The first step in determining fit is to define the parts of an organization that are to be included in the model. My preference is to work with a relatively small number of major organizational features rather than to think in terms of the more complex models that are sometimes used. The major elements of an organization that I think need to fit in order to have an effective organizational system are people, task/technology, information processes, rewards, and organizational structure.

People

The characteristics and abilities of employees are critical in deciding how any organizational practice or policy will affect employee behavior. Particularly relevant is the research on employee motivation, which clearly shows that different employees value different things (Lawler, 1973). This research is especially important for the high-involvement approach to management because the approach depends on attracting and retraining individuals who are motivated by intrinsic rewards such as challenging work, feelings of accomplishment, and personal growth. The approach also often requires individuals who have relatively strong social needs because the work in involvement-oriented organizations often is done in teams. In addition, organizations using the approach typically need individuals who are capable of self-management and have relatively high levels of self-discipline.

What about individuals who need authority, formal power, and hierarchical status symbols? As a general rule, these people are not well suited for involvement-oriented organizations. Managerial jobs in particular need to be filled by individuals who are comfortable with influencing others with their expertise rather than with their rank in the organization.

High-involvement management places substantial demands on employees in terms of their ability to solve problems, contribute to group discussions, and, of course, perform a wide array of technical work-related activities that contribute to the organization's basic effectiveness. Organizations using this management approach also need individuals who are willing and able to continue to learn and develop, since involvement-oriented organizations stress continuous development and improvement.

Critical to having the right employees are human resources systems, including selection, training, and career development systems. These systems are important because, among other things, they determine what kind of people will be in the organization and how adequately individuals will perform the tasks or jobs that are assigned to them. Ultimately, for an organization to be effective, these systems must be used to match the characteristics of the individuals in the organization to the demands of work tasks, the leadership approach, and the information flow. They are the organizational mechanisms that assure that the organization has employees who have the right talents, motives, and orientations to make the hardware of the organization—that is, the task designs, the structure, and the information systems—work effectively.

Task/Technology

A number of researchers have categorized the major types of technologies that can be used by an organization to implement its strategy (see, for example, Woodward, 1965; Thompson, 1967). Most of them identify *process technology* as one major type of technology. In process technology, products or services flow continuously through the organization. Examples of process technologies include electricity generating plants, most chemical plants, and many food plants because products flow through these plants on a continuous basis using automated equipment and sophisticated control rooms. A second type of technology is *sequential production technology*. In this type of technology, parts of products or services are created at a number of workstations and are passed from one individual or area to another. An assembly line is a good example of a sequential production process. In a third type of technology, *custom production technology*, the product or service is individually created, usually by a small number of people, to the specifications of a particular customer.

The kind of technology that an organization uses has a tremendous impact on the type of jobs that are created in the organization. The choice of technology is a critical point because, as will be discussed in the next chapter, high-involvement organizations depend upon creating work settings in which the work itself has characteristics that make it intrinsically motivating. In the absence of these characteristics, it is hard to develop a high-involvement organization. Thus, the members of an organization must make careful choices about which technology the organization uses.

To a degree, the choice of technology is determined by decisions about what products or services the organizations will offer, but it need not be completely determined by this decision. Automobiles, for example, can be produced in a number of different ways (such as on assembly lines as they are produced by most companies and by work teams as they are produced by Volvo), as can many consumer and industrial products. Similarly, services can be delivered in many different ways. Some products and services, however, can be produced economically in only one way. For example, gasoline can only be produced in highly automated production facilities.

Information Processes

The communication flow within an organization is critical to any organization, particularly a high-involvement one. As will be discussed in a later chapter, for a high-involvement organization to operate effectively, information must flow to employees at low levels in the organization. The capability for horizontal communication among individuals at all levels in the organization also is often critical. And many kinds of information, including suggestions and information on employee attitudes, need to flow upward in the organization. Whether this information is conveyed through memos, meetings, electronic mail, videotapes, or the telephone is not critical. It is critical, however, that employees at high levels in the organization receive this information because otherwise they are, in effect, "flying blind."

Rewards

The reward system of an organization has an important influence on the types of employees in an organization as well as on their motivation (Lawler, 1990b). For an organization to operate effectively, the reward system must pay individuals so that they behave in ways that fit the strategic intent of the organization. Reward systems can support and reinforce structures and cultures in an organization or work against them. The two most critical features of an organization's pay system are the degree to which it is tied to performance and how it determines the worth of an individual employee. Later chapters deal with each of these issues.

Organizational Structure

The final element of the fit model is the organizational structure, or design. Organizational structure can best be thought of as constituting the basic architecture or hardware of the organization. Deciding on an organizational structure is like deciding on whether to build a high-rise or a low-rise building, whether to have large offices or small offices, and so forth. The structure is pictured by the organizational chart and, ultimately, is a critical factor in determining how involvement-oriented an organization can and should be. Structures differ vertically as well as in the types of horizontal divisions they make. As will be discussed later in this chapter, some organizational designs simply make it impossible to create an organization that is involvement-oriented, and others virtually demand that an organization be involvement-oriented.

Information, Knowledge, Power, and Rewards

A useful way to think about fit among the different parts of an organization is in terms of how the parts affect the following four features or elements of an organization:

> *Information* about processes, quality, customer feedback, events, and business results
>
> *Knowledge* of the work, the business, and the total work system
>
> *Power* to act and make decisions about the work in all its aspects
>
> *Rewards* tied to business results and growth in capability and contribution

Congruence exists when individuals at all levels in an organization are rewarded based upon how effectively they exercise the power that is associated with their position and they have the information and knowledge to exercise their power effectively. In effective top-down organizations, congruence usually exists because at the lowest levels individuals have little information, knowledge, power, and rewards, and at the top, individuals have large amounts of information, knowledge, power, and rewards. Because congruence exists, top-down organizations can be effective if in fact the type of behavior they produce fits the strategic objectives of the organization.

In the high-involvement approach, congruence is achieved by locating significant amounts of information, knowledge, power, and rewards at low levels of the organization (Lawler, 1986). This approach is not designed to take away these elements from the top of the organization but rather to spread the same kind of information, knowledge, power, and rewards that are present at the top to lower levels of the organization. Researchers have long argued about whether it is possible to spread these four elements, particularly power, throughout an organization or whether they are best thought of in a zero sum sense—that is, as a fixed pie that has to be divided up (see, for example, Likert, 1961). My conclusion from the literature and from my own work is that these elements are not in fact fixed commodities in an organization—they can be expanded so that there is more to share.

Rewards are perhaps the easiest element to expand. If an organization can operate more effectively, rewards can in fact be expanded because more revenue is generated to share among all of the participants in the organization. Knowledge and information can also be expanded in the organization by having better communication systems and making an investment in training and communication.

Perhaps the most difficult of these four elements to expand is power. Some organizational theorists have thought of power as a finite quantity that can only be shared and not expanded (Weber, 1947). Although the evidence is not definitive on this point, my view is that in fact power can be expanded through effective organizational design (Likert, 1961). The argument for this point of view rests partially on the idea that the power that individuals feel they have at the top of a hierarchical organization that is managed in a traditional way is often an illusion. Although they have the power to make a wide range of decisions without consulting others or involving others, these individuals often do not have real power since they do not have the ability to implement the decisions that they make.

If, on the other hand, individuals at the top of an organization share power by involving others in decisions, they may not be able to make the decisions in the same way that they could in a top-down organization. They may feel as though they have lost power. However, when decisions are made in a more participative manner, the decisions are more likely to be implemented and to actually affect the operations of the organization. Thus, if we consider power to be the ability to influence what happens in the organization — as I do — it is possible to expand the amount of power that is available in an organization by involving more individuals in decision making.

If any one, two, or three of the four elements of information, knowledge, power, and rewards are out of alignment, the organization will lose effectiveness (Lawler, 1986). In the case of a high-involvement organization, this argument is perhaps most obvious when only one of the four elements is moved down the organizational hierarchy. For example, simply sharing power with low-level employees in an organization is both foolish and dangerous. It means giving employees the power to make decisions without giving them the knowledge and information to make good decisions and without holding them accountable through reward systems. Moving rewards to low levels in the organization by rewarding employees for organizational performance is not likely to produce any significant gains in organizational performance unless the employees have the power, information, and knowledge to understand what is being rewarded and to influence it. Similarly, training employees in order to develop their knowledge is a waste of money if the employees cannot use the knowledge because they do not have the power and information to use it. Also, giving individuals information that does not affect their rewards, that is not relevant to the power that they have, and that they do not have a great deal of knowledge about is not likely to contribute to organizational effectiveness. Indeed, sharing this information is only likely to contribute to the bureaucratic work load in the organization because someone has to disseminate the information.

I could elaborate on how having two of the four elements in congruence leaves out important parts of what is necessary for an organization to be effective, but the point is obvious. However, the situation is a bit different if three of the four elements are in balance. One pattern deserves special comment because it sometimes results from efforts to create a high-involvement organization.

Often, organizational designs call for moving substantial information, knowledge, and power to low levels in the organization without changing the reward system. This is a precarious long-term strategy because it fails to produce accountability for how individuals exercise their power and few tangible rewards depend upon their learning the necessary skills. This strategy can work, particularly in the short term, because individuals will learn and perform well simply because it is satisfying to do so. However, they may not focus sufficiently on the type of learning and performance that will make the organization economically effective. Long-term equity and motivation problems can also result if rewards are not moved downward.

Congruence between the four elements can be stated in terms of a simple equation. The degree to which information, knowledge, power, and rewards are present at any level in an organization can be expressed on a scale of one to zero, with zero meaning none of the element is present and one meaning that a great deal is present. Rather than adding the amounts together to determine how much involvement exists, it is more appropriate to multipy the scores for each element, since I have argued that if one element is missing the presence of the other three has little or no value in terms of employee involvement. This gives us the following equation:

$$\text{Involvement} = \text{Information} \times \text{Knowledge} \times \text{Power} \times \text{Rewards}$$

Organizational Structure

The formal structure of an organization is a critical component in determining how much information, knowledge, power, and rewards can and will be present at all levels of the organization. As a general rule, "small is beautiful" when it comes to employee involvement (Hammer, 1990; Schumacher, 1973; Boyett and Conn, 1991). The individual entrepreneur has the ultimate involvement in an organization. The challenge is to design organizations that can be big when they need to be to gain competitive advantages but small in terms of letting everyone feel as though they are involved and can contribute to and influence the success of the organization. The smaller the organization, the easier it is to create a setting in which everyone gets all the necessary information about the organization, understands how the organization functions, can influence decisions, and can share in the rewards.

The "tallness," or vertical hierarchy, of an organizational structure is one important element that influences how the organization operates. Equally important is how functions and areas of business are grouped together, or the horizontal dimension of the hierarchy. As we will see, both the vertical and horizontal elements of an organization's structure influence how much employee involvement is possible.

Vertical Design

The number of hierarchical levels in an organization is a particularly critical determinant of how information, knowledge, power, and rewards are allocated. Specifically, the more levels in an organization, the more difficult it is to move information, knowledge, power, and rewards to low levels. Although the amount of these elements can be expanded, there is a point of diminishing returns as far as creating more of the elements. In fact, to create more of these elements, an organization must often have only a few levels of hierarchy. As these elements move down the levels, employees at each level tend to pick off their "fair share," and by the time the elements reach the lowest level in the organization, little information, knowledge, power, and rewards may be left.

The lack of widespread employee involvement is almost inevitable in large organizations. The hierarchies in them rob individuals of the information, knowledge, power, and rewards they need in order to feel that they are an important part of a business. Organizations that need to be large to compete effectively must have flat hierarchies so they will feel small to employees who are responsible for satisfying customers and running a successful business.

Closely related to the tallness of an organization's structure is its *span of control*. This term is used to indicate the number of employees reporting to a supervisor and is very descriptive of the way management is traditionally viewed. With spans of control of five or six, for example, supervisors often can control and coordinate the actions of their subordinates while employees are put in a position of simply following directions. Although six may sound like a small span, it is not unusual. AT&T used to consider six to be the optimal span in most parts of the company, and many organizations I have analyzed have average spans that are smaller. Some organizations have a number of one-to-one reporting relationships.

A small span of control and close supervision creates two problems. First, employees often perform their work poorly because they are not motivated (Hackman and Oldham, 1980). In addition, they are greatly underutilized. Their supervisor is responsible for coordinating their activities and motivating and controlling their actions. If they could do these tasks themselves, a whole level of management would be unnecessary and the organization would save money in labor costs and overhead.

Much of the argument for employee involvement rests on the point that when individuals at the lowest levels of the organization become involved in the business, they can do much of the work that is typically done by a supervisor, making the supervisor unnecessary and leading to superior performance of the work (Lawler, 1988b). Often employees can coordinate their own work better than supervisors can. And when they feel responsible for a whole and meaningful piece of work, employees are motivated to perform better and in more positive ways than if they are rewarded and punished by a supervisor. I am suggesting that with a flat hierarchy, business involvement can be substituted for rules and controls.

There are no simple guidelines that specify the right number of levels and correct spans of control. This is probably for the best because I am regularly surprised to find that organizations have gone further toward flat hierarchies than I would have recommended and it has worked. Some plants, for example, have only a plant manager; everyone else is a team member. I have seen other plants with spans of management of over one hundred. United Parcel Service (UPS) has only six levels of hierarchy, even though it has over 200,000 employees and operates a global business. Union Pacific Railroad has reduced its levels from nine to three, even though it has 30,000 employees. This is in notable contrast to many hierarchical organizations that have twelve or more levels of management.

I believe that most organizations, even very large ones, should be able to operate effectively with no more than six or seven levels of management. Usually spans of management should never be less than fifteen and, in most cases, should be larger. Flat organizational structures do not just happen; they have to be designed. It is easiest to design an organization from the beginning to have a flat management structure. For example, Nucor Steel, which has a headquarters staff of less than 30 and over 5,000 employees, never had a tall structure.

During the 1980s, General Electric worked hard to reduce its hierarchy. It first reduced positions and levels but found that the organization still contained a great amount of hierarchical work, more in fact than the remaining managers could do. The next step was to get the unnecessary hierarchical work out of the organization (Hammer, 1990; Tichy and Charan, 1989). Unnecessary reports, meetings, and approval levels were identified and eliminated. General Electric's 1990 annual report discusses the changes and notes that the company has been "pulling the dandelions of bureaucracy for a decade, but they don't come up easily and they'll be back next week if you don't keep after them. Yes, we've taken out a lot of structure—staff, span breakers, planners, checkers, approvers—and yet we have by no means removed it all." The report goes on to state that by the year 2000 the company will have one-third fewer management positions than it has today.

Horizontal Design

The critical horizontal design decisions begin with deciding how the organization is structured at the very top. If the top levels of the organization are grouped around functional areas such as sales, marketing, manufacturing, engineering, personnel, and so on, it is very difficult to produce a flat organizational structure that develops business involvement at the lowest levels (Nadler and Tushman, 1988). Functionalization, like large size and hierarchy, is the enemy of involvement.

In essence, structure based on function creates a world in which the business only "comes together" at the top. In many respects, these structures are like the planned economies that many communist countries have developed and abandoned. They sound great in theory, but they are impossible to manage. Such a structure creates high need for coordination and integration throughout the organization because no one feels responsible for satisfying the customer and seeing that the business is successful. Thus, the organization creates hierarchy, rules, regulations, and complicated information systems. Employees at low levels of the organization typically are working only on one small part of the total business process. As a result, they are not in a position to supervise themselves and are not doing the kind of work that is motivating and involving because it is clearly related to the success and failure of the organization. Their only "customers" are other functions, their boss, or professional leaders in their field whom they want to impress. Thus, they do not have the full business experience of producing a product or service, satisfying a customer, and being held accountable for revenues and profits.

Organizations structured around function can be effective in dealing with products and environments that are relatively stable and require predictable volumes of output. They are also appropriate when the organization has a single product or service. They get in trouble when behavior cannot be specified from the top and when products and services are diverse. In short, such a structure is best when the organization's task is to do one thing well in a stable environment over a long period of time and, of course, if employees are willing and can be motivated to do a small piece of the total business process.

Even in organizations that need a structure based on function, some employee involvement certainly is possible. For example, a company can establish internal customer relationships by having each function view other functions as suppliers and as customers. This strategy can allow individuals to be motivated by serving their customers and contributing to excellence in their particular function. It can help start a market economy inside the firm and help even the organization with a function-based structure gain some of the advantages of involvement. The organization can also form teams with membership across functions to coordinate the activities of the different functions and, at the same time, give employees a sense of involvement. Still, it is difficult to have a high level of involvement in the organization's business because most individuals in the organization end up without any external customers and any real sense of the financial contribution of their function to the organization's success. It is usually impossible to establish a bottom-line financial measurement system for groups such as accounting, personnel, and sales.

The best approach to developing involvement at all levels of the organization is for the organization to be structured around products, services, customers, or some combination of these three. The key is for organizations to do everything possible to create small profit-and-loss centers, or mini-enterprises, within the organization. Union Pacific Railroad took this approach to reduce levels of hierarchy; it created thirty high-authority field units with customers and bottom lines. This change made many levels of hierarchy and a number of control systems unnecessary because the customers, market, and bottom line took their place. AT&T has even taken a step in this direction by breaking itself up into nineteen business units, most of which have external customers who will "control" the organization.

The idea of breaking large organizations into small mini-enterprises has been carried to an extreme by Mills (1991). He suggests units, or clusters, that vary in size from 30 to 50 employees. He presents case studies from General Electric, Du Pont, Swiss Airlines, and British Petroleum that show how these units can be created and how they can be effective. Supportive data also are provided by the case of Asea Brown Boveri (ABB). This organization has broken its work force of 240,000 people into 4,500 profit centers (Taylor, 1991).

In order to involve employees, a company should usually organize profit centers around customers, for one simple reason: this structure makes it easiest for the organization to align its employees with an external customer who can give feedback and who makes purchasing decisions. Employees can then deal with cost and revenue and identify their competitors. Employees also receive feedback on how their part of the business is doing and gain a sense of the entrepreneurial and business environment in which the organization operates. This in turn puts the competitive marketplace in the position of controlling employee behavior and makes most hierarchical controls unnecessary. The same conditions can usually be created by organizing the structure around products or services, although this approach has its limitations when the organization produces a number of related products that go to the same customers.

Discussing the many variations that are possible in the horizontal design of organizations is far beyond the scope of this book. Thus, I will not analyze which of the many possible approaches is right for particular business situations. My intention here is to emphasize the importance of creating a business experience for all employees. This usually means organizing around customers or products. For example in a large multi-business organization, employee involvement is maximized when autonomous divisions exist that make a particular product or serve a particular group of customers.

Dana Corporation represents an interesting example of a company that is well structured to fit its business and to allow employee involvement. It produces a large number of products for the automobile and truck industry. Basically, it is structured on a product basis. Each of its relatively small divisions has substantial ownership over a product from beginning to end. A division can serve a customer without having any relationship to other divisions in the company. This structure enables the corporation to extend the entrepreneurial experience down to groups of a few hundred employees, which have their own products and, in effect, their own bottom line. Not surprisingly, Dana has an extremely small corporate staff of only a few hundred employees, which does not try to add value by coordinating the different business entities. The corporate staff acts much more like a bank making investments in autonomous businesses and adding up the results. This design is optimal for involving employees but will work only where the business situation allows this type of independent product line or customer orientation.

The key determinant of how far an organization can go in involving employees in all aspects of the business is the degree of interdependency among the different products and services that it offers (Lawrence and Lorsch, 1967). The more interdependency there is, the more difficult it is to involve individuals at low levels in all activities of the business and to have small units that are controlled by the market (Galbraith, 1973). For example, if an organization is selling computer services it may need to offer the customer software services, maintenance services, hardware, and an array of consulting services. In addition, the customer quite rightly expects and wants these services to be integrated, otherwise there is little value in using a single organization to provide them.

A second factor that may influence how far an organization can go toward creating small business units that stand alone is the size and complexity of the products and services that are offered. Because of their size and complexity, products like automobiles and airplanes cannot be economically produced by small, multifunction business units. Certain amounts of functional specialization are required to support the core competence of the organization and a large number of employees may be necessary to produce the product (Prahalad and Hamel, 1990). If integrating the services and products that the organization offers is a key element for organizational effectiveness, the organization needs to put in place some mechanisms that coordinate products and services. Similarly, if integrating large numbers of high level functional specialists is critical, coordinating mechanisms need to be put in place. In these cases, employees at the corporate management level can add value to the products and services of the organization by creating *coordinating structures* such as task forces and project management teams.

An involvement-oriented approach can still be adopted by large integrated organizations, but the opportunity for involvement that is present in the small corner drugstore devoted to offering all services to a defined customer base will not be available. Serving the customer may require the coordinated action of hundreds or even thousands of individuals and may require that individuals get involved in the business at a much greater level of aggregation. As I will discuss next, one alternative is to create a front-end–back-end organization or a network organization, since they can make high levels of involvement possible even when large size is needed.

Front-End–Back-End Organizations

An interesting alternative to organizational structures based on customers or products is the *front-end–back-end organization,* which combines a focus on customers and products at the same level in the organization. The emphasis here is on combining the two at the same level. It is not uncommon for organizations to first divide themselves by products (such as life insurance versus health insurance) and then at the next level down to divide themselves by customers (such as individuals versus businesses) who will be using that particular product. More unusual is the organization that structures itself simultaneously by products or services and customers. In essence, this type of structure can be implemented by creating a "back end" of the organization that produces the products and services sold and marketed by the "front end" of the organization, which is organized around customers.

This type of organization has some definite advantages in involving employees, particularly in comparison to an organization structured purely by function. It creates the possibility of establishing meaningful internal customer relationships between the front end and the back end of the organization and thus allows employees in both the front and the back to have a sense of involvement in the business.

The production end of the organization is focused on developing and manufacturing its products or services and must face the market test of being able to "sell them" to the part of the organization that interacts with the customers. The employees who interact with the customers, on the other hand, have a business experience because they deal with suppliers, all or many of whom usually are inside the organization (it is possible and sometimes desirable to let them use external suppliers), and with customers who have certain needs and demands. Their challenge is to put together combinations of products and services that will satisfy their customers' needs.

The front-end–back-end model can also be applied to many service organizations. For example, one group can be responsible for developing and producing services while another is in charge of marketing and delivering the services to particular customer bases. Customer bases can be determined either by geography or by different market orientations. In financial service businesses, one part of the organization can be charged with servicing financial instruments, credit card accounts, and so on while another part of the organization is focused on selling and marketing to particular customer groups. The front-end–back-end approach to organizing has become increasingly popular in organizations that are trying to sell complex sets of products and services to multiple customer bases.

The computer industry is one in which this approach often makes sense and can be used instead of an approach based on function. The different customers that this industry serves demand different combinations of products and services. In many cases, it is impossible to manufacture specialized computers for each market niche. The solution to this problem is to create a sales, service, and marketing organization that is focused on different customers. For example, the leading computer companies today typically have one group of employees that focuses on the airline industry, another that focuses on banking and financial services, and so on. Meanwhile, the production end of the organization is focused on producing particular computer products.

In front-end–back-end organizations, employees at the corporate level or senior management level face the challenge of facilitating the interaction between the parts of the organization that are producing the products and services and those that are marketing and selling them to defined customers. Although this particular organizational design does not bring the total business experience to all employees, it still can motivate employees in both the customer service or front end of the business and those in the production areas. Both have to meet market tests, even if these tests are to some degree internal market tests. These market tests, however, often are compelling enough to provide employees with a strong sense of motivation and self-control. Thus, some of the types of overhead and management structure that are normally in place in a hierarchical organization are not needed because the market controls operations.

Network Organizations

In the 1980s, a form of organization that has been called *network organization*, or the *value-added partnership*, was developed and became popular (Miles and Snow, 1986; Johnston and Lawrence, 1988). This approach to organizational design has also rather derisively been called the *hollow corporation*. Basically, this approach is built on the principle that in many types of businesses no corporation can do all the steps in the business process well and that the best organizing approach is to do something extremely well and build relationships with others to do other parts of the business process.

The most visible examples of the network approach are

Apple Computer, Reebok, Nike, and Benneton, which do little or no manufacturing. Instead, they have placed themselves at the center of a network of companies who manufacture, sell, and transport products. They do the design, marketing, and advertising for an array of products that go to a particular customer base and serve as integrators of a network of organizations. Other organizations in the network serve as specialists in manufacturing, distribution, and the other functions that are needed to complete the network.

In some cases, network integrators run multiple product lines and are broken into divisions along these product lines. Because so much of the work in the value-added chain is done by others, a very small organization often can produce enormous sales volumes. It is not uncommon, for example, to have hundreds of thousands of dollars of sales per employee. In 1990, Sun Microsystems, with only 12,000 employees, had sales of $3 billion.

Although network organizations do not contain the full array of business functions, they can produce high levels of involvement and are an attractive alternative to large functional organizations. Their structure allows employees to be involved in a business experience. In fact, a much higher percentage of the employees of these organizations can have the experience of dealing with external vendors and external customers than is typically true in multifunction organizations. Although the organization that coordinates the network may not be directly involved in activities such as manufacturing, someone in the organization deals with manufacturing organizations, draws up the contracts, worries about pricing, and in essence coordinates the business from manufacturing through sales. Other organizations in the network that specialize in activities like manufacturing can also offer employees an involving business experience because they face competition when they sell their service or product to the network integrators. Thus, networking can produce a challenging and complete business experience for the employees in a number of organizations, even though no single organization is responsible for all activities with respect to the production and sales of a product or service.

In some cases, using the network approach can make it possible for organizations that otherwise would not be logical candidates to be managed in a high-involvement way to use this approach to management. Network organizations often market and design products that cannot be competitively manufactured in a high-involvement work setting because they tend to require large amounts of low-cost, unskilled labor. This is typically true, for example, in the garment industry and in the athletic shoe market. It is hard to see how many of the manufacturing activities in these businesses can be structured to facilitate high levels of employee involvement. Thus, the best approach often is to place these jobs in low-wage countries and to create simple, repetitive, machine-paced jobs.

Through the network approach, different steps in a value-added chain that goes from raw material to delivered service or product can be managed in the way that is best for the particular step. In addition, each organization has the experience of facing external customers. Different steps can also be managed individually in an organization structured around functions or steps in the value-added chain, but a *double-breasted approach* must be used: some operations are managed in a high-involvement manner while others are managed in a more traditional top-down manner. Such a system can be very difficult to manage. On the other hand, an organization that is at the center of the network can be managed in a high-involvement way, and it can easily deal with suppliers that are managed in either the same or different ways. In essence, networking allows organizations to realize the best management approach for whatever step in the business process they are involved in.

Role of Staff

For employees to feel that they own a particular business and are involved in it, they need to have information about how it is operating, and they need to make the critical decisions that influence its direction. If these decisions are made by the legal, finance, or some other staff group, the line managers and employees who must carry out the decisions will not develop a high level of commitment to the decisions. Thus, for employee involvement to have its desired impact of developing widespread commitment to the success of an organization, staff groups need to be in a strategic support role. They need to provide information and expertise to the actual decision makers, not make the decisions or become obstacles to change and innovation.

The increased use of computers in businesses can help move staff members toward a role of providing strategic guidance and information. Through the use of computers and networking, line employees can have access to more data and can make more of the ongoing operational decisions themselves. This can free staff members to do creative strategic work because they do not have to spend so much time doing basic analysis and support work. It also can help to reduce the number of staff members that are needed, facilitating the move toward a "lean" organization (Savage, 1990).

The need for quick decision making almost mandates that staff members leave the decision making to the line employees and, in particular, to those individuals who have direct contact with the product and the customer. Because staff members are removed from the customer and product, they are not in a position to control decision making and to make many of the ongoing operational decisions that need to be made. If they control decision making, the process inevitably slows down to the point at which the organization cannot be responsive to a dynamic and rapidly changing environment.

Historically, staff members have been asked to develop decision-making rules that will control the actions of the line management group. With the complexities and rapid changes that exist in many business environments, it is impossible for even the best staff members to anticipate all the scenarios that can develop and to prepare appropriate decision-making rules. Inevitably, situations will arise that cannot be programmed and that require effective on-line decisions to be made. This argument strongly suggests that staff members should provide information and advice that will help line managers and employees make decisions rather than impose rules, regulations, and constraints that dictate the decisions made by them. SAS and Nordstrom have recognized this principle and have done away with the procedure manuals that are present in many organizations. They simply tell employees to satisfy the customer (Carlzon, 1987).

In a number of respects, putting staff members in an advisory and support role represents a return to the traditional concept of what a staff member is supposed to do. Early writings on the role of staff members did not view the staff as a control device but as an aide to the line employees, who were to provide critical information and expertise (Weber, 1947). In many organizations, however, the staff has evolved to the point where instead of helping the line, it has become an obstacle to getting things done because it can veto decisions.

Lean Structure

The cost competition that most organizations face puts pressure on them to have relatively lean staffing levels in all areas. In many businesses, labor costs are a major expense, particularly when the organizations operate in high-wage countries. Operating in a high-wage country is by itself a strong argument for limiting the number of staff members who do not directly add value to the product or to the services of an organization, particularly since staff employees often command relatively high salaries.

The argument for a lean staff structure, however, goes further. Staff members can create low-value work or work with no added value that needs to be done by those individuals who actually are in a position to add value to the organization's product or services (Tichy and Charan, 1989). Each staff person, in a sense, should be looked upon as a double cost: not only is there the cost of employing that person, there is the cost associated with the work that the staff member creates for others to do.

Each and every activity carried out by the staff must be subjected to a careful value-added analysis. This value-added analysis should look at the staff work and ask whether its total cost is offset by a comparable benefit. Increasingly, organizations are doing such analyses. In some cases, the analysis justifies the cost of activities that the staff carries out (Ellig, 1989). In most cases, an analysis reveals some activities that the staff is performing that can be better carried out by the line employees or that do not need to be carried out at all. Sometimes, a third set of activities that can best be done by contractors is also identified. Contracting out these activities often reinforces the sense of every part of the organization having a customer and needing to meet a market test because it converts some of the staff activities into services that are purchased.

In many respects, a value-added analysis is not and should not be looked upon as a one-time activity. Most large organizations need to do these analyses regularly because of the tendency of staff groups to grow and add to their numbers. Only by constantly asking and re-asking value-added questions can an organization keep its staff groups at an appropriate size and position.

Once the staff members move from focusing on functional control activities to providing strategic guidance and information, their work load may vary considerably from time to time. The demand for strategic analysis and planning may not be constant throughout the business cycles that an organization faces. At times, additional help is needed to analyze new business areas, new products, new markets, and so on. At other times, there may be little need for this kind of analytical work. Thus, the staff group not only needs to be lean, it also needs to be flexible. An obvious and potentially effective way to make a staff group flexible is to rely heavily on temporary consulting help to carry out large analytical and strategic activities. Another approach is to rotate employees from the line organization into the staff for temporary assignments.

Customer Orientation

The staff should be assessed in terms of the quality and cost of the services that it provides to its customers. The customers, of course, typically are the line employees and in some cases other parts of the staff group. Two trends point toward this assessment of staff departments. One is the movement toward quality, with its emphasis on the importance of everyone having a customer.

The other is the tendency to view staff departments as providing strategic support, information, and analysis rather than exercising control. A customer-focused assessment follows quite naturally from the arguments made earlier that each activity of the staff should be analyzed from a value-added point of view. Once the value-added analysis is completed, it makes sense to ask the line employees how adequately the staff carries out its activities. In essence, once the decision has been made to continue the staff's activities, then the stage is set for the customers of the activities to provide customer satisfaction data and for the staff to provide cost and cost-effectiveness data.

A number of companies, including Corning, Pfizer, and General Electric, are now asking line managers to assess their satisfaction with the various services offered by the human resources department (Ellig, 1989). This process gives the staff members feedback and also allows the line employees to have influence over the behavior of the staff members. It can also be used to trigger a quality analysis of the services offered by the staff if the line employees are dissatisfied with these services. Problem-solving groups can be set up, and work processes analyzed and improved. Such a process has the desirable effect of putting pressure on the staff to improve its performance and to be more accountable. Ultimately, this process can lead to more staff services being contracted out.

Decentralization

Once the decision has been made that many or all of the staff members should be in a support role and that the staff has as its customers the line employees, the logical next step is to decentralize the staff as much as possible. Some organizations do need a strong centralized staff to maintain consistency and competencies in technology, finance, and human resources management (Prahalad and Hamel, 1990). Nevertheless, in most large organizations that are involved in more than one business, most of the staff members should be positioned in a business unit. Such positioning is the only way to ensure that staff members will be close to their customers and that they will be in a position to provide responsive customer service and have a sense of involvement in the business. If the staff is located centrally at the corporate level, there will always be conflicts produced by the staff's distance and lack of business knowledge.

Locating staff members at the business level also creates a possibility for strong business teams that share much of the responsibility for managing the business. The business team approach in turn creates the potential for staff members to become intimately involved in understanding and contributing to the operations of the particular business, which should allow them to provide the kind of ongoing strategic direction and support that the business needs—in essence, to become true business partners.

Chapter Four

Identify
Work Design
Alternatives

Central to the relationship between an individual and a work organization is the nature of the work that the individual is asked to do. A considerable number of research studies have shown that the nature of the task individuals are asked to perform has a strong influence on how motivated they are to do their work, how committed they are to the organization, and, ultimately, how effectively they perform (see, for example, Hackman and Oldham, 1980; Griffin, 1991). Poor work designs can result in dissatisfied, poorly motivated employees, who need to be closely supervised and controlled if they are to do even minimally acceptable work. On the other hand, good work designs can lead to highly motivated, satisfied employees, who, in many respects, are self-managing and require little supervision and direction.

One determinant of the nature of an individual's work is the overall structure of the organization. A second important factor is the type of technology with which the organization operates. Both of these factors are under the control of the decision makers in an organization. Often, however, more choices and options are available concerning organizational structure than are available concerning technology. Nevertheless, in many cases different technological options are available.

Traditional Approach to Work Design

The traditional approach to work design emerged in the early twentieth century and, as was mentioned in Chapter Two, is based on the pioneering work of Frederick Winslow Taylor (1911, 1915). It calls for dividing the production or service process into small subparts, emphasizing standard work procedures, simplifying the tasks to be performed, creating a high degree of specialization, and, where possible, using machine pacing. With this approach, little information, knowledge, and power and few rewards are placed in the hands of the individuals who actually do the work. Taylor reasoned that high productivity and high-quality work will result if each individual repeats a very simple task and if how the task should be performed is carefully specified. Research on the effectiveness of traditional work designs does not, however, support the argument that they necessarily produce high productivity and high-quality work (Cummings and Molloy, 1977). At least four major problems exist with the traditional approach. First, it is an inflexible way to organize work since individuals typically know how to do only one thing and cannot do other activities when necessary. The production process itself is also inflexible because it has been designed to do one particular type of work in a relatively rapid manner. When lower rates of production are needed or a new product or service must be created, the entire production process has to be redesigned and re-engineered.

Second, although the traditional approach would seem to be a very efficient way to work, in fact, it often turns out to be just the opposite. Doing simple, repetitive tasks is not a very motivating activity for most individuals (Lawler, 1973). Most people will not perform such tasks at all much less perform them well unless significant controls and incentives are in place to assure that they do so. In the absence of effective controls, they tend to do low-quality work at a slow pace. Controlling employees involves overhead costs since supervision and measurement systems backed up by rewards and punishments are the predominant ways of obtaining control.

If the work is extremely simple and can be grouped together, as it often can be in assembly-type work and certain service tasks (such as those performed by telephone information operators and highway toll collectors), it may be relatively easy to supervise. However, some individuals will actively work to "beat the system" by producing at low rates and by producing inferior-quality products even when supervision is tight. Indeed, tight supervision seems to encourage some employees to act in this way because it increases the "challenge" (Walker and Guest, 1952; Whyte, 1955).

Third, absenteeism and turnover are particularly difficult to control in a free society and, thus, represent a large problem for traditional work designs. Since individuals working under a traditional system do not find their work very satisfying, they may have little motivation to show up for work, and the cost of absenteeism and turnover end up being high (Mirvis and Lawler, 1977; Mobley, 1982). Traditionally managed automobile plants in the United States, for example, often have as many as 20 percent of their assembly line employees absent on Mondays and Fridays, and in Sweden, Volvo has had over 50 percent of its assembly line workers absent before major holidays.

Fourth, traditional work designs create problems of coordination and accountability. Because each individual knows and performs only one piece of the work, supervision is required to coordinate and plan the work of individuals in any complicated production or service situation. Since no one is responsible for producing an entire product or service, this approach must rely on inspecting quality into the work. Therefore, a number of quality inspectors are placed throughout the production or service process. Inspectors increase overhead, and often the mentality that they produce leads to high rates of scrap and waste and customer irritation and alienation in service situations.

One alternative to inspection is to establish internal customer relationships so that each individual is expected to satisfy the next person or group in the service or production process. This strategy can help improve product quality but is inferior to establishing external customer relationships in several respects. Internal customers often do not provide the same quality of feedback as external customers (they rarely change suppliers, for example). More important, they often do not create the same set of demands for cost, quality, service, and speed that external customers do. They may, for example, place too high a premium on quality because cost is not an issue for them. Thus, employees may develop an inaccurate impression of what the organization needs to do to succeed. External markets are simply more likely than internal customers to demand the right behavior because the organization needs to satisfy them to be successful.

It is easy to see why work designers have searched for alternatives to simplified, standardized, and specialized work. Two major alternative approaches to work design have been developed over the last half century. In many respects, they are not so much competing approaches as approaches that are applicable in different situations. We will first look at the approach of individual job enrichment and then look at work teams. In the next chapter, we will consider the situations in which each of these is most applicable.

Job Enrichment

The idea of enriching the work of individuals in order to improve their motivation, performance, and satisfaction dates back at least to the 1950s. Described in its simplest form, the *job enrichment approach* tries to give individuals a whole piece of work to do and holds them accountable for how well they do it. A considerable amount of research has focused on the question of what will make work so interesting and challenging that individuals will be motivated to do it well without the promise of financial rewards and the fear of punishment (see, for example, Herzberg, 1966; Hackman and Lawler, 1971). The answer to this question seems to rely on putting tasks together so that one individual is responsible for a whole product or service. Much of the early work in this area was done by a noted psychologist, Fred Herzberg, and took place in telephone operations areas at AT&T (Herzberg, 1966; Ford, 1969). Researchers have also developed programs in many service organizations, including Prudential Insurance and Lincoln National Life Insurance (see Hackman and Oldham, 1980, for other examples).

Characteristics of Jobs

Discussions of individual job enrichment distinguish between horizontal and vertical expansion of an individual's job. *Horizon-*

tal expansion refers to assigning an individual additional steps in the production or service process. In a sequential production process, a traditional work design might call for the work to pass from one person to another. In an enriched work design, individuals do the entire process. A complete transformation of the product or a complete customer service activity is in the hands of one individual.

In a manufacturing plant, an enriched work design might call for an employee to assemble an entire product, such as an electronic instrument or the transmission for an automobile. In a customer service organization, an employee may become responsible for all repairs and services for a particular automobile, or a loan officer in a bank may become responsible for all aspects of developing and completing the materials associated with a loan. In most enriched work designs, the employees who have built the product or completed the service put their names on it, test it, and deliver or send it to the customer so that they have direct customer contact.

Vertical expansion involves giving employees responsibility for those control and planning activities that require decision making. It usually means giving employees the responsibility for scheduling work, determining work methods, and assessing the quality of the work done. Vertical expansion must be present for employees to feel that they control how the work is done. Horizontal expansion gives employees the experience of doing a whole and meaningful piece of work. Vertical expansion helps employees to feel that they are responsible for how well the work is done because they make the important decisions.

Most theories of job enrichment stress that jobs need to be expanded both horizontally and vertically for them to have a positive impact on employee motivation and satisfaction (Hackman and Oldham, 1980). This idea is supported by the literature on motivation. For employees to be internally motivated, three conditions must exist (Lawler, 1973; Hackman and Oldham, 1980). First, individuals have to do a meaningful piece of work. Meaningful work exists when individuals do a whole piece of work that involves using some of their valued skills and abilities. To be meaningful, work also has to have a noticeable impact or result. In mission-oriented organizations such as charitable organizations and volunteer organizations, a task may be meaningful to an individual because the individual is committed to the overall purpose of the organization. Even though the task itself, such as sending letters or making telephone calls, is not particularly significant, it can be motivating. In most work organizations, however, a task has to play an important role in the overall success of the organization and the individual has to see the relationship between what he or she is doing and the success or failure of the organization before the task is meaningful to the individual.

Second, individuals must have the autonomy or the freedom to do the job in the way they feel is best. This element is critical because without such autonomy employees do not "own" the products of their labor. If they are simply following a programmed and specified way of performing a task, then the success they achieve in doing the task well is not their success; it is someone else's success. To be intrinsically motivated, employees have to feel that they accomplished the task and that, therefore, the psychological credit for the successful accomplishment is theirs.

Third, in order for employees to be motivated by the work itself, they must receive feedback on how well they performed it. Feedback is critical because it gives individuals information on how they have done, and this in turn allows them to feel psychological success when they have performed well. It also lets individuals know when they are performing poorly so that they can correct their performance.

Job designs need to contain meaningful work, autonomy, and feedback in order for them to motivate employees and meet the job enrichment criteria. All three aspects are necessary; one cannot be substituted for the others. If one aspect is missing, meaningful work is missing and, therefore, so is employee motivation.

Characteristics of Individuals

In order for job enrichment to motivate employees, the individuals doing the work need to have certain characteristics.

They need to value such internal rewards as achievement, competence, and personal growth or what are often called *higher-order needs* in the Maslow (1943) hierarchy of needs. If individuals do not value these kinds of outcomes, then creating work with autonomy and meaningful tasks may frustrate them rather than motivate them.

The job enrichment approach requires relatively skilled individuals and, thus, often a greater investment in training than is required for the traditional approach to job design. The work is made more difficult for the individual, and it requires more skills and abilities to complete successfully. For this approach to work, capable individuals need to be hired, and they need to be trained extensively so that they can perform their work well and feel a sense of accomplishment when they have performed it effectively.

Impact on Involvement

The correctly implemented job enrichment program affects most of the elements of employee involvement, including information, knowledge, power, and internal rewards, but not necessarily financial rewards. These elements are increased in cases where work is horizontally and vertically enriched. Power increases because individuals receive more authority to make decisions about work methods and work procedures. Employees increase their knowledge with broader vertical and greater horizontal responsibilities because they need to know more about not only the production process but also things such as quality control, scheduling, and, sometimes, customer relations. Information is expanded because individuals get increasing amounts of feedback about how well they have performed the work. They receive the feedback because they are given direct customer contact or because they get production or service reports on the particular product or service that they personally produced and delivered. They may also get scheduling information and other business information because of their expanded role in the production process. The feedback usually does not include profit and loss information that is tied to their activities. Typically, they are only doing a small part of the business process and, thus, profit data cannot be generated for their work. However, in some individual sales situations, employees can be treated as profit centers.

Although job enrichment usually does allow individuals to make certain kinds of work-related decisions, it usually does not allow them to get involved in personnel decisions, corporate strategy decisions, and major coordination and planning activities. Usually, managers continue to make these decisions. Simply enriching an individual's work does not lead to involvement in these decisions.

The impact of job enrichment on financial rewards is inconsistent and unpredictable. An employee often receives a small increase in wages because the work that the individual is doing is likely to be evaluated more highly if a traditional job evaluation system is in place. Job enrichment also can help make individual rewards for performance more practical. Since individuals are responsible for a larger piece of work than in a traditional assembly line job, the output of their efforts is more measurable. In some cases, this measurement of output can be converted into an effective individual pay-for-performance system (Mohrman, Resnick-West, and Lawler, 1989; Lawler, 1990b). Job enrichment usually has no impact on rewards that are dependent upon organizational performance. There is nothing inherent in the job enrichment process that helps move the organization toward profit sharing or other pay plans that make more financial rewards dependent upon organizational performance.

Undoubtedly, the greatest impact on rewards that occurs with individual job enrichment is in the area of internal, or intrinsic, rewards. Because of the information, knowledge, and power individuals are given, they can feel a sense of accomplishment and success if they perform well. The focus in job enrichment is on individuals rewarding themselves intrinsically rather than on rewarding them extrinsically when a group or the total organization performs well. If the task an individual performs is very important to how the organization performs, the individual may also feel a sense of psychological success or accomplishment when the overall organization performs effectively.

Research Results

A great deal of literature explores the effectiveness of job enrichment programs (Cummings and Molloy, 1977; Hackman and Oldham, 1980; Guzzo, Jette, and Katzell, 1985; Lawler, 1986). Clearly, when work is enriched, an organization can realize significant savings in a number of areas. Quality in particular improves dramatically because when individuals are responsible for the work they perform, that is, when they psychologically own it, they seem to be more motivated to turn out a high-quality product (Lawler, 1969). Quality also may be improved because employees have a broader perspective on the work process and as a result can catch errors and make corrections that might have gone undetected in a more traditional work design in which employees lacked the knowledge to recognize them. And because they have autonomy to make ongoing improvements, employees can also fine tune and make adjustments in the work process as they become increasingly knowledgeable about how their work can best be done.

Although improvements in productivity also occur with job enrichment, they usually are not as predictable or as large as are the improvements in quality. Productivity may not improve dramatically because of the loss of specialization in enriched jobs. Specialization typically can lead to individuals being highly adept and quick at a very small piece of work, particularly in many assembly processes. By doing the same thing over and over again every few seconds or minutes, individuals can develop highly efficient motions. They can complete a piece of the work much faster than they can complete a part of a more elaborate series of tasks that they have to perform.

I experienced an example of the problems with horizontal expansion in a medical products facility. In making the product, employees had to repeat a very precise manual winding motion every few seconds. Workers reported that they needed to get in rhythm to do it well, and indeed the production data did show that it took ten to fifteen minutes for employees to warm up and reach maximum output. Every time employees needed to stop and do another activity, they had to warm up again. As a result, horizontal expansion lowered productivity.

Although specialization may have some advantages in terms of efficiency, I think that the major reason that job enrichment leads to less significant gains in productivity than in quality is motivational. Improving productivity is simply not as satisfying to individuals as is turning out high-quality products and doing the job correctly. In most cultures, doing high-quality work provides people with more internal satisfaction than does doing a lot of work.

Enriched work can lead to lower absenteeism and turnover because individuals are more likely to be satisfied when they do meaningful work and less likely to look for work elsewhere and to avoid coming to work (Mobley, 1982; Mobley, Hand, Meglino, and Griffeth, 1979). Absenteeism and turnover can be very expensive. They are very disruptive, and the cost of training a replacement can be quite high. Thus, lowering them can have a large financial impact (Seashore, Lawler, Mirvis, and Cammann, 1983).

Job enrichment sometimes creates the possibility for reductions in overhead. While enriched jobs require more training, they often need less supervision. Less supervision is needed because with motivation and control coming from the task itself, individuals do not need to be monitored, punished, and rewarded as closely as they do when work is divided up into small, less meaningful tasks. Also, less coordination may be needed because employees take some of the coordination activities upon themselves by producing a whole product or service. In manufacturing settings, employees also may take on some of the maintenance, set-up, and support tasks that are inherent in the work. As a result, fewer employees, less supervision, and less coordination between the maintenance department and the production department may be needed. The savings in coordination can be significant and may prove to be an important cost advantage.

In some respects, a job enrichment work design is more flexible than a traditional step-by-step production process; it is easier to adjust the rate of production with this approach. Adjusting the rate of production with an assembly line, for example, is often difficult because the line is carefully balanced to maintain efficiency. If the line is slowed down, the number of individuals on the line has to be reduced for the company to realize any savings in labor costs. Therefore, some employees will need to perform multiple steps on the line, a situation that can be difficult. In some cases, it is not physically possible for employees to move up and down the line to perform different tasks. The only way to reduce production may be to operate the line for a shorter period of time, which can lead to reduced work weeks for all employees or layoffs. With enriched jobs, slowing down production often can be accomplished by reassigning some of the employees who normally would be working in the production area or service area to other work. The remaining employees can continue to produce at the same level they were producing at before.

Organizations that use job enrichment often find it easier to change from one product or one service to another than do organizations that use traditional work designs. Their employees have a history of learning, developing, and adding skills to their repertoire. Thus, when a new product or service comes along, they are not as threatened by the need to learn new things. Most likely, their skills from the old situation can be applied to the new one because they have a wider variety of skills to start with than employees in traditionally designed jobs. In simplified, specialized jobs, a change to a new product or service can make all of an employee's skills obsolete.

Setting up a production process can be very expensive when a traditional work design is used. For example, in 1980, Digital spent more than $30 million to set up an assembly line to produce a personal computer. In another case, Kodak invested a great deal of engineering time into setting up a camera production line. In both cases, the assembly line production process proved to be very expensive in terms of capital and design time and poorly suited to production needs.

Both of the products turned out to be relatively slow sellers, and the inflexibility of the production rate of the assembly line was a significant handicap. The lines had to be staffed at all workstations for them to work correctly. When lower production rates were needed, employees had to work on the lines only a few hours a day and were assigned other work when the lines were not running. In both cases, the lines were so inflexible that they could not be staffed efficiently to run at a slow rate. These products could have been built at a substantial savings using either an individual enrichment model or a teamwork model.

Work Teams

Much of the early research on self-managing or semiautonomous work teams was done in Europe and was based on the *sociotechnical approach* to work design (Susman, 1976; Cole, 1989) This work was pioneered by a group led by Eric Trist and was first used in manufacturing settings. Although it has some different theoretical underpinnings, it is very similar to the job enrichment approach in how it regards individuals and work (see Cummings, 1978). The approach is aimed at creating work situations in which teams instead of individuals have a whole and meaningful piece of work to do, receive feedback about the work, and have considerable autonomy in how they accomplish the work. The degree of autonomy of these work groups is one of the key features that distinguishes them from the groups that are used by Toyota and other Japanese manufacturing companies on their assembly lines (Klein, 1991). The Japanese approach gives groups more autonomy than is given to the typical individual on an assembly line (in some cases, groups can stop the line), but the groups are relatively limited in their decision-making power (Womack, Jones, and Roos, 1990).

Even though work teams have been written about and tried as long as has job enrichment, they have never been as popular as job enrichment. A 1987 survey of the Fortune 1000 companies, for example, found that only 28 percent had teams, while 60 percent were using job enrichment (Lawler, Ledford, and Mohrman, 1989; see also, Wellins and others, 1990). Furthermore, virtually all of those organizations that were using teams had less than 20 percent of their work force in teams. A second survey of the same companies in 1990 showed that 47 percent of them used work teams and projected that the use of teams will greatly increase (Lawler, Mohrman, and Ledford, 1992; see also Wellins, Byham, and Wilson, 1991).

Most major manufacturing companies have several plants that use the work team approach as their basic approach to manufacturing products. Much of the original use of work teams in the United States was in new high-involvement plants. These plants were first built in the late 1960s and early 1970s and now number in the hundreds (Walton, 1980; Lawler, 1978, 1990a). The basic building block of these plants typically is the work team. Teams have become an accepted way of organizing and designing work in many manufacturing environments. Organizations also have a growing interest in using teams in service businesses as well as to design new products and do staff work (Hackman, 1989; Orsburn, Moran, Musselwhite, and Zenger, 1990). In some situations, management teams are taking collective responsibility for supervising individuals and teams. In short, teams are not just a way of getting work done on the shop floor, they are becoming a way of getting work done throughout the organization.

Work teams have a number of distinctive characteristics. A brief look at these characteristics will help to define what is meant by the term *work team* and also to highlight the factors that are involved in installing a work team (see Wellins and others, 1990; Lazes and Falkenberg, 1991, for data on how frequently companies use particular implementation strategies).

Work Flow

Work teams, like enriched jobs, are designed so that the task for which the team is responsible constitutes a whole and meaningful piece of work. The literature on the sociotechnical approach provides one way to decide what the appropriate boundaries of a team are. It emphasizes that the team should at least be responsible for the total transformation of a product or a service. Sometimes this transformation is called a *state change*, and it can be conceptualized as changing a raw material to a usable product that is in a different condition and has identifiable customers.

A team must be given responsibility for enough of the creation of a product or service so that it controls and is responsible for a clear input and a clear output. All the factors that influence how successfully a particular transformation is done should be included within its scope of responsibility.

Work team designs may differ substantially in terms of horizontal expansion. A team may take responsibility for only one part of what ends up as a final product that is delivered to an external customer. Similarly, a team may only do one part of a service process and, thus, not have direct customer contact. For example, in a company that makes electrical cable, a state change could involve getting copper from a supplier and converting it into wire. It would not necessarily involve taking that wire and coating it with an insulating substance and then converting that wire into a finished cable. In fact, this particular process involves at least three state changes and is done by three different teams in a plant that was designed by TRW according to sociotechnical design principles.

In the Volvo plant in Kalmar, Sweden, work teams are responsible for completing a whole system in a car. One team, for example, puts the entire electrical system in a particular car while another does all the upholstery. The teams are held accountable for the part of the car they work on and are expected to take ownership over all aspects of its installation. The Volvo teams are different from the groups that are used in most automobile plants; most of these teams do not perform a complete transformation or install a complete system. For example, in the Toyota "lean production system," groups are simply assigned responsibility for a number of stations on the assembly line (Womack, Jones, and Roos, 1990).

On the other hand, teams may complete an entire product and even deliver it to the customer. In Volvo's new automobile plant in Uddevalla, Sweden, work teams build entire cars and have direct customer contacts. Clearly, the more that work can be designed to involve the complete production of a product or service, the more individuals in a work team will experience a sense of responsibility for the product and a sense of business involvement. Only through such a design can individuals have true external supplier and customer relationships, an important key to involving individuals in the business.

Extensive layout changes may be needed in an organization to create work teams. For example, in the typical manufacturing situation, machinery will need to be grouped by product rather than by process. Instead of putting all similar equipment together, an organization must create work cells in which all the equipment that is necessary to produce a particular product is located together.

To increase the sense of shared responsibility as well as to accomplish a number of other objectives, members of the work team are typically cross-trained so that they can do most if not all of the tasks that fall within their work team's area of responsibility. Members usually rotate among tasks on a regular basis. This type of training not only gives the work group flexibility in assigning members but also gives people a sense of ownership and responsibility for the final product. This is the same sense of ownership that comes about in individual job enrichment.

Membership

Work teams typically include all the employees working in an area or on a complete transformational process. Team membership is not optional. If all individuals working on the transformation do not participate and do not agree to be cross-trained and to work flexibly throughout the work process, the whole concept of being a team is defeated. If an individual, for example, simply takes ownership over one part of the process and refuses to do other tasks, the rest of the team members cannot learn that step in the process. This makes it difficult for them to own the entire product or process, and it interferes with the team's growth and development.

There is no one correct size for a team; team size depends on the product or service that is being produced. Small teams, three to eight individuals, are easier to create and manage but sometimes more individuals are needed to produce the product or service. For example, teams in many chemical plants need to be responsible for the entire production process because the plants are based on a continuous flow of materials. In large plants, as many as twenty-five to thirty individuals may be needed to staff all the workstations; thus, these teams have to be this size even though the larger size creates communication and cohesiveness problems.

Decision-Making Responsibilities

For work teams to feel responsible for the work that they are doing, they must make important decisions about how the work is done and must feel in control of the work process (Lawler, 1986; Beekun, 1989). Just how much management-type decision making is usually given to work teams varies considerably (Hackman, 1989). Some of this variability appears in the names that are used to describe work teams. They are sometimes called *self-managing work teams, autonomous work groups, shared management teams, semiautonomous teams,* and so on. In some cases, I think they can best be described as *customer teams* or *market-managed teams* becuase it often is the customers or market that controls them.

Highly autonomous or self-managing work teams make virtually all decisions that are required to run a small business. For example, they hire and fire people, determine pay rates, set and maintain quality standards, specify work methods, manage inventory, deal directly with customers and suppliers, and so on. They are very close to being a small business or mini-enterprise. This type of work team has been created in some new plant environments and in some financial service situations in which individuals are processing claims, managing credit card accounts, managing investments, and providing staff services such as fringe benefits (Orsburn, Moran, Musselwhite, and Zenger, 1990). Highly autonomous teams represent an excellent example of how even a large organization can become small in order to increase employee involvement.

In work teams that are less autonomous, many of the human resources decisions, such as pay and hiring, remain with management, but the work teams still set production goals, manage quality, and determine work methods. To have a reasonable amount of intrinsic motivation, teams must at least make decisions about work processes and work methods and receive considerable feedback and data about the effectiveness of their performance. It is also desirable to give teams a budget so they can make small purchases. In the absence of the power to make decisions, team members are unlikely to feel a sense of ownership over the work output and will not be motivated to perform well.

Training

Two kinds of training are critical to the establishment of work teams. First, extensive technical training is necessary so that individuals can effectively perform multiple functions. This training may go on for years, and often the trainers are other team members. In some of the more complicated team structures, such as those present in chemical plants, it may take team members as long as six to ten years to learn all of the tasks that are the responsibility of the team.

Teaching all members of a team how to perform all the tasks for which the team is responsible may not be practical or desirable. When a great amount of training is needed to perform a task, it may be adequate to have just a few individuals master the task. This is often the case in teams that are doing work that requires high levels of expertise, such as software programming. Cross-training is not an end in itself but rather a means of producing flexibility and group ownership over the results of the collective activity and output. Ownership, in particular, may be produced without a great deal of cross-training if the group is collectively responsible for output and shares power and decision making.

Second, group members need training in interpersonal and team skills. The kind of training that is needed, of course, depends directly on the type of decisions that are given to the work teams. The more they are given responsibilities for making supervisory-type decisions, the more they need group-process training and, of course, technical training. If, for example, teams are given responsibility for their own inventory, quality control, scheduling, and other supervisory-type tasks, then a considerable amount of team development and team training is needed.

Meetings

Work teams need to meet frequently. At least once a week, a team needs to meet to make schedules and to review business results. It may also need special meetings to make decisions about hiring, firing, and other types of management activities. In many manufacturing environments, a team may need to meet daily simply to review how the production process is working. In many plants and offices where work teams exist, the work teams can decide to stop production and hold a meeting if there are significant quality or production problems.

Supervision

In manufacturing settings, the first level supervisor, often called an *area manager* or *management team member*, typically supports several work teams. There may also be a team coordinator or leader who is a working member of the team (Rosow and Zager, 1990). This person handles issues such as scheduling meetings and communicating with other teams and management. The first-level supervisor usually plays a monitoring and support role with respect to the team. It is his or her responsibility to review and approve many of the decisions made by the work teams, particularly the personnel and scheduling decisions. In addition, the supervisor has the major responsibility for assuring that the decision-making processes and the internal operations of the team are effective (Hackman and Walton, 1986). If the supervisor has concerns about either a specific decision or the way decisions are made, he or she has the responsibility to intervene and question how decisions are made.

Supervisors need to be very active as trainers and sup-
porters of group development when teams have just been
formed. Teams need to mature before they can make many of the
more difficult decisions that teams ultimately can make, particularly decisions about who is hired and who gets pay increases
(Orsburn, Moran, Musselwhite, and Zenger, 1990; Wellins, Byham, and Wilson, 1991). Teams may also have difficulty making
decisions about work assignments but usually can master these
decisions earlier than decisions concerning rewards (Lawler,
1981). Teams may not reach full maturity until they are two to
four years old, and even at maturity, they still need a management person to help them solve some of their internal problems
and monitor their decision-making processes (Hackman and
Walton, 1986).

Reward System

The pay team members receive is usually based upon a skill-
based pay system. In this pay system, individuals are paid for the
number and kind of tasks they can perform rather than for the
job they are doing (Lawler, 1990b). As will be discussed in
Chapter Seven, this type of pay system fits quite well with an
employee involvement approach to management. It encourages
and rewards the kind of skill acquisition that is needed in order
to make high-involvement management work.

Characteristics of Individuals

Like job enrichment, work teams are most effective with individuals who desire complex, challenging work (Hackman and
Oldham, 1980). For those individuals who prefer repetitive
tasks, work team environments are highly undesirable. In contrast to individual job enrichment, work teams also require
individuals who enjoy social interaction and who value social
rewards. Meetings are important and frequent, so individuals
who do not like meetings are not likely to thrive in a team
environment. In addition, since social rewards are important

influences on behavior in a group, it is critical that individuals value them and respond to them.

Team members must like to and have the ability to continuously learn. In fact, operating in a team environment often requires an individual to have higher skill levels than does operating alone in an enriched job. Individual job enrichment does not demand that employees have interpersonal skills or group decision-making skills since many decisions are made by individuals, not groups.

Impact on Involvement

In many ways, work teams are similar to individual job enrichment as far as the impact they have on the level of employee involvement. They move significant amounts of information, knowledge, and power to the work force. The increase in power can be appreciable, particularly if the groups are given a considerable amount of supervisory decision-making authority. Indeed, the increase in power can be greater than it typically is with the individual job enrichment approach. There is no counterpart in individual job enrichment to a team's assessment of its members and the decision-making authority a team has about pay increases, p omotions, and work assignments. In addition, work teams can often make scheduling, capital investment, and other types of decisions that affect multiple individuals and move teams toward a total business experience in a mini-enterprise environment.

Perhaps the most noticeable impact of work teams is the degree to which they increase the skills of team members. Team members need a great deal of training because of horizontal expansion. If an organization makes a substantial commitment to vertical expansion so that teams become relatively self-managing, then team members need a great amount of extra knowledge about the business and expertise in group processes and decision making. They also may need to develop skills in quality management. If they are charged with self-inspection, they may need to learn about measurement and statistical process control (Juran, 1989).

To be effective, work teams need considerable information about the business, particularly if they are responsible for coordinating their activities with the activities of other teams and individuals. They need to have access to plans, schedules, and peformance levels in other parts of the organization. If, as is often true, the teams are responsible for their own costs, they need access to budget information. If they play any role in making decisions about new technology or new equipment, they may need information about capital expenditures and the financial condition of the organization. It is usually desirable to give teams access to information from customers and suppliers. Sometimes their customer base is internal, but they always need to receive feedback from whomever uses their products or services.

Moving to teams does not necessarily lead an organization to a change in its pay-for-performance system. Because teams are held responsible for the production of a service or product, it may be possible for an organization to create a small group bonus or other type of group pay-for-performance system. However, most organizations using the work team approach have not done this. As will be discussed in Chapter Eight, work teams are compatible with various types of organizational pay-for-performance plans, such as gainsharing and profit sharing. However, such a pay plan is not a necessary condition for creating teams nor is it an integral part of the team concept as it is usually applied (Lawler, 1990b).

Internal rewards such as feelings of accomplishment and success are the key additional rewards in the work team approach. The team approach aims to create a sense of accomplishment and psychological success in team members when the team performs well. Work is designed to focus individuals on the success of the team rather than on their individual success. For individuals to develop a strong commitment to the team and to care about how successful the team is, organizations must change to a team-based management system. If individuals do not care about their team's peformance, many of the advantages of creating teams are lost, and the organization may be better off with individual job enrichment or traditional job designs.

Overall, work teams typically do make an important difference in the level of employee involvement that is possible for low-level participants in an organization. They receive additional information, knowledge, power, and rewards as a result of this structure. However, just how much additional power, new training, and information they receive varies considerably from organization to organization.

Research Results

The research results for work teams are very similar to those for individual job enrichment. For example, team members have a high concern for quality just as individuals in enriched jobs do (Hackman and Oldham, 1980; Lawler, 1986; Lazes and Falkenberg, 1991). Team situations also provide increased chances to solve problems concerning quality. In most cases, employees have the knowledge to make meaningful improvements in the quality of the product or services that they create.

Instituting work teams can also improve employee output because teams set production goals and get feedback on how well they achieve these goals (Beekun, 1989; Colton and others, 1988; Sundstrom, DeMeuse and Futell, 1990). Production may also increase because of the flexibility of individuals. The cross-training of employees enables them to help each other, and sometimes fewer people are needed to keep a production area operating. Teams may often decide that they can do all of their own support work, thereby eliminating the need for some maintenance and staff support individuals.

When groups are cohesive, social pressure can play an important role in motivating individual performance (Wall, Kemp, Jackson, and Clegg, 1986; Hackman, 1989). Valued social rewards, such as praise from other members of the group and acceptance by the group, depend on satisfactory individual performance. Similarly, punishments are sometimes administered when individuals do not perform well. Groups may be more effective at giving rewards and punishments than are supervisors. Often the reaction from peers is more critical to employees than the reaction from bosses, but perhaps more important, often peers are constantly present and able to give continuous reinforcement while bosses are not always present.

As groups become cohesive, membership in them becomes a very important feature of the work place. Members are hesitant to be absent or quit because they value group membership (Beekun, 1989). They also feel that they are letting down people who are their friends and whose opinions they value. Not surprisingly, members of work teams tend to report relatively high job satisfaction. Work teams can satisfy individuals' needs for social interaction and belonging as well as their needs for challenging work.

Work teams can also have a significant impact on the need for supervisory personnel and staff groups. Work teams can usually take inventory and do scheduling, quality assurance, and even some of the tasks typically done by middle- and upper-level management (Lawler, 1986). Significant cost savings can then be realized by leaner staffing. The higher-level work that is typically done by middle managers at a higher pay rate is transferred to production teams and done by individuals who are paid at a lower wage. This strategy reduces overall labor costs and better utilizes the individuals who are in work teams. In essence, they get to add value to the product or service that they are delivering, contributing to the overall cost effectiveness of the organization.

Work teams are important for organizations trying to operate with a very lean and flat hierarchy. As noted earlier, a reasonable goal for small plants is to have no more than one manager for every fifty to one hundred employees. A recent study by my research center of a regional telephone company found that it was possible to eliminate about half of the supervisors through the use of teams. Cost savings from the reduction of supervision were appreciable, and employee productivity and quality went up slightly with the removal of the supervisors.

Expanding both the horizontal and the vertical aspects of a team's responsibility maximizes the team's accountability and the degree to which it makes supervision and overhead unnecessary. The more a team can handle all the critical interdependencies of the work within itself, the more the organization can operate in a horizontal mode. Admittedly, sometimes not all interdependencies can be handled within work teams and thus some other structures may be required to deal with these areas. The key to making teams work is for the organization to identify the most critical interdependencies in the production of a product or service and encompass all of them within the boundaries of a single team. Even a large organization can look small to an employee in this type of work team.

A good example of the savings that are possible when a white-collar organization switches to a team approach is provided by the Aid Association for Lutherans. In 1987, this insurance company divided itself into regions, each of which is served by four teams. The teams provide almost all services to their customers and are supported by a small group of functional specialists who provide in-depth knowledge on critical issues. As a result of the move to customer-focused teams, supervisory positions were reduced from sixty-two to twenty-two and fifty-seven full-time jobs were eliminated. Shenandoah Life, IDS, and AT&T Credit Corporation have made similar successful changes to the team approach.

As mentioned earlier, decision making and work methods can also improve as a result of using teams. The team meeting format gives individuals a chance to discuss work methods and procedures and to improve upon them. Because employees are cross-trained, they have considerable information about the organization and they are often in an excellent position to solve problems and implement solutions without going through an elaborate and expensive bureaucratic review process.

Chapter Five

Develop
Involving
Work

The job enrichment and work team approaches to work design are congruent with high-involvement management and are definitely the preferred approaches for high-involvement organizations. But they are not necessarily the best approaches to job design for all situations. Thus, before we look at which of them works best in a particular situation, we need to consider in what situations they are likely to be superior to the traditional approach to work design.

Business Strategy

Organizations adopt widely different strategies in their efforts to gain a competitive advantage. As discussed in earlier chapters, some compete more on cost, others on quality and service, and still others by offering innovative new products and services. Since different work designs lead to different behaviors, it follows that different strategies call for different work designs.

Generally, teams and job enrichment fit well in situations in which an organization's strategy emphasizes producing high-quality products. Organizations that adopt such strategies have been shown to produce higher-quality products than those that do not. There is also evidence that they produce the best services. Frequently, they allow customers one-stop shopping and support the development of a relationship between the

101

customer and the service deliverer (Schlesinger and Heskett, 1991b).

Involving-work designs also are indicated for organizations that emphasize innovation. Teams seem to be particularly appropriate for these organizations because, as mentioned earlier, they can speed the process of bringing new products and services to markets. They also can facilitate the quick delivery of services.

Traditional work designs often fit best in organizations that primarily are cost competitive. This approach can lead, at least for a while, to lower labor costs and it can make many manufacturing jobs so simple that they can be done by low-wage employees. Traditional work designs are particularly appropriate for organizations in which labor costs account for a large portion of the total cost of a product or service. In this situation, saving a little bit on wages can make a big difference in an organization's cost. When equipment and material account for most of the costs, however, the key issue is not how much labor costs but how effectively equipment and materials are used. Chemical plants and food processing plants are good examples of situations where labor costs are not critical and, therefore, traditional work designs are not appropriate.

Finally, there are organizations that are trying to be leaders in a combination of innovation, speed, cost, and quality. In most of these situations one of the involvement-oriented approaches is usually the most appropriate. As discussed earlier, when combined with other high-involvement management practices, involvement-oriented work design approaches can create organizations in which individuals or teams produce high-quality products and services in a quick, cost-effective manner.

Nature of the Work

The nature of the work is a vital determinant of whether either of the high-involvement approaches to work design can be effective. For them to be effective, the work must be relatively complex and challenging. If the work is not complex or cannot be made complex in a way that is cost effective, then it will be very hard for an organization to generate the kind of internal motivation in its employees that is critical to the effectiveness of the high-involvement approach (Bowen and Lawler, 1992).

If by its very nature the work can only be done in a highly repetitive, automatic way, employees will simply not feel good about performing it well or feel challenged by the work. In the absence of these kinds of feelings, a major part of high-involvement management cannot be created. If the work does not create intrinsic motivation, then the only alternative is to use a more traditional reward and control approach to motivating employees.

Often the best way an employee can contribute to organizational effectiveness if the employee is performing highly repetitive work is to do a task effectively for a full eight-hour workday. Time that the employee spends in team meetings and problem-solving groups may not pay off in proportion to the employee's lost production time, particularly if the technology is relatively fixed and there is little chance for improving it.

Even in settings that involve repetitive work, it may make sense for an organization to provide individuals with the opportunity to develop ideas about how to perform the work better. As we shall see in the next chapter, capturing these ideas does not require that a company change its approach to work design. An organization can solicit employee suggestions through problem-solving groups and other methods that give individuals the opportunity to use their problem-solving abilities for limited periods of time. Such a strategy does not require restructuring the work in order to create work teams or enriched jobs (Lawler and Mohrman, 1985).

The stability of the work is another critical factor that influences whether a traditional approach to work design or a high-involvement approach is most appropriate. Stable work situations tend to favor more traditional approaches to work design. A stable work situation can be of basically two kinds. *Environmental stability* refers to the situation in which the organization does not need to change its activities to adapt to a continuously changing environment. *Production process stability* means that the organization does not need to adapt to internal variation in its production or service delivery process. If both the production process and the environment are stable, the organization can use highly programmed and controlled ways of producing a product or service. This situation makes the traditional approach to work design practical and, possibly, effective. In this situation, an organization can invest in the measures, work specification documents, and control systems that make for effective use of the traditional approach. If the situation is highly unstable, it becomes extremely difficult for an organization to even predict the kind of problems that employees will face and, therefore, very difficult to write rules and procedures that will cover every situation. Deciding whether or not someone performed well or poorly in a situation that is new and that the individual or the organization has never faced before is also very difficult.

Type of Technology

Technology plays a critical role in determining the nature of the work in an organization. Once an organization chooses a particular manufacturing or service technology, it may have little choice in what the work will be like. In some industries and businesses, few kinds of technology are available. In others, the technology is more flexible, and organizations can determine the nature of the work that they create by the technology that they choose.

The automobile industry provides a classic example of an industry in which the technology is somewhat flexible and in which organizations can determine the kind of work they create (Womack, Jones, and Roos, 1990). Most automobiles are produced on an assembly line, but in some cases—most notably the two Volvo plants mentioned in the previous chapter—they are produced by work teams. In one Volvo plant, work teams produce an entire car for an identified customer. In the other, cars are brought to workstations on pallets and left at the stations as long as the work team needs them in order to complete their step in the production process.

The choice between the workstation technology approach and the assembly line approach is critical in determining the nature of the work that will be present in an automobile manufacturing plant. If the organization chooses the assembly line approach, the work inevitably will be relatively repetitive and standardized. Some of the repetition can be relieved by rotating individuals and by creating work groups along the assembly line. Honda and Toyota use this approach to work groups. As was mentioned earlier, they give their groups limited autonomy and a number of opportunities to make suggestions. However, once an organization chooses an assembly line work process, its options are severely limited.

The Japanese automobile manufacturers have done an impressive job of managing and constructing assembly lines. Their use of groups, total quality programs, and quality circles represents a significant advance beyond the scientific management approach (Womack, Jones, and Roos, 1990). Their strategy clearly has given them a competitive advantage over those U.S. and European car manufacturers who still operate with a traditional scientific management approach. However, it does not represent a move to high-involvement management. The workstation approach, on the other hand, creates work that is high in variety, autonomy, feedback, and meaningfulness. Through this approach, it is possible to create teams that set their own work schedules, control their work pace, and make and immediately implement many changes in work methods and procedures.

In a number of work situations, the technology is not flexible. The organization simply has to use the dominant technology that is available for doing that particular kind of work. For example, companies can use only one technological approach in making gasoline, chemicals, and paper. These products simply cannot be made by an individual in an economically competitive manner. Fortunately, in the case of manufacturing chemicals and paper, and refining oil, the dominant technology leads to interesting, challenging work. The same cannot be said for the technology involved in routing telephone calls, taking reservations, encoding checks, collecting tolls, and sorting mail. In all of these cases, the technology creates quick, highly repetitive work that can be done by an employee in anywhere from a fraction of a second to a minute or two.

Individuals doing work of this nature almost become part of a computer terminal or other machine. This work demands robotlike behavior. Indeed, in many of these situations, the individual ultimately will be replaced by a computer, robot, or expert system. At the present time, these jobs are in a kind of semiautomated state, but as automation becomes more sophisticated, the few steps that are left for human beings to do will be done by machines. However, until we can do without telephone operators, reservations clerks, toll collectors, and so on, the work remains to be done. Unfortunately, this work is not easily redesigned to be interesting and challenging. In fact, these jobs are so highly automated that if an individual were to do the work without the help of automation the work might be more interesting but it would be too costly.

The old telephone switchboard, for example, which was not automated, was much slower but much more interesting and challenging than the machinery operators currently use. Going back to the old "cord boards" clearly is not a viable answer, but neither is job enrichment or creating self-managing teams given the type of work that currently exists. For the time being, the best way for an organization to manage this type of work is to use a relatively control-oriented approach, since little can be done to make the work interesting and challenging.

High-volume car production perhaps is also done most efficiently on an assembly line. Despite Volvo's efforts to develop a viable alternative to the assembly line, the assembly line offers a number of advantages. For example, it aids in material handling and inventory control. Perhaps most important, it facilitates selective automation and the use of robots because it keeps work simple and machine paced. As technology develops, it is easy to replace people on the assembly line with robots, but not people in team environments. The work in team environments is structured to be complex, so robots cannot perform all the functions team members need to perform. Ironically, the move to automation usually creates complex cerebral work that fits a high-involvement approach to management. Often, organizations that have automated are unprepared for this type of work because they have only experienced situations in which control-oriented management is appropriate.

Nature of the Work Force

Both the job enrichment approach and the team approach require individuals who value internal rewards and the kinds of satisfaction that comes from doing challenging work well. Not all people in the work force have these characteristics, and even those who do may not look to the workplace for their intrinsic satisfactions and sense of accomplishment. They may have long ago decided to find their intrinsic rewards in one of the many hobbies and other activities that are available in the diverse economic and social environment that exists today. Those individuals who do not look to their work for this kind of satisfaction simply cannot be tolerated in an organization that designs work to involve employees. They are in a very real sense uncontrollable because they do not respond to the rewards that are counted on to create a motivating work situation for most individuals.

The ability to learn and operate effectively in a high-involvement organization is also a critical characteristic of the work force. Both the job enrichment approach and the team approach require individuals who have or can develop a fairly wide array of skills. These skills include the ability to do relatively complex work as well as the ability to solve problems, interact with others, plan, schedule, and manage work. Again, these abilities are not present in all members of the work force in any country or in any location. Thus, it is important for organizations to find individuals that can meet the ability requirements of a high-involvement organization. If these individuals are not available, then the high-involvement approach to work design is not viable.

The cost of labor also has a critical influence on the type of work design that is most effective. If the cost is high, work design choices become particularly critical. Having a few employees who add a great deal of value often is the only way for an organization to compete when labor costs are high relative to those of a competitor. As mentioned earlier, organizations using the team approach can probably substantially reduce overhead labor costs because much of the work is transferred to the individuals actually peforming the work. However, if labor is inexpensive, the control-oriented approach can be cost effective because the inefficiencies that it creates in terms of extra overhead and even redundant workers do not penalize the organization greatly. When labor is low in cost, an organization can afford to waste it and may not be willing to make the training and other investments in employees that are needed to make a high-involvement approach work.

Sometimes, low labor costs may allow an organization to use an involvement-oriented approach even if it is not the most productive approach. Earlier it was mentioned that in many industries only simplified and standardized machine-aided work can be efficient. If labor costs are very low, however, then the extra labor that might be required to create interesting and challenging work may be acceptable because of the low cost of labor. Instead of employees becoming appendages of machines, employees may be able to do more of the job and the machine do less. This approach is especially appropriate if labor costs are low compared to the cost of the capital that is required for a machine. Such a situation is unlikely in Western Europe and the United States, where labor costs are high, but could be possible in developing countries.

Teams Versus Job Enrichment

Once an organization has decided to use a high-involvement approach to work design, it needs to consider whether a team or individual approach is most appropriate. Individual job enrichment and the work team approach both increase the amount of information, knowledge, and power that are available at the lower levels of an organization. Nevertheless, they are competing approaches in the sense that an organization cannot adopt both in any one work situation. An organization must choose between them based on how much involvement the organization

determines is desirable and on the amount of work flow interde-
pendence that exists in a particular setting.

Work Flow

In many work situations, the technology virtually mandates the
use of a team approach if high-involvement management is to be
implemented. For example, in plants that process food or manufacture glass, steel, paper, or a host of other products, it is not
practical for an individual to take the product from beginning
to end, as might be called for in a job enrichment strategy. A
variety of workstations have to be manned simultaneously in
order for the product to be produced. The use of these workstations produces an interdependency among employees,
which is often called *reciprocal interdependency*, or *simultaneous
interdependency*. To operate these plants effectively, employees
have to be constantly adjusting and changing their behavior in
response to what other employees are doing. In those work
processes that are complex and interdependent, the only way an
individual can get a sense of responsibility for producing the
whole product is by being a member of a team.

In a traditional work setting in which high interdependency exists, supervisors and managers must often spend a lot of
time coordinating the actions of individuals. The traditional
approach usually requires an employee to tell a supervisor of a
problem. The supervisor then has to relay the news to someone
else, often muddling the message and delaying action. Slow
coordination is a serious problem because many decisions
about production processes need to be made quickly. Once
teams become self-managing and individuals understand the
entire production or service process, the teams can often make
adjustments among themselves quickly and effectively. This can
be particularly critical in service situations in which customer
satisfaction requires a quick, high-quality response.

The hierarchical model of coordination also often fails in
product development. Typically, new products are developed by
a process in which the product is handed from one department
to another. Not only is this a very slow process that demands

numerous approvals, it often leads to each department trying to emphasize their aspect of the product: manufacturing wants the product to be easy to manufacture, marketing wants special features, and so on. Often the only way an organization can develop products quickly and make good decisions about the features each department wants is to assign the development process to an autonomous development team that has individuals with all the relevant functional skills. The famous Lockheed "skunk works" has successfully used this process to develop planes, and IBM and Hewlett-Packard have used it to develop computers.

Highly interdependent manufacturing processes that don't use teams often use many supervisors. Oil refineries, for example, commonly employ one supervisor for every six or fewer employees. When employees are formed into a team that does much of the coordination work that was previously done by a supervisor, an organization can reduce its supervisory overhead by at least 75 percent. What is more, when employees communicate horizontally without involving supervisors, communication, decision making, product quality, and raw material yields improve. I have seen this happen in bakeries, chemical plants, paper plants, and a whole string of complex manufacturing environments in which interdependency is high. It also has been shown to work in a variety of financial services, food services, and package delivery situations by Xerox, IDS, and Federal Express (Schlesinger and Heskett, 1991b).

Overall, as work becomes more tightly coupled and interdependency becomes high, using teams gives an organization increasingly greater payoffs. The payoff grows because teams can manage many of the interdependencies themselves and thus can make layers of supervision unnecessary. And teams often simply are better at coordination and decision making than are supervisors.

Work Load

There are a number of service tasks that can reasonably be done by individuals. For example, in the financial services world an individual can be given all the work associated with a certain number of credit card holders. Similarly, in insurance, individuals can be made responsible for the claims created from a certain geographical area or by a certain part of the alphabet. The same relationship can be created in the accounting department of a company as far as a certain number of suppliers or customers is concerned. One viable option here is to use individual job enrichment and create individual customer–employee relationships. This can produce a personalized relationship with customers and can produce high-quality service.

If demand for services from customers is relatively constant and stable, individual job enrichment may be the preferred approach in many service situations. However, if demand varies widely from one time period to another so that one individual may have little to do while another ends up with a great deal to do, it may not make sense to use individual job enrichment. Similarly, if it is important to always have someone available to serve a customer, it may be better to have teams responsible for customer bases because individuals leave or are absent or in training at various times. The same logic also applies to the manufacturing environment in which employees are producing the same products or similar products. Using individual work designs can create a relatively inflexible production system, but using teams allows an organization to reallocate people more easily to adjust to changes in product demand.

Level of Involvement

In some situations, job enrichment can lead to individuals being quite involved in the business of the organization, epecially if individuals have external suppliers and customers. Many of the franchise sales organizations are built on just this principle. Organizations like Mary Kay Cosmetics and Amway create, in effect, individually enriched jobs for their distributors. These jobs involve sales, service, and delivery of the product. The distributors have an external customer, the consumer who buys the products, and an external supplier, the company that provides the merchandise. They are sales specialists in a network organization. This kind of relationship can be extremely motivating, and individuals can be very self-managing because each individual is a mini-enterprise or small business. A somewhat similar situation exists with real estate agents and others who have considerable autonomy and responsibility for a group of customers.

Although job enrichment was initially applied largely to production work, today it seems to be applied most frequently to white-collar sales and service situations. Obviously, it is easier to install the approach in sales and service organizations than in manufacturing plants because its installation does not involve moving equipment or eliminating assembly lines. In addition, sales and service jobs do not involve the complexities of material handling that are found if an individual is to build an entire product. And in many sales and service situations, customers enjoy dealing with a specific individual and may want to develop a relationship with this person. Thus, it makes sense to create a world in which an individual deals with a service transaction from beginning to end. The evidence on service quality also shows that customers prefer one-stop shopping in the sense that they do not like to be passed from one individual to another to have a service transaction completed (see, for example, Bowen, Chase, and Cummings, 1990). These factors all argue for an individual approach to enrichment in sales and service positions, although teams can also accomplish the same thing if the members are cross-trained.

Despite the fact that individual enrichment has important advantages and should be used in certain situations, I think that the preferred work design for most high-involvement situations is the team approach. The work team approach has the potential to create more business involvement than does the individual job enrichment approach. Groups can get involved in more complex decisions and decisions that span wider areas of responsibility than can individuals. Groups can also become involved in more of the steps in designing, producing, and selling a product or service. Hence, with teams an organization will more likely be able to structure itself so that employees have external customers and external suppliers. This, in turn, can provide a market test of how well a team is performing. There is no need to rely on internal customers or proxy measures that simulate a competitive business environment.

Work teams simply allow more decisions and more coordination activities to be pushed lower in the organization than does the individual job enrichment approach, particularly if the production or service process is complicated and involves a number of steps. Even in a complicated process, teams can be used to allow the lowest-level employees to make complete products and deliver total services. Teams can control a product or service from the interaction with an external supplier through the delivery of that product or service to an external customer. They can go far beyond being responsible for a single transformation and can often be market driven and market controlled.

Although work teams have great potential to involve employees, there clearly are costs associated with creating them. They produce much more complicated social interactions and demand much more training than does individual job enrichment (Hackman, 1989). An organization must spend a great deal of time and effort on building effective work teams and training work team members. In addition, supervisors need to be trained to manage groups, which is quite different from managing individuals. Supervisors need to develop goal-setting skills with teams as well as learn skills concerned with group-process intervention and group leadership (Walton and Schlesinger, 1979; Hackman and Walton, 1986).

In some respects, individual job enrichment is the low-cost alternative to designing work that is consistent with a high-involvement approach to management. In those situations in which individuals can be held accountable for a whole product or service, it is often the preferred approach, particularly if the individuals doing the work are not oriented toward social interaction. Although some work in large, complex organizations is best done by individuals, the amount of this type of work is dramatically decreasing. The complexities and interdependencies of modern organizations are such that individuals often cannot do enough of a production or service process for them to experience meaningful work. The only alternative in these situations is a team design.

Toward Team-Based Organizations

The use of work teams has typically been limited to the direct production of products or services, thus most organizations that use teams have them at only the lowest level. Organizations based totally on teams are rare (Lawler, Ledford, and Mohrman, 1989). However, they should and will become more common. An organization can realize many advantages by using teams in staff support and managerial areas (Orsburn, Moran, Musselwhite, and Zenger, 1990). Decades ago Likert (1961) suggested that organizations be made up of overlapping groups so that everyone in the organization would be a member of a work team, but a structure that is totally made up of teams is not appropriate for all organizations. Most organizations today, however, greatly underuse rather than overuse the work team approach.

Management Teams

Some organizations are creating senior management teams at their top levels because of the complexities and demands of the top management role. No one individual typically has all the skills that are necessary to fill this role or the time that is needed to deal with the demands of the role. Management teams usually consist of three or more individuals who take responsibility for the senior management activities in the organization. They often receive limited cross-training so are not as flexible as production work teams. But they do meet regularly to solve problems and work on issues. To some degree, individuals in these teams can substitute for each other when a senior manager is needed to deal with an issue.

Management teams can be developed quite easily in most parts of an organization. I have seen them used in areas in which supervision needs to be flexible and needs to cover a large number of work teams. Instead of having responsibility for a fixed number of teams, the two or more individuals in these management teams have responsibility for an entire work area or plant. They, in effect, are cross-trained and interchangeable in dealing with any one of the teams. Sometimes they develop particular in-depth specialties so that they can bring extra competence to one set of issues. Their responsibilities, however, are for the general work area, and they can support any work team when that work team needs input or assistance.

Managerial teams have numerous advantages. Often, they allow for leaner staffing at the management level just as teams do at the production level. For example, Xerox has used management teams to eliminate one level of management in its sales and service organization. Instead of having a management level that is responsible for a particular geographical area, Xerox simply formed the direct reports of the area manager into a self-managing team and let them run the area. Management teams can be a superior way to provide expertise to employees. Individual managers can develop in-depth knowledge in particular areas of expertise. When employees or teams need help, the manager with relevant expertise can work with them.

Teams are better at handling variable work demands than are individual managers. For example, one newspaper that I studied formed teams of distribution center managers. The teams were unusual because the managers in them were members of a union but the individuals who reported to them were not in unions or in teams. The delivery work done by the employees simply did not lend itself to teams because it was independent work. Teams were appropriate for the supervisory positions because of the variability of the work load; it was difficult to predict which employee would need help at any point in time.

Managerial work teams require considerable meeting time to function effectively, time that presents a significant cost and cannot be dismissed lightly. Team meetings are needed for a very simple reason. If managers are not well coordinated and well informed about how other managers have dealt with a particular work group or individual, they run the great risk of counteracting each other's decisions and being played off against each other. Work teams may try to take advantage of one of the members of the management team who is particularly easy to deal with or weak on some issue. Or a work team may get a decision from one member of the management team, not like it, and try to go to another member of the management team to get a different decision.

Despite some of the limitations of managerial work teams, their popularity seems likely to increase because they offer significant advantages just as do production work teams. In some very complicated production and service situations, business issues really come together for the first time to create a true business experience only at the management level. Although it is desirable to have these issues placed in the hands of a work team, the geographical dispersion, complexity, and speed of the work may make it impossible to have a work team responsible for an entire product or service. Multiple teams, however, under the control of a self-managing or autonomous management team, may be able to take responsibility for the entire product or service. Thus, in many respects, managerial teams can be looked upon as a way to produce integration at a low level of an organization, just as production work teams do it in some situations. If management teams can produce this integration, fewer levels of management and less in the way of overhead support structures will be needed.

Project Teams

Organizations are increasingly using teams to do specific work projects. Often, these teams are expected to operate only as long as it takes to develop a new project or product or to deliver a particular service. Typically, these teams are created because the organization needs to get a project done in a fast, high-quality, integrated way.

As mentioned earlier, in the typical traditional organization, many projects, such as the development of a new product, must go through three or four different functional areas. This process often creates severe speed and quality problems for several reasons (Stalk and Hout, 1990). First and foremost, no one is responsible for the overall quality of the product in a traditionally managed organization, and product quality often suffers. But, perhaps just as important, the process moves slowly because each group has to do its own activity sequentially, and thus the process can only move in a step-by-step method. Often the process is further slowed in moving from one department to another because the hierarchy in each department has to give approval before the process can move on. When this approach to design and development is used, the end product often fails to be suitable because the approach has not considered the many interdependencies between engineering, manufacturing, and marketing that are involved. This cumbersome process is one of the major reasons that companies are slow to bring new products to market.

The obvious solution to this problem is to create self-managing teams that are responsible for developing a product from beginning to end. These teams need to draw members from multiple functions in the organization in a concurrent engineering approach. If the teams are to move quickly, they need to have a high level of autonomy in terms of the work they do on a product or project. If they constantly have to check their decisions with the different functional areas and work their way up the hierarchy in each area, they will fall prey to the same problems that are inherent in a sequential process, and, what is more, the design team members will not have ownership of the end product.

Hewlett-Packard has used what it calls *board of director teams* to coordinate the development of complex new electronic products. A project's board of directors typically includes engineers, technical writers, marketing managers, lawyers, purchasing people, and manufacturing workers. It is their responsibility to coordinate the efforts of different teams and to keep the development of the product on time. Each member of the board influences the decision from his or her perspective, and the team is charged with the resolution of conflicts between different specialties.

In many respects, project teams represent an evolution of the *matrix management model*, which first gained popularity in the 1970s (Galbraith, 1973, 1977; Davis and Lawrence, 1977). It, too, stresses the importance of project teams. In this approach, individuals typically have their "homes" in a functional area and then are assigned to teams for periods of time. Although this approach has many good points, it often does not operate effectively for a number of reasons, not the least of which is that it violates traditional concepts of authority. Violation of these concepts should be less of a problem in a high-involvement culture, particularly if the organization makes a concerted effort to ensure that the project teams have a high level of autonomy and are not controlled by the functional areas. All too often in the matrix model, decision making is slowed because the project team lacks the power to make critical decisions.

The individual members of project teams may not need much cross-training. They are brought together precisely because of their expertise in a particular area. Nevertheless, it is helpful for team members to have some understanding of what goes on in other areas. Over time, the effectiveness of project teams is facilitated by rotational career tracks, which take key individuals through several different functional areas. For example, it is useful for a team to include engineers who have worked in both design engineering and production engineering because these two areas are so crucial to the development of new products.

The practical knowledge about how to actually operate managerial and white-collar teams is still in an embryonic stage. Nevertheless, it seems likely that just as work teams are increasingly replacing individual work designs at the level of production and service delivery in organizations, they will substantially replace individual managerial jobs and individual responsibility for specific functions. Work teams represent a way to give a broad scope to managerial jobs as well as a way to handle some of the speed and coordination issues that are so critical in today's competitive work environment. Many engineers and professionals in accounting and other service firms already work in an environment in which they need to constantly form new project teams and abandon others.

Changes in the demands placed on organizations could

result in high-involvement organizations in which most, if not all, employees are members of a team. Teams potentially can create more adaptive organizations that are able to respond to a business environment that includes short product life cycles and a constant need to improve products and services. In an organization totally based on teams, every employee should feel responsible for and be involved in the organization.

The Mixed Model

In many organizations, the work that needs to be done is not all of the same nature and cannot be changed to be of the same nature. Some work may best fit the individual enrichment approach, some the team approach, and some the traditional control approach. Can these approaches coexist in an organization and, if so, how?

One aspect of this question is relatively easy to answer. It is not difficult for an organization to use both the job enrichment approach and the work team approach. These two approaches are both oriented toward high-involvement and are based on similar assumptions about what motivates people and how people should relate to their work. They both share the same core value of giving information, knowledge, power, and rewards to all employees. Some conflicts may occur because of the different emphasis each approach gives to social skills, social interaction, and individual accountability versus group accountability, but overall, the approaches are congruent and can coexist. The key to avoiding conflicts is to educate employees about why teams are used in some situations while individual job enrichment is used in others.

The situation is quite different when traditional work design is combined with either of the two high-involvement work designs. In a sense, these approaches have coexisted in traditional organizations for decades because high-level managerial work has been highly enriched while low-level jobs have been based on a control-oriented approach. Traditional organizations have been able to use both approaches essentially because the approaches have been used at different, somewhat segregated, levels in the organizations and because the traditional approach has been seen as the only option at the low levels of the organizations. Still, the use of these different approaches has produced problems and conflicts between the haves and the have-nots. In many cases, the use of two approaches has led to militant unions and has produced high levels of dissatisfaction among employees.

In certain organizations, some lower-level employees operate in an environment that has high-involvement work designs and others operate in an environment that is based on a control-oriented approach to work design. In my experience, this difficult situation can be managed if the different approaches to work design are found in different divisions of the company or in different geographical locations. However, it is very hard to manage this situation when the locations are socially interdependent because they are geographically close to each other and when they have work flow interdependencies.

Inevitably, employees in the repetitive jobs want to know why they cannot have the kind of work that exists elsewhere in the organization. The organization has to operate as a double-breasted employer, telling one group that they have to put up with repetitive jobs while other individuals get challenging, interesting, and exciting work. Such a situation makes it very difficult for an organization to develop value and philosophy statements that capture how the organization wants to operate and, of course, makes it difficult for everyone in the organization to have a common sense of purpose and mission. Designing pay and human resources practices also becomes difficult. An organization that operates with just one approach to work design can easily and clearly communicate this approach to all employees and can operate all of its systems in concert with this particular approach to work design. An organization that uses two different approaches has to have two of everything, and this not only is more expensive it may also leave employees with no real sense of how the organization intends to operate.

One alternative approach to designing all jobs the same is to contract out the repetitive and unchallenging work. In manufacturing plants, for example, cleanup and guard duty can be subcontracted to organizations that specialize in these tasks. Airlines can contract out some of the reservations tasks that are hard to make interesting and challenging. Alternatively, it may be best to adopt a network approach to organizing and to let someone else manage the work that does not fit a high-involvement approach. Individuals also can be rotated through some of the repetitive jobs, such as reservations, on a very limited basis so that no one has to do them on a full-time basis. This may not completely solve the problem, but at least it avoids the tendency to create a group of second-class citizens who do the "dum-dum" jobs.

My preference is for an organization to have one approach to work design that it applies universally. This can mean that in some cases work that really should be designed in another manner ends up being designed to be congruent with the dominant approach. In a high-involvement organization, the work that normally would fit the control-oriented model should be done with enriched jobs or teams in order to create a homogeneous internal approach to management.

In most cases, the less-interesting work can be made more interesting even though it may involve some extra labor costs. Again, I have seen this done with reservations jobs in which individuals are given a little extra time to make each reservation so that they can have a more interesting conversation with the individual calling in and develop a better relationship with that person. In other cases, an organization can delay purchase of the latest piece of automated technology in order to leave more involved work in the hands of employees. This strategy may take more labor hours, but it can allow the organization to maintain a consistent work design. If few jobs in an organization are being enriched, even though this is not the most efficient approach, these jobs should not be a serious problem for an organization. The organization simply must accept the inefficiencies of a few jobs that are designed inappropriately in order to gain the efficiencies that are inherent in managing organizations with a single approach to work design.

Chapter Six

Foster Organization- Improvement Groups

The use of improvement groups is closely related to the traditional American practice of written suggestion systems. The group approach simply uses groups to tap the knowledge and expertise that is in the minds of employees and to develop employees' ideas. Groups also can help to assure that ideas are given a fair and reasonable hearing within the organization. This chapter will focus on the strengths and weaknesses of improvement groups and how they should be used in a high-involvement management approach.

Employees' ideas about organizational improvement can be very valuable. They can lead to improvements in work methods as well as to the development of new products and services. The challenge all organizations face is how to elicit, process, and implement these ideas. Although this is easier to do in organizations that emphasize employee involvement, even in these organizations it often requires special attention and programs.

Written suggestion programs are the most common approach organizations use to elicit suggestions (Lawler, Ledford, and Mohrman, 1989). There is little question that such programs can help traditionally managed organizations, but they are very bureaucratic, top-down, and individual in their orientation. Thus they do not fit in high-involvement organizations. More promising approaches are group suggestion programs. A number of organizations in the United States have a long history of creating groups to develop suggestions or ideas that will improve the way the organization operates. Groups of volunteers typically meet for a prescribed period of time and focus their efforts on improving the organization's technical or administrative processes. They submit their suggestions to management, which decides whether to implement them.

Quality Circles

The most popular form of improvement group in the 1980s was the quality circle (Lawler, Ledford, and Mohrman, 1989). In many respects, the adoption of quality circles seemed to be somewhat of a fad, as organizations rushed to improve the quality of their goods and services in order to compete more effectively with Japanese companies (Lawler and Mohrman, 1985). In just a few years, the United States went from a country with a few hundred people participating in quality circles to a country in which hundreds of thousands of employees participated in them.

In some cases, quality circles have been introduced as a stand-alone program. In other situations they are introduced as part of a *total quality program*. Total quality programs are based on the work of Juran, Deming, or some other quality expert and have become increasingly popular for a variety of reasons, including the belief that they have contributed to the success of many Japanese organizations. The creation in the United States of the Malcolm Baldrige National Quality Award has also focused attention on them, particularly since some of the winners of the award have used receiving the award as a marketing tool. When quality circles are part of a total quality program, they are usually combined with work process simplification, work cells, cost-of-quality measurement, self-inspection, and other features that are targeted at helping an organization improve the quality of its performance. In these programs, quality circles are usually seen as the means of involving people in the quality-improvement process.

A study of the Fortune 1000 companies found that 70 percent of them used quality circles in 1987, although they tended to use them on a limited basis (Lawler, Ledford, and Mohrman, 1989). For example, those companies reporting that they used quality circles typically involved less than 20 percent of their employees in a circle at any point in time. The study also found that most of the organizations had started to use the groups during the 1980s. A later survey of the Fortune 1000 showed a small increase in the use of quality circles from 1987 to 1990 (Lawler, Mohrman, and Ledford, 1992).

Although quality circles are the most frequently adopted and visible approach to creating problem-solving groups, infinite variations of these groups exist. Many organizations have tested the basic idea of problem-solving groups over time and have modified it to best fit the kind of issues that they face and their management approach.

In many respects, quality circles are just the most recent manifestation of the view that groups can be used to develop ideas that will improve an organization's operations. An earlier application of this view is the use of productivity-improvement groups as part of the installation of Scanlon and other gainsharing plans that combine them with plant-wide bonuses. As will be discussed further in Chapter Eight, these plans typically combine the use of financial incentives with the creation of groups to process suggestions about how work methods and procedures can be improved.

Characteristics

It is worth briefly reviewing the characteristics of the typical quality circle to clarify the basic elements and rationale that underlie this approach to organizational improvement.

As with any management practice, the actual characteristics of quality circles differ from situation to situation. This is because companies adapt the basic model to their particular circumstances. Nevertheless, the different approaches have enough similarities that it is possible to talk about a general model for quality circles.

The membership of most quality circles is composed of volunteers from a particular work area or department. Rarely are all the members of a work group or area involved. Typically, more people volunteer than there are spaces available in the circle (frequently, about 80 percent of the people in a work area volunteer). As a result, some people have to be refused the opportunity to participate, at least initially. Over time, membership typically changes; in many cases, circles stop meeting and new ones are formed in the same work area. Most individuals who want to participate eventually can do so.

Most of the early applications of quality circles were in blue-collar, nonmanagement areas. Currently, organizations use quality circles in white-collar and technical areas as well, and they are now used throughout some organizations. They usually do not involve managers.

Quality circles are told to focus on improving product quality. In some organizations, they are also instructed to look at issues of productivity and cost reduction. However, they are not given a broad mandate to look at ways in which the organization could operate more effectively and improve the quality of work life. This is in contrast to the union-management quality-of-work-life programs that will be discussed in Chapter Twelve and some other participative management techniques (Lawler, 1986). Overall, the agenda of most quality circles is very clearly stated and programmed so that it is limited to discussions of quality and perhaps productivity. Most circles have no budget or ability to spend company or organizational resources, but they can study the financial implications of their recommendations and are often expected to do so.

In most quality circle programs, employees do not receive direct financial rewards for coming up with good ideas or cost savings. People typically are paid for participating in the meetings since they are held on company time, and highly successful groups often are given nonmonetary recognition awards. To an extent, this practice follows the Japanese model in which pictures, awards, banquets, symbols, and so on are given to quality circles that are particularly effective (Cole, 1989). It is amazing to see the variety of awards that companies give to their quality circles. I have seen enormous creativity go into the development of T-shirts, logos, hats, and awards ceremonies. In the Northrop

Corporation, for example, awards have been emblazoned with team names, including "Tiger by the Tail" and "Team Hornet." Xerox runs an elaborate corporatewide "team day" that recognizes the contributions of teams.

Some companies reward individuals and circles for the number of suggestions they develop and even have quotas for suggestions, a clear example of the control approach being applied to a participative activity! Occasionally, companies allow quality circles to receive a cash award through their already existing suggestion programs. These rewards are typically based on an estimate of the savings that will result from the suggestion during the first year. In their "pure" form, however, quality circles do not receive financial rewards; usually, great stress is placed on the fact that the rewards for participating in the circles are intrinsic, not financial.

Most quality circle programs place a heavy emphasis on training. Particularly at the beginning, circle members are trained in group-process and in problem-solving techniques. This training often does not include the kind of statistical quality-control methods that Deming (1986) made an integral part of the Japanese quality-control approach. In the United States, the training for quality circles emphasizes techniques such as how to identify a problem, how to brainstorm solutions, and how to present solutions to others. It is common for a quality circle program to involve ten to twenty hours of training per individual and for companies to buy a prepared training package from a consultant.

Quality circles typically meet on a regular basis, often at two-week intervals, and meetings last from one to two hours. As people become involved in problem solving and in developing particular solutions, they may meet for longer time periods. Sometimes quality circles meet on their own time to develop their ideas and presentations for managers. However, in most cases, since it is required by law, circle members are paid by their company for all the time they spend on quality circle activities. In Japan, quality circles almost always meet on the employees' time!

Most quality circles are not led by the manager in the

work area where they operate. Instead, a facilitator is provided to meet with the groups. This person usually has been trained in group-process techniques but is not necessarily technically knowledgeable with respect to the work procedures and methods. This facilitator's job is to help the group prepare its solutions, work effectively as a team, and, ultimately, present its solutions to management.

Quality circles are typically installed in a top-down manner; that is, someone at the top of the organization decides that quality circles are attractive and mandates that they be tried in the organization. Next, volunteers are requested at the lowest level of the organization. Many of the middle levels of the organization and the staff support people are ignored in the early phases of the installation of the quality circles, which are typically handled by the facilitators. After being trained by consultants, the facilitators form the groups, organize the presentations, and handle the upward flow of communications.

Quality circles have no formal authority in the organization except to meet and make suggestions. As such, they are not particularly threatening to the basic management prerogatives in the organization. Many consultants market quality circles on the basis that they do not require a change in most top-down management styles.

An important part of every circle's activity is presenting its ideas to management for approval. This presentation is usually carefully planned and involves several different levels in the organization. The employees usually have only their expertise and the credibility of their arguments to help them. In a few cases, however, I have seen top management order acceptance of the initial suggestions of the circles in order to get them off to "the right start."

Impact on Involvement

We can now look at quality circles in terms of how they affect information, knowledge, power, and rewards. No systematic communication program is associated with quality circles to move information downward in the organization. However, since circles often involve people from different areas of the organization, circle members may develop a broader understanding of the product or service and they may come to appreciate other people's problems and perspectives. In addition, as the members develop solutions, figure out the cost of the solutions, and present their solutions to management, they often learn a considerable amount about the constraints and issues that their organization faces. They may also learn something about costs and about the role of capital.

Quality circles do facilitate the upward flow of ideas for improvement, which is probably their major contribution. Since circle members present their ideas to higher-level managers, the program typically leads to a new upward flow of communication that is quite important, with a positive impact on both management and the employees who present their suggestions. I have seen a number of top managers who were positively impressed by the presentations of quality circles. Managers find out that the rank and file have ideas and can get involved in the organization in the same way that they do. Presenting their ideas to upper management is understandably a big event for most circle members; it involves using skills that they do not usually use and meeting with high-status people.

An organization's training program for quality circle members usually increases people's problem-solving skills as well as their communication and interpersonal skills. As such, quality circles typically lead people to feel more competent and to be more skilled in certain areas. However, participants do not usually learn much about particular work methods or procedures such as scheduling and inventory. Instead, they learn how to solve problems, how to interact, how to make presentations, and how to deal with others. These are important skills to learn if the organization plans to move to other forms of employee participation, such as work teams. However, employees use these skills infrequently in quality circle programs (once a week for an hour or two at the most). As a result, their development of the skills is limited, and this can be as much a source of frustration as satisfaction.

Quality circles have little power to affect most decisions

that are made in organizations. In fact, they represent a parallel structure to the traditional hierarchical authority; that is, all the traditional power relationships remain in place when quality circles are installed. For an hour or two every week, people have the chance to meet in a special situation that involves a free exchange of ideas and thoughts about improvement. Employees also have the opportunity to present their suggestions to the traditional hierarchical structure, which usually has no mandate to accept the suggestions.

A subtle change in the power structure of organizations may occur when quality circles are used. Since knowledge and information are a kind of power, some power may shift to low-level circle members. This shift can be quite dramatic if top management mandates that the circles' suggestions be taken seriously. However, most companies simply give circles their "day in court," and, thus, their only power is the power of their ideas and presentation skills. Since few quality circle programs involve sharing financial rewards, with a few exceptions, the financial reward systems in most organizations go unchanged.

Overall, quality circle programs do not change organizations substantially. They do not represent a major move toward involving employees psychologically or financially in their organizations (Lawler, 1988a). They fail to create external customer relationships and often fail to give individuals a real sense of the business realities that their organization faces. They leave unchanged promotion, selection, and pay systems. They do change the training system in ways that give people new skills and expertise. Their major impact is in developing suggestions and providing a vehicle for processing suggestions that come out of the problem-solving sessions. Thus, they help assure that the ideas will be heard. This is important, but it is far short of the type of participation that occurs when work teams are created or jobs are enriched.

Effectiveness

Quality circles initially can and usually do produce useful ideas about how to improve quality and productivity (Lawler, 1986;

Ledford, Lawler, and Mohrman, 1989). The literature on quality circles is full of stories about how circles have saved companies millions of dollars by ideas as simple as changing suppliers or as complex as new work processes. Quality circles also can establish employees' desire to participate in the problem-solving aspects of the company. However, they are an approach to problem solving and idea generation that has high costs associated with it and questionable long-term effectiveness.

Quality circle programs have a definite life cycle (Lawler and Mohrman, 1985, 1987a). Organizations need to understand this life cycle in order to assess quality circles and to make recommendations concerning their use. The initial concern in the life cycle of a quality circle is membership. Since quality circles are staffed with volunteers, management is always concerned about whether there will be enough volunteers. This concern is usually quickly eliminated when the call for volunteers produces many more volunteers than can be incorporated in the circles that are planned.

The circle members' initial enthusiasm usually carries through the training and the first meetings of the quality circles. In most circles, it also carries through the identification of solutions to several important problems. The few quality circles that fail at this stage do so because they find the problems they are dealing with intractable and insolvable. But these groups are the exception rather than the rule.

Groups usually continue to be successful through the development of the presentation of the solution and initial meetings with members of management about implementing the suggested solutions. A major problem can develop at this point: management rejection of the ideas. Management may reject the ideas for a wide range of reasons, one of which is simple resistance to the change because management did not participate in the problem solving. Often, individuals who need to accept and implement the suggestions are not in the program and thus do not feel they own the changes. In some cases, they may be threatened by the changes. And some groups may work on issues that are not of concern to management. For example, I have seen groups focus on lighting the parking lot and slowing the use of paper towels in bathroom. Sometimes the ideas cost too much or management is already planning a less-expensive solution to the problem.

If the ideas are accepted, the organization often publicizes them and praises the ideas that have come out of the quality circle program. Projected savings of hundreds of thousands of dollars are often mentioned at this point. For example, one company I worked with estimated savings of $300,000 a year from a suggestion that called for buying a new set of tools (which cost $40,000) so that the employees would not have to slow production while they searched for tools.

The next phase in the life cycle of the quality circle program is often an expansion of the program; more groups are formed and trained. In many companies, this is the high point of the program. It appears that the ability of quality circles to improve the company's performance hinges simply on creating more groups and letting them go to work. During this phase, success is often measured by the number of groups and the number of people involved—more is always better. One manager I interviewed called this the "by-the-numbers phase," in which many managers do the right things (start participation) for the wrong reason (the push from top management to have a program).

Additional important complications and problems occur during the expansion phase. First, implementation of many of the ideas suggested by the groups proves to be difficult. It often requires middle-level managers and staff support groups (such as engineering and maintenance) to implement change or to accept changes in procedures and practices that they developed and that are under their control. Not only do these ideas for change mean extra work for these people, they also often imply that these individuals have not done their job correctly in the past. Furthermore, as mentioned earlier, these individuals are usually not part of the quality circle process and may even find out about quality circles for the first time when the circles suggest some changes in their area of expertise. Not surprisingly, resistance is extremely common when this occurs.

It is difficult to institute change in organizations under

any circumstances, and the difficulty increases when the change is spearheaded by a group that has no formal authority, that typically comes from the lower levels of the organization, and that is asking people who have "professional expertise" to change things that they have been doing for many years. Perhaps the best way to summarize this point is to stress that quality circles are often seen as a significant threat to both the ego and the jobs of certain people in organizations. As a result, the ideas that they suggest often are not implemented, which disillusions and angers quality circle participants.

"Irrational" resistance is not the only reason why suggestions from quality circles do not get implemented. Sometimes the suggestions simply prove to be impractical. Because of the limited information and knowledge most circle participants have, they can develop ideas that look good to them but that are impractical given conditions they are not aware of. For example, groups often develop solutions that call for significant expenditures of money (such as buying new equipment) only to find out that the money is not available. In one case I observed, a circle's suggestion could not be implemented because management had already bought a major piece of equipment that changed the manufacturing process.

If quality circles get beyond the hurdle of developing and suggesting solutions that are actually implemented, the program enters a new phase. At this point, it comes up against a design feature that is common to most quality circle programs: only certain members of the organization can be involved at any one point in time. Those employees who are not involved become upset that they are not participating. An organization can rotate membership in quality circles, but members often do not want to leave after experiencing success. They often argue that the company should not liquidate their highly successful quality circle. I have literally seen members cry when they have to leave their circles. I have also seen circles continue for months longer than they should have simply because people enjoy the social aspects of meeting. For a while, Motorola tried to deal with this issue by letting everyone who wished to be in a circle be in one.

If the program is expanded, the organization must increase the number of facilitators and commit more and more resources to the program. Ultimately, this expansion leads to the phase during which most programs decline or end. Costs are high because so many groups are meeting, and substantial opposition has built up among those who feel they have lost power. In addition, many of the easy problems have been solved, so the problem-solving activity does not go as well in later groups as it did in the initial groups. And, usually, some of the savings that were initially projected have not been realized.

The parallel structure that is created to manage a quality circle program can be quite large in a well-established program. It often includes a program director, facilitators, and trainers who are assigned full time to support and manage the program. No studies show just how many employees it takes to run a quality circle program. My observation is that at least one full-time person is required for each six to ten circles. For example, in 1985, Northrop reported having eleven staff people and close to 2,000 employees involved in quality circles and associated activities. Obviously, these figures indicate the significant costs associated with quality circle programs, but I have never seen a good study of all the costs.

The history of Florida Power and Light highlights the cost and bureaucracy these programs can produce. An early adopter of the total quality approach, the company won the prestigious Deming Award for total quality. They are the only company based outside of Japan to win this Japanese award. However, in 1990, they began to dismantle the extensive bureaucracy they had developed to support their program. According to a letter sent to all employees in June 1990 from Jim Broadhead, their chief executive officer, the program placed too great an emphasis on charts, graphs, reports, and meetings. He went on to add that the organization had become too focused on quality and was not balancing it with the need to control costs and respond quickly.

Perhaps the most serious long-term problem with quality circle programs is that they may raise expectations that cannot be filled by the design of the typical quality circle program. To the degree that people feel competent and powerful in their quality circle activities, they may challenge a number of basic assumptions about the way that their organization is run. Because quality circles are a parallel structure, they leave the day-to-day work activities of individuals intact. People can be absolute geniuses in their quality circles, but when doing their regular job, they are still expected to perform the same repetitive, boring, mindless task. In addition, they may be told that their idea saved the company hundreds of thousands of dollars, but they are not financially rewarded for this saving. It all goes to the company and not to the person making the suggestion.

A kind of catch-22 operates with respect to financial rewards. The success of a program depends on positive feedback, and management needs to report savings and give credit to the quality circles. This feedback, in turn, highlights the advantages of the program for the company and raises the issue of financial payoffs for the employees. Ironically, this issue rarely comes up in unsuccessful efforts or where no savings are claimed—the programs simply end.

Quality circle programs can also change people's ideas of their own competence, and this development often calls for changes in the organization's career system. Management careers often look more attractive and attainable to those who have done well in problem solving. Since many quality circle participants are not trained in management skills, they ask for career tracks and training that will lead them into management.

Overall, a quality circle program may lead to a demand for movement toward a more participative management system. If management is prepared to change, quality circle programs can be an effective way to move toward high-involvement management. However, if management is not ready to change, a quality circle program can alienate and disappoint those people who are most effective in the program—the people who come up with good ideas and who develop their skills.

In a very real sense, the major weaknesses of quality circles occur because the circles are a parallel activity to the regular work activities. Because of this, a number of inefficiencies and overhead costs are built into their operation. The obvious extra costs include training and meeting costs. Less

obvious costs include the hierarchy of facilitators and adminis-
trators that needs to be maintained to operate the program.
And it can be expensive to process suggestions if they have to be
recorded and processed for approval. All too often, the focus
becomes the number of suggestions produced rather than the
cost of processing them.

Several years ago, a consultant told me with great pride
that in one of his programs an employee was producing eight
suggestions a day and that the implementation rate of her
suggestions was over 90 percent. While I applaud the employee's
energy and creativity, I cannot help wondering if all these ideas
really needed to be processed and approved; could not some of
them have just been implemented by the employee or her work
team?

Alternatives to Quality Circles

A number of companies that have tried quality circles have
reduced their use of the circles while increasing their use of a
variety of targeted problem-solving groups (Lawler, Ledford,
and Mohrman, 1989). Task forces and improvement groups
created by management and asked to look at and evaluate
specific elements of the organization's work process or practices
are, in fact, used more frequently than are quality circles according to a 1990 survey of the Fortune 1000 companies (Lawler,
Mohrman, and Ledford, 1992). These groups can be effective in
producing suggestions and also can be useful in the transition
to the high-involvement approach.

By targeting what groups focus on, an organization gains
a number of advantages, although group members may view this
focus as decreasing their power. In fact, a clear focus often
increases the power of a group because it assures that the issue it
deals with is one that is central to the organization and one that
the organization plans to act on. In addition, because management has sanctioned and sponsored the group's work, the group
often has high levels of energy to work on the issue and can
usually draw upon staff and outside resources to support it as it
solves problems and designs solutions.

The challenge for any improvement group is to be sure that it gathers all the information it needs to make good decisions and that it is well linked to the rest of the organization so that when it comes up with its recommendations the organization is, in a sense, presold. The group needs to be sure that individuals throughout the organization are generally familiar with the direction that its recommendations take and are in agreement with them. Some organizations help to ensure this agreement by assigning a senior management sponsor to work with each improvement group.

Increasingly, organizations that have total quality programs are using improvement groups. The use of these groups reflects the frustration that these organizations feel with the inefficiencies of the quality circle approach and their desire to maintain more control over group activity. In many cases, these improvement groups fit in well with total quality programs. Most total quality programs espouse employee involvement, but they are very structured and controlled so that only low levels of involvement are possible. Targeted improvement groups, however, are one vehicle that allows these programs to involve a number of employees and to focus the organization on improving the work process activities that involve many people and are so critical to quality improvements.

In many respects, groups that are focused on a particular area of the organization that needs improvement can do more to move an organization toward employee involvement than can quality circles. If they are correctly targeted at the key issues that need to change, they not only can train individuals in skills that are needed for a high-involvement approach to management but also can design specific management practices and policies that move the organization toward high involvement. Of course, the groups may be focused on only technical and production issues that do not directly affect the move to employee involvement as a management approach.

Despite their limitations, targeted problem-solving groups and targeted quality circles can play a role in making traditional organizations more effective because they help mitigate the effects of traditional work designs. They allow types of coordination, idea generation, and problem solving to take place that cannot normally take place within the traditional structure. Hence, the parallel model makes sense in organizations in which a high-involvement approach to management does not fit. Indeed, in many traditional manufacturing situations, parallel problem-solving groups may be the only way to get most employees involved in even minimally participative activities. These groups can at least provide individuals with a chance to improve work situations and use their problem-solving skills where more extensive forms of involvement are not practical.

Work Teams and Improvement Groups

One approach to implementing employee involvement is to progress from the use of parallel groups like quality circles to an approach in which employees solve problems and generate ideas as a regular part of the work process. Integrating these activities into employees' jobs should produce a substantial cost savings because the overhead that it takes to run the quality circles is saved. It also should lead to quicker implementation of ideas since they will not have to be reviewed and screened at higher levels of the organization.

The creation of work teams would appear to be the ideal way to make most quality circles unnecessary. Quality circles are needed primarily because individuals do not have the power to change work processes and work methods and they do not have the time and skills to solve problems unless this special structure is created. Quality circles often counter some of the most negative effects of the traditional organizational design; that is, they allow individuals who have improvement ideas to spend time solving problems and working on issues that go beyond their narrow jobs.

In organizations that create effective work teams, individuals do control work procedures and work methods for the production of a whole product or service. Through routine meetings and training, they should have the opportunity and the skills to do the type of problem solving that is usually done in quality circles. An organization based on well-designed work teams should integrate the activities found in quality circles into the ongoing work activities of work teams and should not need to create an extensive parallel structure.

Quality circles and similar problem-solving groups may be useful as the starting point for a movement to work teams. They can provide just the kind of training individuals need to operate effectively in work teams (Lawler and Mohrman, 1987a). They also are somewhat less threatening to the existing management structure than are work teams, and managers typically do not resist them as much as they resist work teams.

The success of problem-solving groups often can help convince reluctant managers that, in fact, it is useful to involve employees in this manner and thus can facilitate the overall movement of the organization toward employee involvement. As a first step, these groups can often "pick the low-hanging fruit"; that is, they can quickly solve some of the more obvious problems an organization faces and produce some good immediate gains for the organization. Because these groups do not take as long to form as work teams, they can provide some immediate help to an organization that is not available through the work team process.

Improvement groups can facilitate an organization's movement from a traditional structure to a high-involvement structure, but are they useful once an organization has moved to a high-involvement approach based on teams? As with most questions about organizations, no answer to this question is universally true, but, generally speaking, the need for improvement groups in most high-involvement organizations is limited. However, improvement groups can accomplish certain things that are not easily and naturally done by work teams. Indeed, it is possible that this type of group can be a valuable complement to work teams precisely because these groups help an organization deal with issues that do not naturally fall within the responsibility and capability of a particular team.

Once work teams are formed, they are very good at dealing with work-improvement issues and even policy issues that fall within their area of responsibility, particularly improving their product or their service. Indeed, as mentioned earlier, they are much more efficient at making changes than improvement groups are simply because they do not have to go through a formal approval process to implement the changes. In addition, their members often are much more knowledgeable about the work process and, thus, develop better ideas. In general, the research evidence suggests that work teams are a superior approach to involvement in comparison to improvement groups (Beekun, 1989). But what about those issues that do not fall within a team's boundaries or only partially fall within them? For example, a customer relationship may require coordination between delivery and sales, product development issues may affect teams in engineering and manufacturing, or issues concerning the facility may affect everyone at a location. Some sort of overlay or other structure is needed to deal with these inter-team issues.

Organizations with work teams can use temporary improvement groups to address issues that affect multiple teams and are, therefore, beyond the boundary of any one team to correct. Members of these groups can be drawn from those teams that are likely to be affected by the issue. Because the team members have been trained in team skills and problem-solving skills, these groups should be able to operate quite effectively and start up quickly. In most cases, these improvement groups should be asked to address a specific issue because it does not make sense to have them simply begin to meet in order to decide what problems they will address.

By using targeted improvement groups and work teams, a high-involvement organization may be able to operate effectively without using any traditional quality circles. I do not want to totally rule out the use of some traditional quality circles in even a high-involvement organization, however. They may still play a limited role in certain work areas in which high rates of change exist and there is a heavy need for ongoing improvement of work methods. If the rate of change in a work situation is very high, it may be difficult for work teams to find the time to do open-ended problem solving. Also, they may have trouble identifying those issues that cut across teams and that need to be resolved. Sometimes quality circles that have members from many related work groups can, in fact, identify these issues and make progress on them when work teams or targeted improvement groups cannot.

Groups for Organizational Assessment and Renewal

Most high-involvement organizations definitely need task forces and improvement groups that constantly evaluate how effectively the organization is operating as a system and culture. Complacency is a potential problem with any high-involvement organization that is based on work teams. Teams tend to become cohesive and to want to maintain their identity and their ways of operating. In addition, sometimes teams get stuck at a particular level of development and need a push to improve and further develop their effectiveness (Hackman, 1989).

One way that high-involvement organizations can keep constantly focused on improving and developing is for them to regularly commission task forces and teams to look at how effectively the organization is operating. Groups that have a wide-ranging membership, often covering multiple levels in the organization, can be valuable in assessing the current effectiveness of the organization. They also can plan for organizational change and the adoption of high-involvement management. These groups are often called *diagonal task forces* to reflect the fact that they draw people from multiple functions and multiple levels in the organization. They can be assigned to study the pay, production, and information systems or any number of issues that the organization must act upon to improve its effectiveness and to progress toward high-involvement management.

If possible, these groups should use the organization's competitors as a basis for comparison and assessment. Such a benchmark can help bring an element of specificity to what it means to be a world-class competitor and how the organization needs to improve in order to achieve this status.

As will be discussed in Chapter Ten, an organization should conduct attitude surveys and interviews and gather other data to help groups looking at how effectively the organization is operating. For example, work teams can be given data on how effectively they are operating and asked to solve problems around their operations. If they fail to solve these problems successfully on their own, the organization may need to intervene and emphasize the need for continuous improvement of the group's skills and performance.

The examination of specific systems in the organization (such as the pay, selection, and information systems and the organization's design and structure) by diagonal task forces is consistent with the high-involvement concept of moving information, knowledge, and power down the hierarchy. Indeed, ongoing maintenance and operation of these systems may also appropriately be placed in the hands of groups that rotate membership over time and are constantly asked to assess and evaluate the systems.

Forming teams and task forces to work on issues of organizational effectiveness is not simple. The groups must be carefully planned, and they need to receive a clear charter. The charter should specify what they should work on and clearly delineate their constraints. These groups need to be given decision-making power that usually is not given to quality circles. They should be told that their recommendations will be accepted and implemented if the recommendations fall within the constraints. This strategy is highly consistent with the high-involvement model of management and it usually contributes to the groups having high energy for their activities. They, in effect, know that their recommendations will make a difference and will be accepted. Thus, they do not spend an inordinate amount of time worrying how they can make their recommendation acceptable to senior management. In addition, the organization does not run the risk of having the group's ideas rejected and having group members feel disillusioned about the process.

Management teams may be the best groups to work on some issues, for example, decisions about finances. The key tests of whether issues are best dealt with by a management group or by a diagonal task force are who has the expertise to solve the problem and how important it is that the work teams accept the solution in order for it to be effective. Clearly, the more the expertise to solve the problem lies with the work teams and the more their acceptance is critical to the implementation of the solution, the more important it is that a diagonal task force be used. Also, who has the time available must be considered. Sometimes members of work teams have more time to be involved in problem solving than managers do, particularly if the organization has been structured in a very lean manner.

One other advantage of having work team members involved in high-level strategic issues is that it creates a different kind of educational experience for the members. They learn what is going on in other parts of the organization and expand their understanding of work activities and processes. They also often gain a much greater understanding of customers and the competitive environment.

A good example of the use of diagonal improvement groups is provided by a Digital team-based plant that makes electronic boards for computers. When changing to manufacturing a different product, the plant needed to look at how the change should be managed and how it would affect the production teams. A diagonal task force was created to study the implementation of the change and, among other things, it recommended restructuring the teams and the organization.

Because acceptance of the new structure by the work teams was very important, the diagonal task force was the logical and correct way to address the implementation of the change. The management had no choice as to whether to accept the new technology (the old one was simply obsolete) but had a great deal of choice about how the new technology would be introduced and what its impact would be on group structures and work processes. Thus, it was vital for the management to involve employees extensively in this redesign process.

The same organization, incidentally, has constantly monitored its own effectiveness through attitude surveys and improvement groups that study the effectiveness of the organization in comparison to its competitors. This monitoring helps give the organization's improvement groups a good sense of how the organization is performing and where it needs to improve, which has stimulated them to solve problems and work on specific issues when needed.

All organizations should try to continuously improve. They should always be questioning how they do work, with an eye toward making substantial improvements. Improvement groups and task forces can be effective vehicles for achieving these improvements. It may be particularly important to have these groups in a control-oriented organization, but high-involvement organizations should selectively use them as well.

Chapter Seven

Pay the Person, Not the Job

How an individual's pay level is determined has a number of important effects on an organization. In this chapter, the focus will be on how the determination of pay level affects organizational culture, employees' motivation to learn new skills, and the attraction and retention of skilled individuals. In Chapter Eight, motivation to perform and the degree to which performance has an impact on pay will be considered.

In most traditional control-oriented organizations, the major determinant of individuals' pay is the type of work they do. Organizations hire people for their individual qualities, but once they join an organization, the amount they are paid is primarily determined by the type of job they do. Why this switch from the person to the job? Basing pay on a person's job is a well-established practice that has a long history in the United States. It fits well with bureaucratic management approaches that exercise control by developing job descriptions, assigning individuals to them, and holding individuals accountable for how well they perform (Lawler, 1990b). In this approach, employees are, in many respects, actually worth what their job descriptions say they do because this is all they are asked to do. They also may be viewed as being replaceable by another individual who is assigned to do the job; hence, organizations have little need to focus on the individuals and their market value.

The major alternative to job-based pay is person-based

pay. It focuses on one or more characteristics of an individual in order to determine his or her pay. In Japan and many other countries, age and seniority are major determinants of pay. Family situations may also be important. As will be discussed later in this chapter, paying a person based on what he or she can do is the approach to person-based pay that fits best in a high-involvement organization.

Job-Based Pay

Job-based pay typically rests upon the foundation of a job evaluation system. Frequently, this job evaluation system takes a *point factor approach* to evaluating jobs (see Lawler, 1990b). The point factor approach starts with a carefully written job description that is the basis for the job evaluation. Job factors are then identified and given a relative weight. Typical plans include four job factors that differ substantially in their weight; that is, some carry the potential for earning more points than others. Commonly used factors include working conditions, problem-solving ability needed, knowledge required, and accountability. Jobs are assessed, usually by a job evaluation committee, as to how much of each factor they contain. The committee then assigns points for each factor and a total point score is produced for each job.

Usually, every job in the company ends up with a score. Point totals can then be compared to salary survey data that show how much other organizations pay for jobs with similar point totals. The point score is then translated into a salary level. Thus, through a series of subjective decisions, an organization can translate the tasks that it asks individuals to perform into an "objective" quantified result and a pay level. This "objectivity" is often facilitated by some mathematical manipulations of the data and the use of computers, which give the results an appearance of scientific precision.

Advantages of Pay Systems Based on Job Evaluation

Perhaps the single most important reason why organizations adopt pay systems based on job evaluation is that the evaluation helps them determine what other organizations are paying and can help an organization assess whether it is paying more or less than its competitors. Job evaluation can do this because it allows apples and oranges to be compared; that is, it allows jobs from one organization to be measured and scored on measures that are identical to or at least comparable to those used by another organization. Thus, even though organizations have different ways of organizing and end up with different jobs, the approach still can be applied and pay levels compared.

The second major advantage of job evaluation systems is that they allow for centralized control of an organization's pay system and of its pay levels. It is not by accident that consulting firms sell job evaluation to companies by focusing on senior management. In their presentations to senior management, consultants stress the important advantages that job evaluation gives in terms of being sure that the pay rates of all divisions and groups are in line. They also point out that job evaluation gives the corporate compensation staff the ability to audit any part of the organization for comparability and "equitable" pay rates. With a centralized pay structure and a good job evaluation system, all jobs can be slotted at a pay rate that can be audited by a corporate staff group. Audits can be used as a way to keep pay rates down and may be needed if there are no other reasons to keep pay costs at a reasonable level. Often, in large bureaucratic organizations, most managers and employees experience little pressure to control costs because they do not have responsibility for profit and do not have to face market tests of their labor costs.

Job evaluation is a proven technology. It has been used for so long that it has few mysteries and little research and development needs to be done on it (Rock, 1984; Rock and Berger, 1991). It is a ready-made approach that is relatively easy to use and that can be computerized in order to save labor. The approach is especially efficient if many individuals in an organization do the same job; only one evaluation is needed and the differences among individuals can be ignored. In contrast, person-based pay, which will be discussed next, requires an organization to develop the methods, procedures, and formulas that are needed to support it. In addition, person-based pay involves focusing on each individual and what he or she can do.

Sophisticated systems of job evaluation also make it possible for organizations to compare jobs internally. Thus, for organizations that desire to have high levels of internal equity, job evaluation is a useful tool because all the jobs in the organizations can be paid according to a single system. An organization can pay people the same amount for comparable job duties, regardless of which division, nook, cranny, or far reach of the organization they are in. Many large organizations see this as an advantage because they have a commitment to internal equity, fairness, and comparability of pay rates, regardless of where people are located in the organization.

Internal equity has some practical outcomes for an organization. For example, it facilitates employees' movement from one part of an organization to another. It helps an organization avoid situations in which the organization desires to promote someone but finds the pay system to be an obstacle because it calls for a pay decrease or no change in pay. With a good job evaluation system, a move to a "bigger job" will almost always result in a pay increase for the individual; therefore, movement up the hierarchy does not require major changes in the pay system or special treatment of the individuals who move.

Disadvantages of Pay Systems Based on Job Evaluation

Many of my criticisms of job evaluation rest on the argument that it is more than a way to pay employees; it is an integral part of the control-oriented approach to management. Because of this, it has limitations and it does not fit with a high-involvement approach to management. The fit between job evaluation and management style, however, often is not obvious to organizations when they first look at job evaluation. They see only a "fair" way to pay people, but job evaluation is more than this; it is an approach to thinking about work and people's relationship to their organization.

Bureaucratic Orientation

The first indication of the bureaucratic nature of job evaluation is its starting point: the job description. Basic to the bureaucratic approach to management is the idea that an individual has carefully prescribed activities to perform and that the individual should be held accountable for how well he or she performs those activities. The approach emphasizes control and individuals doing what the organization tells them to do.

Inherent in any job description system is a message to an individual about what is not included in his or her job responsibilities. Again, this message fits well with the traditional management idea of holding people accountable for certain specified duties. It does not fit well, however, with an orientation that says that an individual should do what is right in the situation rather than what is called for by a job description. Admittedly, job evaluation is only one small part of the problem, but it is a part of the problem. Sometimes an emphasis on job description is carried to its extreme and employees refuse to do things because they are "not in their job description." They demand a pay increase when they are asked to do more because they have accepted the value system that says that you are worth what you do; therefore, if you are asked to do more or to do different things by an organization, you obviously should have your job reevaluated and upgraded.

Emphasis on Hierarchy

Traditional bureaucratic management depends on a steep, well-reinforced hierarchy for its effectiveness. Orders and directions are provided by people at high levels in the hierarchy, and effectiveness depends on other employees doing what they are told. Job evaluation fits into this system quite well since it measures jobs in terms of their hierarchical power, control, and responsibilities. Large numbers of points are typically assigned to factors concerned with level of responsibility and number of reporting relationships. As a result, job evaluation scores clearly say to everyone in the organization who has the most responsible job, the next most responsible, and so on. The approach has the capability of differentiating among people who are at the same management level and have the same titles. This distinction has some obvious advantages when jobs are being evaluated internally and externally, but it also may have some severe negative consequences.

Job evaluation can create unnecessary and undesirable pecking orders and power relationships in the organization. In several organizations that I have studied, it has contributed to groups being hierarchical and power oriented. Research confirms that a rigid hierarchical structure is the last thing that is needed in professional and high-technology organizations (see, for example, Schuster, 1984; Von Glinow and Mohrman, 1989). Indeed, the key to success in these organizations often lies in utilizing the technical knowledge and the innovations that come from the bottom of the organization. Thus, employees need to operate in an organizational culture in which individuals are respected and rewarded for their expertise and ideas, not the "value" of the job they hold.

The principle that people are worth what they do may not be the most desirable cultural value for an organization. It tends to depersonalize individuals and equate them with a set of duties rather than with who they are and what they can do. It de-emphasizes paying people for the skills that they have and for their ability and willingness to grow and develop. A high-involvement organization needs to emphasize employees' growth, development, and performance as well as their value as total human beings. In organizations whose key assets are employees, a system that focuses on people rather than on jobs would seem to be a better fit than job evaluation.

Market Orientation

A focus on what other companies are doing in the marketplace and using these companies as a benchmark for performance are becoming increasingly important parts of involving employees in the business and giving them feedback about how they and the business are doing. In the ideal case, pay rates should be part of this external comparison process. Indeed, some companies (for example, TRW) try to target their salary levels to how the companies perform in comparison to their competitors. Job evaluation tends to focus pay on the internal relationships among jobs. It purports to provide a common measure (points) that is comparable across all jobs in the organization. This makes it possible for individuals to look across the organization and determine how they "should" stack up in terms of pay.

Thus, instead of focusing on the competition, employees often end up focusing on how other individuals within the organization are paid and on how they can improve their relative pay position. This focus takes them away from key business issues. What is more, it also tends to lead to inflation of internal pay rates. With such a system, the natural tendency of employees is to find a job internally that is relatively highly evaluated and to argue that it should be used as the benchmark that drives the internal pay structure. This is a virtually inevitable consequence of individuals being able to compare their jobs with other jobs on a common point system, and it can lead to higher and higher pay levels.

Inflexibility

In several ways, the job evaluation approach discourages organizations from changing. First, the amount of work it takes to create a job description and do a job evaluation generates a high investment in the status quo. Organizational change and reorganization become major issues in this system; it is no small task to rewrite all the job descriptions and reevaluate all the jobs.

A major factor in any change is the potential effect the change may have on the pay of individuals. Most major changes involve some individuals giving up responsibilities and accountabilities while others gain them. For example, in a move to a high-involvement approach to management, managers often need to give up some of their formal control and power and reduce the number of management levels below them so that employees can be more self-managing. If job evaluation is used, employees who give up responsibilities and reduce reporting levels receive lower pay. This system sets up a competition among individuals for responsibilities and creates resistance to reducing the levels of hierarchy and moving decisions to lower levels in the hierarchy. In short, job evaluation systems often end up as servants of the status quo rather than as stimulants for needed organizational change.

Bad Data

After organizations have used job evaluation systems for a while, employees become quite sophisticated in knowing how to get jobs evaluated highly. They realize that writing inflated job descriptions as well as changing their job duties can lead to increases in their pay. Employees may spend a considerable amount of time and effort on rewriting job descriptions so that their jobs will be scored highly.

Because enhancing job descriptions can lead to higher pay levels, the job evaluation system encourages and rewards dishonesty. It is all too easy for employees to learn that the way to beat the job evaluation system is to write overly flamboyant and inclusive job descriptions. This kind of corporate misinformation can be destructive to the long-term credibility of the organization. Most job evaluation systems have an internal audit to catch supervisors who lie about their duties and the duties of their subordinates. In some ways, this problem is not a fault of the system so much as it is a fault of the individual managers, but the system does tend to encourage this kind of misreporting.

Over time, inflating job descriptions can become standard operating procedure in an organization, and this can have three important negative consequences. First, because of inflated job evaluations, the organization simply ends up paying everyone too much. No data exist on how common this inflation is, but my guess is that it is very common. In some extreme cases, organizations find that the only cure for inflated pay rates is to start over again with a new job evaluation system. Second, inflated job descriptions can contribute to an organizational culture in which it is okay to provide misinformation to the human resources department. Third, they can lead to an adversarial relationship between the compensation department and the rest of the organization if this department tries to audit and correct the pay rates.

Empire Building

Job evaluation systems can also lead individuals to grab added responsibilites in order to get more points. The responsibilities employees grab can include extra budget and more subordinates, items that can add to the cost of doing business. In a rather direct although unintended way, point factor systems reward individuals for creating overhead and high costs because these lead to bigger, more highly evaluated jobs. This is exactly the opposite direction from the one in which high-involvement organizations need to move if they are to have low costs and to respond quickly to the environment and customer needs.

Hierarchical Career Development

Because most job evaluation systems assign a heavy weight to level of responsibility and reporting relationships, these systems typically strongly reinforce the idea of hierarchical careers. Virtually every point factor system creates an internal wage structure in which the major way to increase compensation is to be promoted.

A hierarchical approach to pay makes considerable sense in organizations that want the best and the brightest employees to move up a steep hierarchy. It encourages individuals to develop managerial skills because those skills lead to higher rewards. It nicely reinforces a "linear career orientation," in which people see their career as moving onward and upward, and fits well with traditional top-down management. The organization with a traditional management approach needs to have most if not all individuals striving for upward mobility. This can help assure that the most talented individuals end up in the top management positions, thus the right employees fill the critical positions in the organization.

The importance of senior management was clearly recognized by AT&T during its days as a regulated monopoly. The company did a number of things to assure that it had a large supply of well-qualified senior managers. It had extensive management development programs, assessment centers to determine who the best managers were, and, of course, a hierarchical pay and perquisite system that encouraged competent people to try to get to the top. In a system in which the people at the top make most of the important decisions and guide the rest of the organization through numerous policies, the best and brightest people need to be at the top if the organization is to be effective.

The situation is quite different, however, in professional and high-technology work organizations. To be successful, organizations involved in these kinds of work need individuals who have technical excellence (Von Glinow and Mohrman, 1989). They also need individuals who prefer to make horizontal or lateral career moves that develop in them the type of broad-based understanding of the organization and its technology that will allow them to operate as integrators, team members, and effective problem solvers. Often, the key to effectiveness in these organizations is lateral relationships and individuals who have lateral careers.

The technical specialist career and the horizontal career are not reinforced by the typical job evaluation approach. Individuals choosing these types of careers can look forward to static and potentially declining compensation if their organization uses a point factor approach. This approach can be disastrous for the organization that needs technical excellence to compete effectively because it drives the best technical people into managerial roles in which they may not be successful. In addition, it does nothing to encourage employees who stay in technical and professional jobs to develop their technical skills. It can have similar dysfunctional consequences in high-involvement organizations that deemphasize hierarchy.

Because the hierarchies of high-involvement organizations are by design flat and lean, employees have considerably less opportunity to move up the hierarchy than in traditional organizations. If little upward mobility is available in an organization, it is not as important to motivate people to try to achieve upward mobility. Indeed, it may be counterproductive to strongly motivate this kind of behavior in high-involvement organizations because it will produce large numbers of frustrated and disillusioned individuals.

Emphasis on Promotion

Inherent in the job evaluation approach is the idea that a promotion warrants a significant pay increase. It warrants an increase not because a person is necessarily more valuable or skilled or has accomplished anything worthwhile but rather because the person has taken on additional job responsibilities. Indeed, in many organizations, whether a career move is considered to be an upward move or not is dictated by the number of additional job evaluation points that the new job involves. This can lead to individuals refusing job moves because they are not worth many additional points. Some organizations become relatively inflexible in their career moves because people have learned to look for a certain number of additional points before they make a move. If this attitude becomes too strong a part of an organization's culture, employees arbitrarily rule out certain desirable moves and important learning opportunities.

The whole logic of someone receiving a pay increase simply because he or she has moved to a higher-level job can be challenged. An alternative approach is for an organization to wait until the person has demonstrated that he or she can do a new job before giving that person an additional amount of money. Money that is given to someone simply because that person has taken on new responsibilities is a reward that is not contingent upon performance. Thus, many organizations end up spending a great deal of their payroll dollars to reinforce job changes rather than to reinforce outstanding performance or growth in skill. Is it any wonder that individuals often spend more time worrying about what their next job will be than they spend worrying about how well they are performing their present one?

Misuses of Job Evaluation

In many organizations, the points developed by the job evaluation approach end up getting used for a number of nonpay purposes, including determining who gets parking spaces and other perquisites, who gets included in certain meetings, and who gets critical communications. In short, a whole host of benefits get attached to achieving higher and higher pay levels. Job evaluation systems were not designed to be a multipurpose evaluation of who should engage in a wide variety of organizational activities and get a wide variety of organizational perquisites and benefits. Particularly in high-involvement organizations, other factors need to be considered and hierarchy needs to be downplayed, not highlighted.

Job-Based Alternatives

There are alternatives to the job evaluation approach. One possibility is for an organization to stay with a job-based approach and simply compare all or virtually all jobs to the market individually (see Schuster, Zingheim, and Dertien, 1990). This strategy solves some of the problems with job evaluation approaches like the point factor approach but falls short of what is optimal for high-involvement management. It can help to focus the organization externally and may produce more competitive overall compensation costs. However, basing pay on comparisons with other organizations is unlikely to change the hierarchical nature of an organization's pay system since organizations in the market also are hierarchical. Comparing jobs to the market will lead an organization to install a pay system that looks like those in other organizations—job based and hierarchical—but it also should lead to a pay system that is more market oriented. Thus, although comparing jobs to the market is an improvement over job evaluation, it still creates major problems for an organization that wants to practice high-involvement management. What such an organization needs is a system that breaks out of the bureaucratic approach and focuses on individuals.

Skill-Based Pay

Paying individuals according to their skills is a system that leads to a focus on people and their value. This approach fits well with high-involvement management as well as with how labor markets operate. It is people that change jobs, it is people that develop skills, and it is people that are important assets. Paying them based on their value reflects this, while paying them for the job they hold may not.

A pay program that focuses on skill, knowledge, or competency development, or what I call a *skill-based pay system*, can help an organization to actively manage the skill-acquisition process by directly motivating individuals to learn specific skills. Being able to do this is critical in a high-involvement organization. The effectiveness of a high-involvement organization depends on individuals with a wide variety of skills, some of which may be horizontal to the work they are doing. Since high-involvement organizations have a flatter hierarchy than traditional organizations, they need to develop career tracks that do not depend on linear, vertical movement. Again, skill-based pay systems can make this possible.

Characteristics

To design a skill-based pay system, an organization must first identify those tasks that need to be performed in the organization. Next, the organization identifies the skills that are needed to perform the tasks and develops tests or measures to determine whether an individual has learned the skills. The number and kind of skills that each individual can learn need to be specified. Specifying the skills that each individual can learn is a key decision because it determines how the skill-based pay system should be structured. The type of skills chosen need to fit the type of work design the organization has chosen and the organization's business strategy and core competencies. Employees then need to be told what they can learn given their positions in the organization and how learning skills will affect their pay. Individuals are typically paid only for those skills that they currently can and are willing to perform.

Most skill-based pay plans I have seen give individuals pay increases when they learn a new skill. In a few cases, individuals are given a lump sum, one-time payment when they learn a skill. This approach is appropriate where pay rates are already high and the organization wants to encourage individuals to learn new skills. A somewhat different approach is used by Volvo in Sweden and one U.S. company with which I worked. They give every employee in a work area a pay increase when the employees in that area prove they can operate without a supervisor. Obviously, this provides a powerful incentive for groups to make their supervisor unnecessary.

There are several keys to successful skill assessment. As I have already mentioned, an organization needs to identify blocks of skills and develop tests and standards to define what constitutes acceptable levels of the skills. Team members need to be trained in how to do assessments if this is one of their responsibilities. If team members are not knowledgeable enough to do the assessments, experts from staff groups or other areas need to be identified as assessors. A skilled team leader or manager is also usually needed to make a skill-based system work. The leader is needed to help the group with the initial assessments and to challenge the group if it is not performing the individual skill assessments well.

In many respects, the application of skill-based pay to manufacturing jobs and production line service jobs is the most clear-cut and straightforward use of the concept (Ledford, 1991). Typically, in these situations, individuals simply learn to perform a number of tasks that might be considered horizontal to the tasks that they otherwise would perform. That is, they learn jobs upstream and downstream from their jobs in the production or service process. The skill-based pay plans usually require that employees learn a certain minimum number of skills and that they be willing and able to perform any skill for which they are paid. Some plans, such as those in Digital,

Procter & Gamble, Mead, and Corning, also reward individuals for learning skills that are normally possessed by managers and staff professionals. These upwardly vertical skills may include taking inventory, checking quality, scheduling work, and leading a team. They are particularly important skills to include in a plan when self-managing teams and high-involvement management are used.

Most organizations recognize the need to have some individuals with multiple skills. For example, companies that have assembly technologies typically have *utility workers*, or workers who are trained to do multiple assembly tasks. Usually, only a small percentage of the work force is trained in this way. There is an important difference between having a few utility workers and having a fully developed skill-based pay system. In a skill-based system, all individuals are trained in many skills and can work at many points in the production or service process.

Skill-based pay systems do not necessarily need to include or exclude the idea of paying for individual performance. They are, in a sense, neutral on the point of whether individuals should receive more pay depending upon how well they perform a particular skill. They deal only with the issue of whether someone can perform a job, while pay-for-performance systems focus on a different issue—how well someone performs a job or task over a period of time. As will be discussed in Chapter Eight, it is quite possible to assess how well individuals perform each of the skills for which they are being paid. This type of assessment can be combined with a skill-based system. In this respect, skill-based pay is identical to job-based pay; it allows organizations to vary the amount of total compensation that an individual receives according to the individual's performance. An important difference remains, however. In skill-based pay systems, the starting point for pay is determined by the mix and depth of an individual's skills rather than the job to which the person is assigned.

Skill-based pay for the managers and professionals in an organization can take several forms. Managers and high-level professionals can be paid for learning skills that are horizontal to their jobs, just like a production worker can. That is, a personnel manager can learn accounting and so forth. This approach makes particularly good sense when management teams are used. Managers also can be paid for learning skills that are lower in the hierarchy than their job is; that is, downwardly vertical from their job. Examples of these skills include manufacturing production skills and typing skills. They also can be paid to learn skills higher in the hierarchy than their jobs, such as higher-level management skills. Finally they can be paid for learning the skills that are needed to perform their job in greater depth. If the person is an accountant, he or she could, for example, learn more about the tax code.

The development of a skill-based pay system for managerial and professional employees in an organization involves a number of often complex and difficult decisions about which skills it is desirable for individuals to learn. An organization must determine whether it is useful for each individual to learn particular vertical skills or horizontal skills or to deepen the skills he or she already possesses. This decision needs to be driven by how individuals are organized and, of course, the nature of the work.

Employees in high-technology organizations and research and development employees typically should be rewarded for developing greater depth in their skills. Skill depth is often a critical competitive factor because being at the forefront of technology is essential to the success of the organization. It is usually apparent that it is to everyone's advantage to have at least some employees develop a real depth of skill in those technical areas that support the core competencies of the organization. It is often less clear which horizontal skills managers should learn. In most high-involvement organizations some horizontal learning is desirable because it helps build understanding, coordination, and adaptability.

Earlier it was mentioned that any skill-based pay system needs to be based on measures of skill acquisition or competency. These measures can be difficult to develop for managerial and professional employees. Sometimes the only way to assess skills is to have the person perform the job and then evaluate a sample of the person's work. Although many of the systems that currently operate in plants use peer-group assessment of skills, this particular approach does not have to be part of a skill-based system. Skill-based pay systems merely require some test of skill acquisition. Depending upon the situation, this test can be based on a supervisor's judgment, written questions and answers, an outside testing agency's assessment, or peer-group appraisal, to mention some of the more obvious possibilities.

Applications

A 1987 study found that 5 percent of 1,598 companies reported having a skill-based pay system (O'Dell, 1987). Most companies reported that they had recently installed the plans. Another study found that 40 percent of the Fortune 1000 service and manufacturing organizations report having skill-based plans (Lawler, Ledford, and Mohrman, 1989). In this study, most of the companies that indicated they used skill-based pay also indicated they used it for only a few parts of their work force.

The Fortune 1000 study found greater use of skill-based pay systems, in part because of the different definitions of skill-based pay used by the two studies. The 1987 study limited its definition to pay for the number of jobs a person can do and related it to the team concept. The Fortune 1000 study used a more general definition. Both studies suggested that the use of skill-based pay systems was likely to increase, a predition that was confirmed by a restudy of the Fortune 1000 companies (Lawler, Mohrman, and Ledford, 1992). In that study, 51 percent of the companies reported using a skill-based pay system, a 10 percent increase that corresponds to the increase in the use of teams.

The most widely used systems of skill-based pay are probably technical ladders. Through the use of technical ladders, organizations pay individuals for the depth of skill they have in a particular technical specialty. These ladders have been used by many organizations and are most commonly found in the research and development areas of large organizations and in the apprenticeship systems that are used for skilled tradespeople. Technical ladders are also found in such diverse organizations as universities, where they are used for the payment of faculty, and corporate law departments, where they are used to recognize the development of legal skills.

Technical ladders have been around a long time but are not always identified as a form of skill-based pay. Rather than being called skill-based pay, a technical ladder is usually treated as part of a job-based pay system; different job descriptions are written for different positions on the technical ladder. Nevertheless, in most cases, the ladder is a form of skill-based pay, one that is based on an employee's developing depth in a skill rather than developing horizontal or vertical skills.

Skill-based pay is the most common method of paying production workers (sometimes called *associates, technicians,* or *team members*) in new high-involvement or high-performance plants (Lawler, 1986). These plants, which will be discussed in detail in Chapter Thirteen, have been built since the early 1970s and now are relatively common. In most of these high-involvement plants, skill-based pay is used for the production employees; however, it is not used for managerial and other employees. Thus, the typical high-involvement plant has both a skill-based pay system and a traditional job-based pay system.

Procter & Gamble started using skill-based pay in the late 1960s, and by the 1980s, at least twenty of its plants had production employees who were paid through skill-based pay systems. As is true with most organizations, the original installations of skill-based pay systems in Procter & Gamble were in new plants that made extensive use of teams. Recently, the company has installed the system in all of its manufacturing facilities. In the Procter & Gamble system, production employees are paid for horizontal skills and, in some cases, upwardly vertical skills. In a few cases, they are also paid for learning downwardly vertical skills, such as cleaning and routine production tasks. The major purpose of the plan in the Procter & Gamble plants is to support the development of work teams.

Advantages

The single most obvious advantage of skill-based pay in a production situation is flexibility. When individuals can perform multiple tasks, organizations gain tremendous flexibility in using their work force. A number of conditions can make this flexibility extremely desirable, including the need to replace absent or terminated employees. If the organization's products frequently change, the organization needs a highly trained work force that can smoothly adapt to transitions in the production process. This type of work force is likely to become increasingly important in the future because of the tendency for products to have short life cycles and the increasing demands for product customization.

Flexibility can also be important if an organization needs most of its employees to be working at a particular stage or particular point in the production process. For example, manufacturing organizations commonly face shortages of parts and the need to rework products. If everybody can do all portions of the production process, then all employees can work on the problem. This situation is often far superior to one in which only a few individuals can work at each phase of the production process, a situation that can bottleneck production until the relevant individuals can correct the problem or install the missing part. The increasing use of "just-in-time" manufacturing systems that have low inventories of parts is consistent with the increased use of skill-based pay (Womack, Jones, and Roos, 1990). This approach can lead to temporary shortages of parts that are more easily handled when skill-based pay is used.

The flexibility that comes from a skill-based pay system may lead to slightly leaner staffing among production employees. Often, a company does not need to have as many extra employees on hand to cover for absenteeism and other activities such as training and meetings that take people away from direct production work. And sometimes employees discover that some jobs can be eliminated because two individuals can do the work of three or because employees can do some of their own maintenance and material handling.

Much of the flexibility inherent in a skill-based pay system can be gained by simply having a significant number of individuals cross-trained, as in the utility worker concept. Thus, often the advantages of skill-based pay must extend beyond simple flexibility if in fact it is going to offer a significant advantage over a traditional job-based approach to pay.

When combined with a high-involvement approach to management and work teams, skill-based pay can produce benefits other than those that stem from having a flexible work force (Ledford, 1991). This seems to be particularly true when the system encourages production employees to acquire upwardly vertical skills. When employees learn both horizontal and vertical skills, they gain an entirely different perspective on the organization's operations, the way in which it is managed, and the information that supports the organization. This perspective allows them to do a number of things that they could not do in the absence of this breadth of understanding.

First, it allows employees to solve systemic problems more effectively. Their broad perspective helps employees to be innovative in improving operations. Thus, they become more effective in a quality circle or any other problem-solving group. Too often I have seen employees come up with ideas for improvement that look great from their perspective but that are not usable because of roadblocks that are present elsewhere in the organization, roadblocks they were not aware of because they did not know what went on outside their limited area of work. Similarly, a broad perspective helps employees who are working on a particular phase of the production process; they are often more effective because they know the entire process. They are not limited to the perspective that comes from doing just one step in the process and can make operating decisions that reflect a broad understanding of the organization and the external market.

Second, employees often become more committed to seeing that the organization operates effectively when they have an overview of the entire operation. Feedback about such things as product quality, production rates, costs, and customer satisfaction becomes more meaningful to them, and, thus, their intrinsic motivation to perform increases. The result for the organization can be improved quality and better operations.

Third, skill-based pay is an important reinforcer of a participative culture. When skill-based pay is widely used in an organization, it has the potential to dramatically change the entire culture of the organization because it can separate pay levels from levels in the hierarchy. It can, for example, lead to employees with valued technical skills making more than most or all managers because of the depth of their skills. It can also lead to employees making more than their manager if they are broadly knowledgeable about the organization and its activities. Thus, the system can create new career tracks that do not depend on upward mobility. With the flat hierarchies that are typical of high-involvement organizations, this feature of skill-based pay systems is particularly important because it provides a new "nonlinear" way for people to grow and succeed in their career.

Fourth, skill-based pay is a concrete way that organizations can back up their commitment to participative management and to such statements as "people are our most important resource." It delivers a tangible reward in return for the employees doing just what the organization says it believes they can do: grow, learn, and develop. Therefore, organizations that use a skill-based pay system typically have cultures that are seen as valuing human development and are optimistic about the capability and potential of the people who work in the organization. Although sometimes difficult to quantify, these attitudes are nevertheless a very real and important advantage of skill-based pay.

Fifth, and perhaps most important, when employees are broadly knowledgeable about the operations of an organization, they can increase their self-management; that is, they are in a better position to control their own behavior, coordinate with others, and participate in a self-managing team that operates a particular part of the organization. They also can communicate more effectively with employees doing other parts of the production or service process because they understand what these other people are doing. This communication can lead to better problem solving because employees know about each other's job and can discuss problems and devise good solutions for problems. Such problem solving is particularly important in a production process that is highly interdependent. Coordination and problem solving can be achieved by using managers, or they can be achieved by knowledgeable employees talking to other knowledgeable employees. The latter approach is often less expensive and more effective than the former.

Because skill-based pay systems aid in self-management, they make significant savings possible. Such a system supports the reduction of levels of management and the reduction of staff and support personnel. Reduced management overhead is particularly likely when upwardly vertical skills are included in the system so that individuals learn some of the staff support roles and are able to perform them. Thus, employees are able to solve problems without the help of a staff specialist, and the organization may not need a specialist at all because the individuals can do the work. This feature of skill-based pay is particularly important when, as part of a total quality program, organizations move toward self-inspection and direct customer contact. These require that individuals learn new skills, and skill-based pay is a way to help assure that they learn these skills.

Disadvantages

Skill-based pay systems have some disadvantages that need to be considered, the most obvious of which concerns pay levels. The very nature of the system is to encourage individuals to become more valuable to the organization and as a result to be paid more. In most skill-based pay systems, nonmanagement employees are paid more than they are under a traditional pay system, which limits how much more they can grow, develop, and be paid. Total wage costs do not have to be higher with a skill-based system; however, an organization has to be sure that individuals are using the skills for which they are paid. If the organization can make use of skilled people in ways that add significant value to the product, then, in fact, total labor costs can still be lower than with a traditional pay system.

An organization using a skill-based pay system typically commits to giving everyone the opportunity to learn multiple skills. In this case, the organization has to make a large investment in training, and, of course, training is expensive. Because employees are regularly learning new jobs, the organization can have production losses and problems due to inexperienced people doing the work. It must constantly make trade-offs between production and skill acquisition. Indeed, in the worst-case scenario, an organization can have many people who know how to do every job but still find that at a particular point in time all jobs are being done by individuals who do not know how to perform them at a high level of competence.

Skill-based pay also makes market comparisons of jobs difficult. It is hard for an organization to go to the market and get a pay rate for a skill when it is looking at the skill in the context of someone who has several other skills and who may only be peforming that skill part of the time. Thus, in many cases, the pay rates that organizations using a skill-based pay system develop for individuals have to be an estimate of what it takes to attract, retain, and satisfy somebody with a particular skill mix.

Even in the most ambitious skill-based pay system, individuals can "top out"; that is, they can learn all the skills that the program calls for them to learn. They may then be dissatisfied because they have become accustomed to learning, growing, and receiving pay raises. They are still better off than they would be in the typical pay system, but, nevertheless, they may be unhappy about reaching the limit of the system.

Increasing the vertical learning opportunities for employees is a way to solve the problem of topping out. In many respects, this problem is an artificial one created by management systems that assume that only a limited amount of vertical skills are desirable. One qualification is necessary here, however. Extensive training of employees in vertical skills is likely to make sense only in a company that practices an advanced form of high-involvement management because otherwise the company is likely to underutilize these skills.

Skill-based pay systems involve a certain level of administrative complexity. Keeping track of exactly who is qualified on all of the different tasks and of the different pay rates certainly requires a good information system. In addition, since individuals can move at almost any time into a new skill and master it, pay changes occur throughout the year and not just once a year as in pay systems based on merit or seniority.

Although employees may be paid for having multiple skills, they may not be able to perform all of them as well as when they originally learned them. Most skill-based pay systems require that an individual regularly perform the skill in order to be paid for the skill. This is a good principle, but it can often get lost in the desire of an organization to maximize production and to operate effectively. It is all too easy to forget the importance of rotating people and being sure that they still have certain skills when the people are currently needed at a different point in the work process.

Major technological changes can mean that certain skills are no longer needed in an organization, which raises the question of what happens to the individuals who are being paid for skills that are now obsolete. Technological changes can have the positive effect of emphasizing that learning on the job is a continuous process and of motivating employees to learn new skills when their work changes. However, they can also create transition problems as old skills become obsolete. Not only can certain skills become obsolete, combinations of skills that at one time made sense may no longer make sense. Thus, individuals can find that their skills no longer fit the way work is organized. As a result, the organization may have to make extensive revisions in its skill-based pay system, and individuals may have to learn a number of new skills. The same thing is likely to be true if the organization has a job-based system; that is, the organization will need to write new job descriptions, and individuals will need to learn new jobs. Both approaches have rigidity built into them, but I think that in most situations organizations with skill-based pay systems are likely to be more flexible than those with job-based systems. Why? Because skill-based pay systems tend to produce organizations with cultures that value learning, growth, and change and employees who are not as protective of their particular areas of expertise.

Impact on Involvement

Skill-based pay is the right approach for high-involvement management organizations. This conclusion has already been demonstrated in the case of many plants and production work teams (see, for example, Ledford, 1991). Although they have some drawbacks, skill-based systems are also superior to job-based systems for employees involved in managerial and staff support work in high-involvement organizations (Lawler, 1990b). An organization should use a skill-based pay system for all employees because the system puts everyone on the same footing and creates a homogeneous culture. Such a system is also the best way to deal with the problems of career progression that are created by a flat organizational structure. Applying skill-based pay systems to managerial jobs has the desirable effect of eliminating pay increases for promotions. Large pay increases can instead be used to encourage individuals to learn the skills associated with a new job.

I think that if an individual does not want a promotion because the new job does not result in an immediate pay increase, it is probably best for all concerned that the individual not take the job. Among other things, this attitude suggests that the person wanted the promotion primarily for the money involved. In a high-involvement organization, I would rather see individuals take a job, particularly a managerial job because they want to do the work rather than because they want a pay increase. Too often, good technical people become poor managers because they cannot turn down the lure of an instant pay increase.

Skill-based pay for managers makes particular sense if an organization has a *matrix* or *network structure* such as those discussed in Chapter Three. These approaches work best when the individuals in them have had experience in a variety of functions and business areas. Skill-based pay encourages people to learn horizontal skills. This allows these individuals to see things from other people's viewpoints, which is especially important in a horizontally oriented organizational structure.

If skill-based pay systems are to be widely used in organizations, approaches need to be developed that will reduce the administrative complexity associated with the systems and that will effectively tie them to the external pay market. Early skill-based systems often simply priced each skill and then added up the skills to get to a pay rate. This approach is effective in production jobs but may not fit managerial jobs.

An approach that makes more sense for managerial jobs is a pay band approach that starts by placing individuals in one of a very few management pay ranges or bands in the organization. For example, the ladder might include a pay rate for first-level supervisors, a rate for unit managers, and a few other rates. To provide for meaningful growth for employees, the pay ranges for each level should be much wider than is typical of the ranges in traditional multigrade systems. For example, the top of the range might be twice that of the bottom. General Electric, Monsanto, and Northern Telecom have adopted pay approaches for management somewhat like this.

The rate of pay for each range is determined by what the market pays someone with the skills that are needed at that level of management to join an organization, or, in other words, a *replacement-cost approach*. This approach requires shifting the salary survey process from looking at what others are paying for jobs to looking at what they are paying to hire particular kinds of individuals. In a system with wide pay ranges, individuals can progress a great deal in pay by learning additional skills of whatever type fit the situation. Horizontal and vertical learning can be rewarded. The organization can manage each individual's growth by asking individuals to establish a learning plan and get this plan approved by their manager or work team.

Alternatively, an organization can write descriptions of groups of skills and can compare individuals to these descriptions to determine which pay range the individuals should fall into. These descriptions can be taken to the market and priced on a replacement-cost basis. I helped Polaroid develop a plan like this, called a *pay-for-applied-knowledge plan*. The plan asks managers to plot their skill growth with their supervisors.

A slightly different plan is being used by 3M for their "new venture" managers. The 3M system focuses on depth of skills by rewarding managers for getting better and better at managing new ventures. It was installed because too many new venture managers moved on to higher-level positions in order to advance their career. This situation was not desirable in an organization that prides itself on starting new businesses.

Theoretically, all employees in an organizational unit could be given the opportunity to earn all of the skills in the unit. Production employees could in fact become indistinguishable from managerial and white-collar employees. And somebody doing a production task may be among the highest-paid employees in the organization. At first glance, this sitaution seems a bit radical, but if a production employee had the most knowledge about plant operations, then in fact he or she could deserve the highest pay. The issue remains of whether or not such extensive training would be the best use of this person's time, but it is possible that it might be in certain situations, particularly if it helps the person better understand the organization's overall operation and condition.

Impact on Organizational Change

Skill-based pay can potentially help organizations make the move from a traditional to a more participative form of management. It can be an incentive for veteran employees to acquire new skills and to allow others to learn their skills. The reason, of course, is that both veteran and new employees can earn higher pay by learning each others' job. Thus, veteran employees who refuse to let others learn "their" skills harm both themselves and other employees.

Problems can arise in a skill-based system if the higher-seniority employees are already highly paid and it is difficult to offer them more money to learn additional skills. Furthermore, these employees may feel that their job security is in their skills, and they may not want to train others or allow others to do their job. Also, they may have progressed through the other jobs and have no interest in doing them because they are lower in status and less interesting than their current job.

I know of no easy solutions to these problems. Some organizations have used a "red circle" approach in which the high-paid employees are guaranteed their existing pay rate for a period of time but then have to learn new skills or take a drop in pay. This approach is not always accepted happily by high-paid employees, but it can be successful. Sometimes, a company can pay a one-time learning bonus. This approach has the advantage of motivating employees to change without creating pay annuity.

One General Electric plant I worked with simply decreased employees' pay when it started a skill-based pay system. This strategy had the desirable effect of immediately motivating everyone to learn new skills. It did not produce a major employee uprising because the business was failing and the employees knew that if they did not take a pay cut the plant would be shut down. Short of this kind of situation, I would not advise starting a skill-based pay plan with a pay cut.

Some plants have used a *simplified pay-grade structure* as a way of changing traditional work settings. In this approach, a few generic job descriptions and pay rates are established, and individuals are simply told that they are expected to do anything that needs to be done in their work area. Several unionized General Motors (GM) plants have adopted this approach as have the U.S. automobile plants of Honda and Nissan. In these plants, individuals are put into teams and told to learn all the skills it takes to operate their part of the assembly line. In some cases, this approach is supported by very general skill descriptions for each of the two or three pay levels that exist in the production area. This method simplifies the pay-for-skills approach but removes much of the direct incentive for learning new skills. Thus, although it may be the best approach in certain situations, I generally think of it as the best choice only when political opposition, complexity of work, rapid change in technology, or some other reason makes it impossible to create a more targeted skill-based system. In most situations, I think a skill-based pay system is the best way to motivate employees to improve their skills and knowledge because the system directly rewards employees for learning.

Chapter Eight

Reward
Performance

.

Bonus payments based on the performance of organizations and individuals are an old and potentially effective way to improve organizational performance. They can improve employee motivation, build a high-involvement work culture in which people are committed to and care about the organization's effectiveness, help focus organizations on the competitive environment, and adjust the labor costs of an organization to its ability to pay (Blinder, 1990). However, in many traditionally managed organizations pay-for-performance bonus plans that are based on organizational performance do not have a major positive impact (Lawler, 1990b). The same is also often true of employee ownership plans. The reason for this is simple: most employees do not have the information, knowledge, and power to understand these plans and to influence the amounts of money that they pay out. Furthermore, because most employees do not see how their work influences the organization's performance, they do not feel it is fair for their rewards to be tied to the organization's performance.

In a high-involvement organization, part of the pay of individuals should be dependent on how well the organization performs. Research shows that the most successful efforts at employee involvement use financial rewards (see, for example, Beekun, 1989; Blinder, 1990; Lawler, 1986). Financial rewards are vital to a proper balance of power, information, knowledge, and rewards in an organization. If such rewards are missing,

172

individuals have no financial accountability for how they use the information, knowledge, and power they are given to improve organizational performance. Lack of financial rewards also can raise major equity issues that can harm an organization's culture. When, as a result of employee efforts, organizational performance improves, employees expect to share in the gains. If they do not share in these gains, they feel exploited and ultimately reject management systems that give them more information, knowledge, and power and ask them for better performance but do not reward them for their performance.

There are literally thousands of approaches to paying employees for organizational performance, and companies must deal with many complex organizational issues if a plan to pay employees for performance is to be successful. Decades of research have pointed out a number of things that must be done if pay plans are to be successful, and, as a result, designing a plan or plans that fit a high-involvement management approach does not have to be an unguided trip for an organization.

Three major approaches to rewarding individuals for organizational performance exist. The oldest is the approach of paying bonuses based on the profitability of the organization. This is undoubtedly the most widely accepted approach around the world (O'Dell, 1987; Lawler, Ledford, and Mohrman, 1989). This approach has important advantages as well as some very important limitations. Employee ownership represents a second way to be sure that employees gain when organizational performance improves. An approach that is not as well known as profit sharing or employee ownership but that is increasingly popular is *gainsharing*. Gainsharing is strongly associated with employee involvement and will be discussed next. Consideration will be given later to the use of individual pay-for-performance approaches and team-based rewards. These approaches can be very effective in some high-involvement organizations, particularly when they are combined with rewards based on organizational performance.

Gainsharing

Gainsharing has been around for at least forty years and has been successfully applied by hundreds, perhaps even thousands, of organizations (O'Dell, 1987). Employees and companies have both profited from gainsharing—companies in the form of reduced costs and employees in the form of bonus payments and improved job satisfaction. The original and best-known gainsharing plan is the Scanlon plan (Frost, Wakeley, and Ruh, 1974; Graham-Moore and Ross, 1983). Other well-known gainsharing plans include the Improshare plan and the Rucker plan. Many companies have their own gainsharing plans that are specifically designed for them.

In the typical gainsharing plan, an organization uses a formula to share financial gains with all employees in a single plant or location. The organization establishes a historical base period of performance and uses this to determine whether or not gains in performance have occurred; hence the name *gain-sharing*. Typically, only controllable costs are measured for the purpose of computing the gain. Unless a major change takes place in the organization's products or technology, the historical base stays the same during the entire history of the plan. Thus, the organization's performance is always compared to the time period before it started the gainsharing plan. When the organization's performance is better than it was in the base period, the plan funds a bonus pool. When its performance falls short, no bonus pool is created. In the typical plan, about half of the bonus pool is paid out to the employees, and the rest is kept by the company. Payments are usually made on a monthly basis, with all employees receiving the same percentage of their regular base pay.

No one has an accurate estimate of how many gainsharing plans are in place in the United States and Europe. The number is at least a thousand—some companies, such as Dana, Motorola, and General Electric, have ten or more plans. Undoubtedly, the popularity of the plans has increased tremendously in the last ten years. A 1987 survey of the Fortune 1000 companies found that 26 percent used gainsharing somewhere in their organization but that most used it in only a few situations (Lawler, Ledford, and Mohrman, 1989). The resurvey of these organizations in 1990 found that 39 percent used gainsharing, a significant increase in just three years (Lawler, Mohrman, and Ledford, 1992). Another survey of a larger and more diverse sample found that 13 percent of the respondents used gainsharing and went on to claim that the use is growing rapidly (O'Dell, 1987). The White House Conference on Productivity, the U.S. General Accounting Office, and the President's Task Force on Industrial Competitiveness have all endorsed gainsharing (see, for example, U.S. General Accounting Office, 1981).

Until ten years ago, gainsharing was used primarily in small manufacturing organizations, many of them with a history of participative management. Much has been written in the United States about the success of gainsharing in two companies that adopted it prior to 1950, Herman Miller and Donnelly Mirrors (see, for example, Frost, Wakeley, and Ruh, 1974). During the 1970s, an interesting and important trend developed: large companies such as General Electric, Rockwell, Motorola, TRW, Dana, 3M, and Monsanto began installing gainsharing plans in some of their manufacturing plants. The trend of large corporations defining organizational units that have their own gainsharing plans appears to be continuing, and, therefore, more organizations are adopting gainsharing plans.

Gainsharing moved beyond the factory environment during the 1980s as it was adopted by a number of service organizations, including hotels, restaurants, insurance companies, hospitals, retail stores, and banks. Schlesinger and Heskett (1991a) argue that gainsharing can help break the cycle of failure and low wages that is so common in a variety of retail businesses. They cite Au Bon Pain, a quick-service French cafe chain as an example of a company that has done just that. Gainsharing plans have also been adopted by high-technology companies to encourage employees to be cost effective and to do high-quality work. Rockwell, Motorola, and TRW have plans covering pieces of their defense contracting businesses.

The increased popularity of gainsharing relates to an important feature of most gainsharing plans. They are more than just pay-incentive plans; they are a way of managing and a technology for organizational development. To be specific, they are a participative approach to management and are often used as a way to install or reinforce participative management.

Joe Scanlon, the creator of the Scanlon plan, emphasized that gainsharing fits a participative management style (Frost, Wakeley, and Ruh, 1974). As a general rule, an organization needs a participative system for the plan to work at all and, in all cases, they are needed in order for the full potential of the plan to be realized. In the absence of a change in employee behavior, an organization has no reason to expect a payout from the kind of formula that is typically developed in gainsharing plans. A payout requires an improvement in employee performance, and that improvement requires more effective behavior on the part of the employees.

Employees may improve their performance somewhat simply because the organization motivates them through tying pay to performance. This effect is particularly likely in small organizations in which the work is not highly skilled or interdependent and, as a result, employee effort is directly related to measurable performance. In most situations, however, a gainsharing plan will not produce an appreciable improvement in performance without participative management (Blinder, 1990; Lawler, 1990b).

The motivational impact of a gainsharing plan usually is not large because most gainsharing plans aggregate a number of people. Therefore, a plan at best produces only a small increment in the perceived relationship between individual performance and pay. This lack of impact on motivation is particularly true in traditionally managed organizations because employees can only influence a few of the factors that determine organizational performance. The formula used to measure the gains is also a factor in employee motivation. Some plans use very simple formulas that focus on the relationship between labor input and productivity (such as the Improshare plan), while others use a comprehensive set of financial measures (such as the Rucker plan). Simple labor-based plans are more likely to affect motivation because with these plans, even in a traditionally managed organization, employees may see a relationship between their efforts and their bonuses. Despite their attractiveness, however, simple plans are not always best in terms of organizational effectiveness, as will be discussed later.

In many cases, effort and good intentions are not enough to improve the performance of an organization. What most organizations need to improve results is employees who are working harder, smarter, and more effectively together, and sharing their ideas. An organization often needs a formal participative system that converts the motivation to improve performance into changes in the operating procedures of the organization.

In traditional gainsharing plans such as the Scanlon plan, the key participative approach is a formal suggestion system with written suggestions and shop-floor committees to review the suggestions. Often, these plans also include a high-level review committee that looks over the recommendations that involve several parts of the organization or large expenditures. This parallel system of committees is one way for an organization to try to assure that new ideas will be seriously considered and, where appropriate, implemented. In many respects this approach is like a quality circle program. However, there are two important differences. Committees are typically given the authority to implement ideas if they affect only their area and are within certain budget limitations. Everyone in the organization gets much more business information than is shared in a quality circle program because the bonus system leads to information being widely distributed within the organization.

Research Results

The most important thing we know about gainsharing plans is that they work (Lawler, 1981; 1990b). The following are some of the common results that have been found in the hundreds of research studies of gainsharing plans (Lawler, 1981):

- Coordination, teamwork, and sharing of knowledge are enhanced in the organization.

- Employees' social needs are recognized via participation and mutually reinforcing group behavior.
- Attention is focused on cost savings.
- Acceptance of change due to technology, market, and new methods is greater because higher efficiency leads to bonuses.
- Employees change their attitudes, and they demand more efficient management practices and better planning.
- Employees demand better performance from each other.
- Employees try to work smarter.
- Employees produce ideas as well as physical work.
- When unions are present, union-management relations become more flexible.
- When unions support the plan, they are strengthened because a better work situation and higher pay result from the plan.
- Unorganized locations tend to remain nonunion.

Research supporting the positive results of gainsharing has been around for decades. We know somewhat less about the frequency with which gainsharing plans achieve these positive results, but evidence suggests that they achieve such results about 75 percent of the time (Bullock and Lawler, 1984).

A number of books and articles describe in some detail how to put together gainsharing formulas, how to introduce plans, and how to manage the development and implementation of a plan (see, for example, Moore and Ross, 1978; O'Dell, 1981). The Scanlon plan in particular has been well researched. Indeed, careful reading of the literature on this plan can make it possible for an organization to develop and install a plan without the help of a consultant. However, in my experience, most plans are installed by consultants. The research evidence also shows that the following situational factors favor gainsharing plans (see Lawler, 1971; 1981; 1990b):

Organizational Size. Gainsharing plans are based on employees seeing a relationship between what they do and their pay. As organizations get larger, employees have difficulty seeing this relationship. Most successful gain-sharing plans cover fewer than 1,000 employees.

Performance Measurement. In some organizations, good performance measures and a reasonable performance history simply do not exist and cannot be established, especially organizations in which rapid technological and market changes occur. In these organizations, formulas for gainsharing are difficult to develop.

Measurement Complexity. Often performance can be measured only in very complex ways. The more complex the method of measurement, the more difficult it is for an organization to make a plan work because there is no clear, easily understood connection between an individual's behavior and rewards.

Worker Characteristics. Successful gainsharing depends on workers who want to participate and want to earn more money. Most workers have these goals, but not all do. Unless a substantial majority of the employees want the benefits the plan offers, it cannot succeed.

Communication. For gainsharing to work, employees must understand the plan and trust it enough to believe that their pay will increase if they perform better. Employees will not have these beliefs without a great deal of open communication and education. If an organization does not have communication and education programs already, they must be started if the plan is to succeed.

Management Attitudes. Unless managers favor the idea of participation, gainsharing will not fit the management style of the organization. In some organizations, the plan has been tried simply as a pay-incentive plan without regard to management style, and it has failed.

Supervisory Skills. Successful gainsharing requires supervisors to change. They are forced to deal with many suggestions, and their competence is tested and questioned in new ways. Unless supervisors are prepared for and accept these changes, the plan can fail.

As this list demonstrates, gainsharing does not fit every situation. It is easy to see why the installation of gainsharing plans was limited for so long to manufacturing situations, since they are most likely to have these favorable conditions. Although a great deal remains to be learned about how gainsharing plans should be designed for service and professional work environ-ments, it appears that they can be designed to work in these settings. Indeed, gainsharing may prove to be more effective in service organizations than in manufacturing organizations be-cause labor costs are so important in service settings and perfor-mance is so easily controlled by the people doing the work. As long as some critical design features can be built into a plan, I believe gainsharing can work in any organization.

Critical Elements

The design of a gainsharing plan for an organization is part science and part art. Because there are so many different gain-sharing plans available, an organization can easily lose track of what the key elements are that make for a successful gainsharing plan. Perhaps the vital issue in the design of a gainsharing plan is that of fit. The formula for the plan and the organization's participative management approach need to fit each other and the situation. Given the variety of situations in which gainshar-ing plans have been tried, it is appropriate that a wide variety of plans have been developed. Different situations require differ-ent designs; different designs require different practices. How-ever, any plan needs some general elements if it is to be suc-cessful. Let us turn to a consideration of each of the elements and look at how an organization can achieve them.

Credible, Trusted Development Process. Gainsharing plans vary widely in how they are developed. In some cases, a knowledge-able expert convinces the organization that an already devel-oped plan will work for it. Probably the majority of the plans I have seen have been installed in this manner. For example, the Improshare plan is typically installed by an expert who begins with a standard formula. The expert adapts the formula to the organization and then asks the employees to vote on whether or not they want the plan. In other cases, the organization creates a task force that is representative of the employees to investigate different plans and ultimately make a recommendation. The task force may even take responsibility for developing a custom formula that fits their situation. All the plans that I have installed followed this approach.

No one right process for developing a plan exists, but unless the development practices lead employees to believe in the plan, the plan has little chance of success. A gainsharing plan can only be successful when employees believe that if they perform better they will be paid more. Initially, this belief requires a leap of faith because employees receive no payment until their performance improves.

There is no question that in some cases an outside expert can effectively install a plan. In my experience, however, a participative development process that uses a task force is more likely to lead to a high level of employee acceptance and trust of the plan. This approach typically results in a much slower development process, however, than when a plan is installed by an outside expert. But once an organization has gone through this type of self-design process, it usually is in a position to operate and maintain the plan without the help of a consultant (Mohrman and Cummings, 1989).

Bonuses That Employees Can Understand and Influence. If a gainsharing plan is going to increase employee motivation, employees must understand and be able to influence their bonuses. They must be able to see how through their behavior they can influence the size of the bonus. Helping employees to achieve this understanding is not easy, particularly in a complex organization. It takes education, communication, the use of participative management practices, and the development of an appropriate measurement approach to determine the size of the bonus.

A formula typically is used to calculate the size of the bonus in gainsharing plans. Using a formula is much more objective than using a discretionary decision about how much the bonus will be. I cannot rule out discretionary judgment as a possible vehicle for deciding the bonus, however. This method appears to be gaining in popularity, in situations of rapid change or complexity where a formula cannot be used. If an organization can develop a valid and trusted decision process, it still can have an effective plan without a formula. In some cases, organizations have used committees to successfully make bonus decisions. In others, trusted managers have set performance goals for organizations and have tied specific bonus amounts to the achievement of the goals.

Credible Standard. Every bonus plan must have a standard that triggers payment. Many profit-sharing plans use a financial break-even point or a certain return on investment as their standard. As noted earlier, gainsharing plans typically use a historical performance level as a standard. Using historical performance as a standard has a number of advantages, particularly in terms of credibility. A historical performance level is a credible standard because employees know it can be achieved and they understand where it came from. It is not an "arbitrary number" based on some economic concept like return on investment or an estimate by someone of what performance should be. Organizations often use such a standard because improvement beyond it represents real improvement in organizational performance, and it is thus possible to argue that bonuses are self-funding because without improvement there are no bonuses. Historical performance is not, however, the only correct basis for a standard.

    If an organization is on a learning curve, historical performance may be too easy to achieve, and, therefore, some projection of future performance on the learning curve may be needed. Typically, I recommend against gainsharing plans if the organization is on a steep learning curve because it is too difficult to establish a valid curve. Most plans I have seen that are based on future projections of performance have failed, but a few have worked. The successful ones were in organizations that understood their technology well and had the trust of their employees so that they could make credible changes in the standard.

In organizations that experience a dramatic change of products or technology, history may no longer be a relevant basis for setting the standard. Some other, more subjective, approach such as a committee decision may be required.

If an organization's historical performance is very low, it may not make economic sense for the organization to use it as a permanent standard. It might simply be too expensive to use this standard if the organization is already at a cost disadvantage. Continuing to pay bonuses for performance that just gets the organization to a competent level may not solve the organization's problems because labor costs go up along with performance. The organization may need either a moving standard or a cut in base wages. I have seen both of these approaches work, but they need to be fully, carefully, and openly justified on the basis of business need.

In some plans, managers make annual adjustments to the performance standard based on their estimates of how the organization should perform. This approach seems to be gaining in popularity. An increasing number of chemical, paper, and other manufacturing organizations adopt this approach. Although this approach can work, I see it as the approach of last resort because of the position in which it puts management. If the managers make a poor estimate of what the goal should be, employees may see them as villains. Instead of people worrying about how to improve the organization's performance, they focus on management's poor decision. Management is also often in a difficult situation if it needs to raise the goal from one year to the next. Employees can easily see raising the goal as an attempt to squeeze out more production for no more pay. As the employees I interviewed in one plant noted, "Nothing gets punished around here like good performance because it raises our performance standards."

Timely Bonuses. Gainsharing plans typically pay bonuses on a monthly basis, but there is no magic in monthly payments. The important principle is that bonuses should be paid as soon after the performance as possible. In organizations where the work process is simple, a month may be the right time period or even too long a period. In organizations with complex work processes, however, a month may not be long enough for the organization to complete the production of the product or the delivery of a service. In this case, quarterly or even semiannual bonus payments may be more appropriate.

Comprehensive Measures. Any discussion of gainsharing formulas raises the question of what to measure. Some advocates of gainsharing push strongly for simple plans because of their belief that it is always best to keep plans simple. Time after time, I have heard advocates of this approach use the saying "Keep it simple, stupid" to convince companies that a simple plan is best. In this spirit, some plans simply measure the number of units of output per labor hour. These plans may be effective if labor costs are the key issue for the organization and the business is a very simple one. In most cases, however, ignoring other costs such as materials and supplies can be quite dangerous and counterproductive. Similarly, ignoring product quality and customer satisfaction also can be dangerous because it gives employees an incorrect message about what the market is like and what their organization needs to do to be successful.

I have seen many gainsharing plans cause problems because employees have reduced measured costs at the expense of unmeasured costs. Commonly, labor costs go down (people work faster) but material and supply costs go up (people are less careful in their use of consumables). This happened when Donnelly Mirrors introduced their original Scanlon plan, which covered only labor cost. The employees who ran the diamond grinding wheels quickly discovered that they could increase their productivity by running their machines faster and discarding grinding wheels when they started to wear out. Therefore, labor costs went down but supply costs went up, with the net result being higher costs (diamond grinding wheels are expensive).

In most cases, gainsharing formulas need to include multiple costs precisely because employees control multiple costs, and the success of a business depends on an organization performing well in a number of areas. Usually, keeping a plan simple is stupid because the organization will get simple performance in a situation that requires complex performance. Complex situations call for high levels of employee involvement, and involvement can make the complex understandable and controllable. Stated another way, it is risky to try to protect employees and gainsharing plans from the true complexity of the business because they will not perform as they need to in order to make the organization successful.

Involvement Opportunities. Employees need to be able to influence the measures that are used as the basis for calculating the bonus. Their ability to have an influence has direct implications for the fit between decision-making power in the organization and the bonus formula. If the bonus is based on labor cost only, then often the kind of suggestion program that is used in the Scanlon plan is quite appropriate, as is the use of quality circles. Through written suggestions, employees can devise improvements in work methods that speed production and reduce labor costs.

If an organization's production process is complex and involves multiple costs, more advanced forms of employee involvement are needed so that employees can influence the payout. Employees need to be able to influence not only direct production decisions but also decisions involving other costs, such as materials, supplies, inventory, and so forth. Work teams, task forces, new communication systems, and training in business economics usually are needed in these situations.

Maintenance. All gainsharing plans require maintenance. Businesses and environments change, and, as a result, formulas and involvement approaches need to change. The key to a successful change in a gainsharing plan is that it is timely and is done in a way that employees see as credible. Typically, a change in the plans is best handled by an ongoing task force that includes representatives from all levels in the organization. This group needs to regularly review the plan and recommend changes. It needs to be staffed by trusted, knowledgeable individuals who understand the business and are capable of making good decisions and communicating them to the rest of the work force.

The alternative to an ongoing task force is an outside expert who comes in and updates the plan on a regular basis. This approach can work, but it has the disadvantage of making the organization dependent on an outsider, and employees may not view the outsider to be as credible as an internal group.

Profit Sharing

Profit sharing is better known, older, and more widely practiced than gainsharing (Weitzman, 1984; Blinder, 1990). In 1987, about 15 percent of the Fortune 1,000 companies covered all employees and over 60 percent covered some employees with a profit-sharing plan (Lawler, Ledford, and Mohrman, 1989). Profit-sharing plans typically are much less effective than gainsharing plans in influencing employee motivation and in producing the kind of social and cultural outcomes that are associated with gainsharing (Nalbantian, 1987; Blinder, 1990; Lawler, 1990b). This lack of effectiveness is particularly apparent in large organizations because the connection between individual performance and corporate profits is virtually nonexistent in these companies, even with high levels of involvement. Furthermore, in the typical profit-sharing plan, profit-sharing bonuses are put into retirement plans. This makes it more difficult to clearly relate rewards to controllable performance. Thus, most profit-sharing plans have little impact on the motivation and behavior of most employees. Because their profit-sharing plans have little impact on employee motivation, organizations often express disappointment with such plans.

Before we dismiss profit sharing as being completely useless in terms of improving organizational effectiveness, I need to stress that even a deferred profit-sharing plan in a large corporation can accomplish three things. First, paying all employees based on organizational performance has some symbolic and communication value. It can effectively point out to everyone that they are part of the organization and that cooperative effort is needed. Since the salaries of corporate exeuctives are often based on profit sharing, a profit-sharing plan can help assure that the rewards received by top management and those received by people throughout the organization are in balance (Foulkes, 1991). Thus, an organization can avoid the all too common problem of executives getting large bonuses while low-level employees receive no bonuses. This disparity may not be a serious problem if the organization is traditionally oriented in its approach to management, but it can be a significant problem in a high-involvement organization. It makes a mockery of the idea of pushing information, knowledge, power, and rewards downward so that all employees will be involved in the business.

Second, some companies, notably Hewlett-Packard, have effectively used their profit-sharing plans as vehicles for educating employees about the financial condition of the organization. When employees are actually sharing in the profits, the meaning of profits and how they are calculated come alive for them, and they become interested in learning about profits and organizational effectiveness. Hewlett-Packard does a number of things to reinforce the communication value of its plan. It makes cash payments to employees on a semiannual basis and involves employees in numerous meetings and discussions about the payments. In addition, it educates employees in the economics of the business.

Third, profit sharing makes the labor costs of an organization variable and adjusts them to the organization's ability to pay (Weitzman, 1984). In a profit-sharing plan, when profits go down, labor costs go down. This is a particularly desirable feature for organizations that are in cyclical or seasonal businesses. In most Western countries, changes in labor costs are handled through increases and decreases in the size of the work force. This approach is a necessity when wages are high and fixed because there is no other way to reduce labor costs to reflect the organization's ability to pay. With profit sharing, an organization can reduce costs significantly without reducing the number of employees or using work sharing. Most Japanese companies have used profit sharing to vary labor costs for decades. It allows an organization to make a much stronger commitment to employees in terms of job stability and helps it gain the advantages that are inherent in having a stable work force. As will be discussed further in Chapter Ten, it is important for a high-involvement organization to provide this for its employees.

As long as an organization does not develop unrealistic expectations about what a profit-sharing plan can do, the plan can be successful. The challenge for an organization in many cases is to manage its own and employees' expectations. An organization needs to clearly understand that regardless of how the plans are structured, they are unlikley to affect motivation. At times employees will be disappointed with the payment they receive because something they could not influence reduced profits. This too has to be expected, and employees need to understand how difficult it is to predict and contol earnings. If expectations are managed well, then profit sharing can have an overall favorable impact on an organization.

Employee Ownership

A number of pay plans exist that help get some or all of the ownership of a company into the hands of employees. These include *stock option plans, stock purchase plans, stock grant programs* and *employee stock ownership plans* (ESOPs). These employee ownership plans are increasingly popular (Blasi, 1988; Rosen, Klein, and Young, 1986; Rosen and Young, 1991). Avis and some other companies use employee ownership as part of their advertising. According to one study of U.S. companies, some eleven million employees in over eight thousand businesses now own at least 15 percent of the companies employing them (Blasi, 1988). Another study reports that in 1990 employee ownership plans in the U.S. controlled $60 billion in assets (Rosen and Young, 1991). It is difficult to generalize about the impact of these plans because they vary widely in how much ownership employees receive and what employees have to do to receive stock. Also their impact is likely to depend on a wide variety of conditions.

Much of what I have said about the impact of profit-sharing plans and gainsharing plans is relevant to stock owner-ship plans. In some situations, a stock ownership plan can have much the same impact as an effective gainsharing plan. Re-search has shown that in a small organization that practices high-involvement management, a stock ownership plan has a good chance of increasing organizational performance (Conte and Tannenbaum, 1980). It might even make profit sharing and gainsharing unnecessary if it is combined with an appropriate approach to employee involvement. The key to the effectiveness of such a plan is combining it with the right approach to employee involvement since stock ownership plans typically produce a weaker visible connection between performance and rewards than does gainsharing or even profit sharing. The con-nection is weaker because it depends on an additional uncon-trollable factor: the value that the financial markets put on the stock of a company. Every time that it seems as though stock prices are fair, reasonable, and predictable, large swings in value occur (who can forget October 1987 or the last half of 1990?) that make the process appear uncontrollable.

In a large organization, employee ownership can do little more than have a positive effect on organizational culture by creating integration across the total organization if, of course, all employees are included in the ownership plan. For this reason, Pepsico, Merck, and other large organizations give stock options to all employees. Many companies have subsidized stock purchase plans for their employees. If most or all employees are not included in the plan, employee ownership can have a nega-tive influence on employee involvement by separating or dis-tinguishing some employees or levels of management from others. Unlike a profit-sharing plan, an employee ownership plan does not automatically adjust costs to reflect the organiza-tion's ability to pay.

Design of Systems to Reward Organizational Performance

My analysis so far suggests that gainsharing, profit sharing, and employee ownership can be very important contributors to the success of organizations using high-involvement management.

Interestingly, it also suggests that they ought not to be looked at as competing approaches but as compatible approaches that accomplish different, important objectives.

Gainsharing, if correctly designed, can increase motivation and produce a culture in which people are committed to seeing their organizational unit operate effectively. Profit sharing can have the desirable effect of creating variable costs for an organization, thus allowing the organization to adjust its costs to its ability to pay. It can also affect the communication pattern and culture of an organization in ways that emphasize the performance of the total organization. In some organizations, employee ownership can motivate employees to improve their performance. In a large organization, its impact on motivation is limited, however. Like profit sharing, it can influence organizational culture and help employees to understand the business. If the stock is held in trust or paid on a delayed basis, employee ownership can help with employee retention.

The ideal combination for many large corporations that want to practice high-involvement management would seem to be a corporatewide profit-sharing plan and a corporatewide stock ownership plan. For example, Corning, Lincoln Electric, and Science Applications International Corporation use a combination of profit sharing, a stock ownership plan, and a stock option plan to focus all employees on the financial performance of the business. Where appropriate, organizations should also use gainsharing plans in major operating plants or units.

The combination of gainsharing and profit sharing deals directly with an organization's need to have variable labor costs. It also helps to move financial information and knowledge throughout the organization. Gainsharing alone does not create variable costs or move information throughout the organization because it tends to be based on subunits of the organization and measures that do not include all the operating costs of the business. Thus, a gainsharing plan could pay out a bonus when the organization is performing poorly. Paying a bonus under these circumstances could be important for employee motivation if the employees are performing well against the things that they are measured on and can control. However, employees may erroneously feel that the organization is in good shape since they are receiving a bonus. The addition of a profit-sharing plan in such situations can help the organization call attention to the fact that the organization's performance is not satisfactory. It also can adjust labor costs according to the organization's ability to pay.

Employee ownership can tie the interests of the employees and other stockholders together so that they do not have competing agendas. This is particularly important if senior managers have stock options and other stock-based incentive plans. Unless stock is widely owned in the organization, these plans can separate the interests of top managers from those of other employees and make it difficult for senior managers to provide the type of leadership that is needed in a high-involvement organization.

Some organizational conditions must be considered in the design of performance-based pay systems. The more interdependent the different units of an organization are and the smaller the organization is, the more profit sharing and employee stock ownership should come into play. The logic here is that the extent of these conditions affect how easy it is and how important it is for employees to focus on organizational performance. At the other extreme, in highly diversified organizations such as Hanson Trust, ITT, or Westinghouse, stock ownership and corporate profit sharing may not be important except for top management. This type of organization has no need to integrate the organization and give employees the feeling of being part of a single entity. Thus, the best approach may be to base pay on the performance of each business unit.

The amount of profit-sharing and gainsharing money that is paid to individuals probably should not be the same at all levels in the organization. At the lowest organizational level, gainsharing should potentially produce larger payouts than the profit-sharing plan does. The emphasis here is on potential payouts since the actual amount should be determined by performance. Most employees relate to and can control gainsharing more easily than profit sharing, and a significant amount of money must be involved for gainsharing to motivate employees.

Among top management, the situation is different; profit sharing should have the greatest potential payoff.

    In most cases, the best pay system for a high-involvement
organization is one that has several pay-for-performance plans
that affect most employees, including profit-sharing, stock
ownership, and gainsharing plans. Senior managers should not
have all the special incentive plans they have in the typical
organization; they should simply have the same profit-sharing
and stock ownership plans that affect other employees so that
their rewards will be aligned with those of other employees and
with the performance of the organization. Thus, the high-
involvement approach basically turns the organization upside
down in order to move performance-based rewards to employees at all levels. This strategy is appropriate because in the high-
involvement approach employees at all levels can make a difference, and, thus, it is important to hold them accountable
through the reward systems for how they and the organization
perform.

Rewards for Individual and Team Performance

Tying pay to individual performance is a basic management
practice in traditionally managed organizations. It fits with the
idea of having a job description and potentially provides a
positive motivational force. In many relatively uninteresting and
unchallenging jobs, it is particularly important to tie pay to
performance because, in the absence of pay as a motivator, there
may be little or no reason for individuals to perform their jobs
effectively. At best, they may be motivated to do the minimum
necessary to avoid punishment.

    The situation is quite different when high-involvement
management is practiced. Work is designed to be motivating
and interesting, and, as a result, paying for individual performance may not be as important or as possible as in a traditionally managed organization. This is particularly true in team
environments when effective programs are used to reward individuals for skill development and gainsharing, profit-sharing,

and stock ownership plans are used to reward them for organizational performance.

Even though it may not be as important to reward individual performance in a high-involvement organization as in a traditional organization, there still are some potentially good reasons for doing so. Many employees feel that being rewarded for individual performance is an issue of equity and fairness (Lawler, 1971). And, of course, these rewards can motivate employees if the systems are well designed—most organizations can always use improvements in employee motivation. Individual rewards can also help to attract and retain individuals who are high performers. Individuals who perform well tend to have a high market value, and they need to be paid well in order to assure that they will be motivated to join and remain with an organization. If pay can be related to individual performance, it seems foolish to ignore this kind of reward and to miss the opportunity to assure that better performers are in fact more highly paid.

Rewards for Individual Performance

The amount of literature on the issues that are involved in rewarding individuals by tying pay to measures of individual performance is enormous. The advantages of rewarding individual performance, as has already been discussed, are significant, but the pitfalls are many and potentially quite serious. It is clear from the research literature that an organization needs to meet certain conditions for an individual pay-for-performance strategy to be effective (Lawler, 1971). Perhaps the most important of these conditions has to do with the design of the employees' work.

Obviously, if the interdependency of the work is such that teams need to be created in order to allow meaningful work to exist, rewards for individual performance essentially are ruled out. On the other hand, if an organization uses an individual job enrichment strategy and individuals can be assigned to whole and meaningful jobs, then these rewards can and, in most cases, should be an important part of an organization's strategy. This relationship holds whether the organization is committed to high-involvement management or not. If a high-involvement approach to management is practiced, it may be easier for an organization to make a pay-for-performance strategy work effectively, even though it may be less important to do so.

A pay-for-performance strategy may work better when paired with job enrichment and high-involvement management because of the difficulty of measuring individual performance. In a pure top-down organization, supervisors and subordinates may not easily develop the kind of communication, trust, and information sharing that is required to adequately assess an individual's performance (Mohrman, Resnick-West, and Lawler, 1989). It is also often difficult for an organization to establish a credible link between individual performance and pay changes, whether they are bonuses or merit salary increases. Thus, even though traditional organizations need pay-for-performance systems to motivate individuals to perform well, they have great difficulty establishing credible measures of performance and credible links between performance and pay.

The key to a successful pay-for-performance plan for individual performance is the establishment of a good system to measure performance and a clear relationship between performance and rewards. Let us start with a discussion of what is needed to measure performance.

System to Measure Performance. Measures that focus on traits such as honesty, reliability, and communication skills almost always make employees defensive and produce poor communication because these are value-laden traits rather than actual behaviors. To be effective, the performance appraisal needs to focus on behaviors that can be translated into quantifiable measures. A note of caution is in order here: it may not be possible to identify a large number of levels of performance. Sometimes the best that can be done is to identify three levels of performance, such as outstanding, acceptable, and failing. Requiring the appraiser to go beyond this will produce invalid data and unhappy and resentful employees.

It is important that the goals and measures that will be

used to assess performance be clear and be understood by both the appraisee and the appraiser and that they be subject to discussion and mutual influence. The individual being appraised must feel that he or she has had fair input in the establishment of the goals and that the goals are reasonable.

Performance appraisals often compare individual to individual and ask which person performed better. This approach is not appropriate in a high-involvement organization. Even if individual behavior is the focus because the jobs have been designed with the individual job enrichment approach in mind, it is important that people not be put in competition with each other. The kind of competition that is engendered by peer comparisons is unlikely to produce the kind of sharing, cooperation, and trust that is needed to make a high-involvement organization operate effectively. Therefore, the performance appraisal process should be one in which people compete against absolute standards so that all can win or all can lose if they fail to make the standard.

In top-down organizations, the manager should be the one appraising employee behavior. In a high-involvement organization, the manager still has responsibility for seeing that a valid appraisal occurs, but he or she may gather data from many sources. It is not automatically assumed that the boss is fully knowledgeable about a subordinate's performance or that the boss can be trusted to provide valid data. Peers, customers, subordinates, and high-level managers may all contribute data to the appraisal process. The key to the process is identifying who has knowledge of the person's performance and gathering data from these individuals. For example, in the evaluation of a manager, the appraiser may need to gather data from her peers in order to see how she works with them and from subordinates in order to judge how she manages others.

The literature clearly establishes that most individuals want regular career discussions that focus on their long-term development (Mohrman, Resnick-West, and Lawler, 1989). These discussions should be separate from the discussions that focus on current performance results and how these results are related to changes in pay.

Training both the appraisee and the appraiser in the performance-appraisal process is critical in making the process effective. Most appraisers are uncomfortable doing appraisals, just as most individuals are uncomfortable being appraised: both need to practice and develop skills. In a high-involvement organization, it makes sense to train the appraiser and the appraisee together so that they understand what is expected of each other and they can practice the appraisal process in a supportive environment.

Even in the best-managed organizations, employees sometimes are treated unfairly by unreasonable or misguided supervisors. Thus, it is critical in all organizations, but particularly in high-involvement organizations, that individuals have a chance to appeal the outcome of their performance appraisal. This appeal must allow them to get a fair and impartial hearing from an individual whom they trust. It also must occur in a climate in which their supervisor cannot and will not punish them for questioning his or her decision.

In a high-involvement organization, it is important that supervisors be held accountable for how well they deal with the performance appraisal process and, indeed, with all their management responsibilities. The best way to hold supervisors responsible for the appraisal process is by looking at how well the appraisal itself was done and by asking the individuals who were appraised how they felt about the appraisal process.

Relationship Between Performance and Rewards. A few simple principles need to be kept in mind in order to successfully relate pay to the results of individual performance appraisals. First, the relationship between pay and performance needs to be a clear one. The best way to make the relationship clear is to make public the actual pay rates and the relationship between pay and performance. In traditional organizations, this suggestion is usually immediately rejected because it is seen as too threatening and too potentially explosive. In a high-involvement organization, pay rates and the relationship between pay and performance should be public because keeping them secret is contrary to the idea that all employees should understand and be able to question how they are treated, understand the business, be involved in the business, and be in control of their career and development.

Second, in order for pay to be a motivator, a meaningful amount of money has to be "at risk" when an individual performs. Merit pay plans that make small changes in base pay rarely put enough compensation at risk. Also, with these plans it often takes a long time for high-performing individuals to move to the point where their pay actually reflects their individual performance. To solve these problems, organizations can and increasingly are giving lump-sum merit payments or bonus payments of 10 percent or more to individuals instead of giving individual merit increases. This approach allows organizations to substantially vary the pay of individuals according to their current performance and does not make past salary increases annuities that cannot be used to reward future performance.

Deming and others associated with the research on Total Quality reject entirely the idea of basing pay on individual performance (Deming, 1986). Although I agree with many of their arguments, I still think that pay that is based on the results of performance appraisals can be a positive factor when work is designed for individuals and the appraisals follow the approaches discussed here. There are no guarantees when relating pay to individual performance, but it can work if the situation and the process are right. If they are not right, then it definitely is best to avoid trying to tie pay to individual performance.

Rewards for Team Performance

When teams are an organization's chosen approach to job design, it often makes little or no sense for the organization to create systems that reward individual performance. Particularly destructive are performance-appraisal systems for individuals that require a fixed number of positive and negative ratings or provide fixed pots of budget money that need to be divided up differentially among the individuals in a group. These practices put team members in competition for rewards.

Rewarding team performance works well in situations in which team performance is easily measurable and where the work calls for high levels of team-oriented behavior. However, strong emphasis should be placed on rewarding team behavior only if teams are operating in a relatively autonomous way. If the teams have complete responsiblity for a product or a service, an organization may be able to create a gainsharing plan for each team. Motorola and some financial service firms have used this approach and it has worked. An organization can also give teams merit pay based on performance appraisals. The same measurement and reward issues that apply to appraisals of individuals are relevant to appraisals of teams. To appraise the performance of teams, managers need to be able to set team goals, measure team performance, and give feedback to teams. Team-based rewards also ensure that all team members get the same size bonus or salary increase.

If the level of interdependency among team members is low, it may not make sense to reward teams. However it still might make sense to do something to assure that individuals are good team members and do not focus only on their individual performance, such as including measures of their contribution to the team in their individual performance appraisal. A good source of data on an individual's contribution to the team usually is another member of the team. Team members can be asked to rate each other on teamwork, cooperation, and contribution, and this rating, in turn, can have an impact on the level of individual rewards that employees receive.

It may make sense to single out one or two individuals from a team for special rewards if they have been particularly valuable contributors to the team. In most cases, the other team members should select the individuals to be rewarded. Sometimes, recognition can be a very powerful reward for those individuals who are particularly important contributors to teams. Formal recognition programs often use articles in newspapers or newsletters, ceremonies, and posted pictures to reward individuals.

Congratulations and social recognition from other team members are often the most valued rewards. They are particularly likely to occur when the team is held accountable for its performance and no rewards from management go to individual team members. When management rewards individual team members, other members are not as motivated to provide rewards themselves because they do not see it as their responsibility. Thus, individual rewards from management may discourage team members from giving individuals what they want most: recognition from their peers.

Several reward strategies combine a focus on individual performance and team performance. Again, these strategies are particularly appropriate when individual performance can be measured and high team cohesiveness is not critical. One strategy that can be effective is to create a bonus pool based on the performance of the overall team. This bonus pool can be divided up among the individuals who are members of the team based on how well the individuals performed. In order to be sure that individuals do not compete unfairly or destructively, input can be solicited from the members of the team on how much each team member contributed. Another alternative is for an organization to have two separate reward systems operating in tandem. One system provides bonuses to teams based on their performance; the second rewards individuals based on how well they have performed. These systems can be based on separate budgets so that they do not compete. They should vary in how much impact they have on the pay of individuals according to how much focus in the organization should be on individual performance and how much should be on team performance.

Although teams are generally designed to be relatively freestanding and to control the production of a whole product or service, sometimes they are interdependent with other activities in the organization. A classic example of this interdependency is a multishift plant where what one shift or team does has a strong impact on what the next shift or team can do. In this kind of environment, I have often recommended that only a few rewards be given to teams and that the major focus be on rewarding employees for the performance of the organization or plant. Too many rewards for individual teams can cause them to focus on their own performance at the expense of the overall organization's performance.

If an effective gainsharing plan is in place, often a good approach is for an organization to use recognition-type rewards to motivate teams and reinforce their good performance. These rewards can include write-ups in the company newspaper and tickets to entertainment events. Teams can be rewarded for a variety of results, including setting new quality records, having perfect attendance, and suggesting improvements. The key is for an organization to find a balance between team and organizational awards that encourages teams to excel and, at the same time, causes them to focus strongly on how their actions affect the overall performance of their business unit.

Mix of Organizational, Individual, and Team Rewards

It takes considerable thought, planning, and some design skill for an organization to identify the right mix of individual, team, and organizational rewards. A number of factors need to be taken into consideration, but none is more important than the kind of interdependency that exists among the members of teams and among the teams in an organization. This interdependency must determine how many rewards are based on the performance of individuals, teams, and the organization.

High-involvement management and the kind of culture that it creates can be quite supportive of properly designed pay-for-performance systems. It can make possible the kind of open communication, valid measurement, and trusting relationships that are necessary to clearly relate measures of performance to reward levels. Thus, it is possible to have highly effective individual, team, and organizational pay-for-performance systems. Indeed, the effectiveness of high-involvement management depends on the creation of these systems. They produce accountability for how information, knowledge, and power are used and they encourage individuals to take responsibility for their actions and the performance of their organization. However, if poor decisions are made about how to design these systems, they can be powerful deterrents to effective organizational performance and can be very destructive in a high-involvement organization. They can, for example, work strongly against the kind of teamwork that is needed to make self-managing work teams operate effectively, and they can discourage individual initiative if not enough recognition and rewards are directed to individuals.

Fortunately, individuals in most organizations often have a good sense of what the right mix of rewards is, and, thus, if a participative design process is used, they can contribute substantially to designing a reward system that has the right mix of individual, team, and organizational rewards. Using this type of design process is also highly consistent with an employee involvement approach to management.

PART THREE

Managing

Information

and Human

Resources

Chapter Nine

Promote Open Information Channels

An organization's information systems must promote the open flow of information if the organization is to successfully practice high-involvement management. Employees must have information to be able to direct and manage themselves, operate with a reduced hierarchy, and be involved in the business. This chapter will look at some of the critical information flows that must exist for an organization to operate in a high-involvement manner. It will also discuss some of the technologies that organizations can use to facilitate the needed creation and movement of information.

Moving Information Downward

Creating a culture in which employees do the "right thing," not just the prescribed thing, sounds great. However, for employees to act in ways that support organizational effectiveness, they must understand the organization's mission, how the organization measures performance, and what they can do to contribute to the mission and influence performance. If they do not understand their organization's mission, employees cannot know how to behave, even if they want to do the right thing. Equally critical is information about how the organization is performing; without it, employees cannot get the feedback they need to correct their behavior and improve upon it.

205

How the mission is developed can influence how well communicated and accepted it is. It is helpful for employees to participate in the development of the mission by commenting on drafts and attending meetings (Weisbord, 1987). The mission needs to be communicated in as many ways as possible. Johnson & Johnson and other organizations that do a good job of communicating their mission post the mission statement throughout the organization. Management should also repeat it in newsletters, speeches, help-wanted advertisements, annual reports, new employee training programs, and other sources of information about the company. Senior managers need to constantly repeat the mission and refer to it when they announce strategic decisions so that employees will see how it is being used to guide the overall direction of the organization.

Employees also need extensive training to help them understand financial and performance results. This training can and should be facilitated by a skill-based pay system. Economic literacy is fundamental for employees because unless they understand how to interpret business results, it is hard for them to understand how to direct their behavior and be motivated and intrinsically rewarded by the success of the organization. Working in an organization and not knowing how its performance is measured is roughly equivalent to going to or participating in a sports event without knowing how to keep score: although you might be briefly interested in the pageantry, it quickly runs the risk of becoming boring because you do not know how well the teams are performing and why others are cheering!

Performance Results

When important events occur in the operations of an organization and when performance results are available, it is critical that management communicate these as quickly as possible to all employees. Along with training in understanding performance results, this information is fundamental to giving individuals a sense of success when their organization performs well. It is needed to help move such nonfinancial rewards as the joy of winning, feelings of being competent, and feelings of being part of a successful organization to individuals throughout the organization. It is also critical to the success of profit sharing, gain-sharing, and other organizational pay-for-performance plans. Without this information, individuals throughout the organization cannot be expected to care about the organization's performance.

Nothing makes an employee feel more like an outsider than to hear of important events, results, and activities in the organization through the grapevine or the local newspaper. Employees' feelings of being involved and being an important part of the organization are reinforced by communication patterns and policies that get information to the employees as soon as legally possible. I include the word *legally* here because publicly traded companies have limitations on how quickly they can release information to employees.

Organizations have a legitimate concern about competitors gaining access to their plans and financial results if they communicate these items to employees. From my experience, however, most organizations are far too conservative in sharing sensitive information with employees. They assume that no one can be trusted with information but the top few people, thereby reinforcing a hierarchical approach to management. Employees need to be educated to understand that information is a competitive advantage and that they are hurting themselves and their organization if they share it with outsiders. When they understand this, employees are capable of behaving responsibly and not putting the company at risk because of leaks of information. If a profit-sharing or stock ownership plan is in place, employees are less likely to share information because it will hurt them financially.

Communication Approaches

Effective communication of financial and strategic information is a primary responsibility of senior management. Managers need to build into the organization information systems that allow them to regularly and effectively disseminate business results and information about critical events in the organization. A number of technologies can be used to facilitate this type of communication. Indeed, because of some new technologies, organizations can regularly give employees throughout the world an ongoing sense of how they are doing and what their strategic direction is. By the use of electronic mail, voice mail, live television programs, videotapes and, of course, speeches and personal contact, managers can move information rapidly and effectively around most large organizations. Increasingly, organizations are taking advantage of these technologies to improve their communication practices. IBM, for example, has its own internal television network, and Digital and Sun Microsystems use electronic mail to communicate with their employees. Incidentally, one good guideline is that any important message or piece of information should be communicated in at least two ways and probably through all the communication channels that are available in the organization.

A simple first step in facilitating communication about business results is for an organization to send all employees copies of the reports that are sent to stockholders. Of course, if the organization makes all employees stockholders, this will happen automatically. If employees are not stockholders, giving them this information is still important, even though it is a small step in opening up communication channels. It seems obvious that most companies should do this, but, in fact, a 1987 survey of the Fortune 1,000 companies showed that a significant number (50 percent) do not even take this basic step (Lawler, Ledford, and Mohrman, 1989).

Something as important as business results should not only be communicated by written reports but also should be supported by both personal communications and electronic communications. Some of the most innovative practices I have seen involve the use of videotapes to communicate business results throughout the organization. For example, McDonnell Douglas sends a half-hour videotape to the home of every employee at the end of every quarter. This videotape, which features the company's president, discusses the company's financial results, new products, and future. The videotape costs a little over $3 per employee, but so far it seems to be worth the cost. According to data gathered by McDonnell Douglas, over 80 percent of the employees watch the videotape and they particularly appreciate the opportunity to show their family what is happening in their organization. Incidentally, the employees are told how to erase the tape so they can use it for recording television shows.

Some organizations create live television hookups around the world to announce major events and financial results to employees. This method of communication can be a tremendous aid to getting individuals involved in the events, particularly if it involves two-way communication. The two-way communication need not involve individuals asking the president or chief executive officer to clarify his or her comments; in a large organization this may not be possible. Instead, this communication can be in the form of local question-and-answer sessions that follow the broadcast of the corporate television program.

Electronic mail is a very quick way to send announcements about business results and critical events throughout an organization. If the organization is connected by a network as are IBM, Sun Microsystems, and Digital, electronic mail is perhaps the best way to get information to individuals throughout the organization (Savage, 1990; Zuboff, 1988). If individuals can ask for clarification and interpretation of the communication, it can be more effective. At Digital, questions to the chief executive officer (CEO) are answered on an electronic mail system that is open to all employees so that there is a continuous, open discussion and flow of information about business events and results.

Levi Strauss has developed an interactive computer information system that provides employees with a wealth of information about benefits, compensation, training, and development opportunities. The system, named *Oliver*, has the capability of personalizing information and helping employees choose benefits. It allows employees to perform a number of functions, such as projecting retirement income and completing enrollment forms for training courses.

Some airlines and other organizations that have employees widely scattered throughout the country find it very difficult to get employees together at any one point in time to announce performance results and discuss business events. To overcome this problem, several major airlines have national toll-free numbers so that individuals anywhere in the country can call in and find out about critical company events. This system can be an effective way to spread information and to eliminate the unfounded rumors that often circulate in a company. It clearly demonstrates to employees that the organization wants them to understand and be informed about how the business is doing.

The oldest and potentially most effective method of communication is the face-to-face meeting. Every information system needs to include this approach to disseminating business information. A good time to begin the practice of face-to-face communication is when an individual joins an organization. Some company presidents insist on meeting all new employees. They spend anywhere from half an hour to several hours talking with new employees about how the organization is managed and what goals, objectives, and strategies it is currently pursuing.

Meeting with a company president who is a charismatic and effective leader can be a tremendously powerful experience for new employees. First, it shows the company's concern for them, and, second, it helps them understand what the organization is trying to accomplish. It can also be important for other managers to see senior managers engaging in this kind of behavior.

The number of employees that senior managers can personally meet with on a regular basis is limited. Thus, for large organizations to have the necessary personal communications, managers throughout the organization must hold meetings, discuss results, and effectively communicate with employees. It is vital that managers, particularly in large organizations, talk about division results, plant results, and work group results on a regular basis with employees throughout their units. Often, this communication can be combined with organizationwide communications that focus on the plans, objectives, and results of the total organization.

If the appropriate technology is in place, an organization

can give employees ongoing, almost continuous information about how their particular part of the business is performing. For example, Frito-Lay has computerized its entire product distribution system so that everyone in the organization has an ongoing sense of sales volumes across all product lines. This system allows employees who are calling on stores to immediately identify when they have a problem and suggests how they should direct their sales activity in that location.

The Honda plant in Marysville, Ohio, uses a simple system for providing ongoing feedback. The plant has large scoreboards that show the production schedule for the day and give ongoing information about performance. This system does not take a high level of technology; indeed, all it requires is a commitment on the part of management to post data and keep the information up-to-date.

Statistical process control, a method for detecting out-of-control work processes, is another good example of a technology that can help give employees the kind of feedback on performance that they need to make ongoing adjustments in performance. Through this system, particularly if it can be supplemented with cost data, individuals can continuously receive information about how their particular piece of the organization is operating. Ultimately, it is information about employees' local operation that has the most powerful effect on their behavior. Although it is important to give individuals information about how the total organization is performing, this information is not a substitute for providing good local financial and businesss data.

A basic component of the work team and job enrichment strategies is for an organization to provide individuals with ongoing information and feedback on performance. Without this feedback, employee motivation falls dramatically as does the ability of individuals to direct their behavior in an effective manner. Thus, an organization must strongly emphasize local communication practices that provide individuals with information about how their work team and work area is performing. Often, a simple bulletin board can do the job. In some plants and offices, I have seen bulletin boards used to provide data about competitors and, of course, ongoing performance results. They also can be used to communicate with employees on different shifts and at different levels of the organization. All too often, bulletin boards are covered with commercial posters containing trite slogans instead of business information.

A guideline with respect to the downward flow of information is that it is virtually impossible for an organization to communicate its mission, strategy, and performance results too often. This is true in any organization, but it is particularly true in high-involvement organizations. They rely on individuals knowing the right thing to do since they do not have traditional job descriptions and controls. Furthermore, these organizations rely on individuals being motivated in part because they care about the success of the organization. To care about an organization, employees must have an understanding of the organization and must receive performance feedback.

Moving Information Upward

Three kinds of information need to move up the hierarchy in a high-involvement organization. The first is business information about operating results and performance levels. The second is employees' ideas and suggestions about how to improve or change the effectiveness of the organization. The third is information about employees' views of how their organization functions and how they are being treated and about their general feelings toward the culture and climate of the organization. As with the downward flow of information, the upward flow of information needs to be supported by a number of different technologies.

Performance Results

Increasingly, the results of business activities are being communicated upward by the use of electronic data. Federal Express has connected its entire organization through a computer network so that senior managers and employees can quickly and easily find out about work activities and performance throughout the organization. Federal Express's computer network has data not only about all the packages and letters that the company is moving but also about the individuals who work for the organization. Thus, it is possible for management to quickly have access to the profiles of individuals working in the organization and find out what skills they have, what jobs they have held, and what their performance goals are for a particular time period.

Having performance data available on a computer network is obviously an advantage for upper-level managers because it gives them a sense of how the organization is operating below them. As will be discussed later, easy access to this information may also be vital to individuals who are at the same level in the organization; it can support the horizontal coordination that is needed in carrying out complex manufacturing and service processes and in developing complex products (Savage, 1990; Walton, 1989).

Electronic reporting of performance can allow senior managers to know a great deal about how people throughout the organization are performing and to quickly identify areas with problems and low productivity (Pava, 1983). Consequently, it can be used in the service of an authoritarian top-down approach to management. If senior managers use this information to overcontrol and overdirect behavior at low levels of an organization, they will defeat any attempts to use high-involvement management (Zuboff, 1988). On the other hand, if senior managers use the information as part of a process to identify and solve problems and if they use it to give individuals a greater opportunity for self-management, this information can be a tremendous boon to employee involvement.

Researchers disagree about whether using information technology to provide performance data is inherently more compatible with a top-down approach or an employee involvement approach to management. However, the most common conclusion is that the use of this technology is most compatible with a high-involvement approach to management (Pava, 1983; Zuboff, 1988; Walton, 1989). A major reason that researchers reach this conclusion is that once the information is collected and available in the electronic information system of an organization, it seems to find its way to individuals throughout the organization, regardless of what management does to limit employees' access to it. With information comes the power to influence; thus, efforts to keep power at the top often fail. Employees also seem to find ways to falsify this information in a top-down organization so that management does not have the accurate data it needs to control and direct behavior at lower levels in the organization.

Suggestions for Improvement

There are many ways that organizations can move ideas for improvement up the hierarchy so that they can be effectively developed and implemented. As has already been discussed, improvement groups are a viable way, as are written suggestion programs. Written suggestion programs are obviously badly needed in traditional top-down organizations and have been popular for decades. I question, however, whether these programs are useful in involvement-oriented organizations. Many of the ideas that are processed in written suggestion programs could effectively be implemented by a local work team without the help of the large bureaucracy that needs to be in place to handle written suggestions.

Organizations may outgrow the need for formal written suggestion programs as they develop other communication and problem-solving processes. Written suggestion programs can create conflicts about who gets credit for a particular suggestion and the value of the suggestion. If an organization uses a gain-sharing plan or other kind of pay-for-performance plan, many of these conflicts are eliminated because everyone shares in the gains that are produced by the suggestions and only suggestions that actually have an impact on operations are rewarded.

A low-tech suggestion system is used by the Milliken Company plant in Marietta, South Carolina. At the end of each assembly line is a bulletin board plastered with notes. The notes contain handwritten suggestions by employees. The foreman in charge has twenty-four hours to acknowledge that he or she has read each note and seventy-two hours to respond to each note. Often the solution to a problem or an answer is provided by another employee who sees the note and volunteers to respond to it.

One alternative to the traditional written suggestion program that I have already mentioned is the electronic mail system, used at Digital and Sun Microsystems, in which employees throughout the organization can raise issues with senior management about how the organization is operating. In its U.S. operations Honda makes effective use of a written "channel two" system that allows employees to get answers directly from top management ("channel one" is open discussion). Some companies have started using television to facilitate the upward flow of ideas for improvement. The companies make videocameras and videotapes available to individuals or groups so that, if appropriate, they can make a short videotape to capture their idea.

In all of these suggestion systems, the organization typically commits to getting back to the employee in a few days with an answer to his or her suggestion. The answers can either be made public or, if desired by the individual, kept confidential. These communication techniques can be used both to deal with technical problems and suggestions and to raise concerns about personnel policies and management actions.

It may also make sense for organizations to establish communication channels that allow employees to raise tough issues involving personal risk without the fear of retribution. In one case, a work team used such a "hot line" to blow the whistle on a management group that was falsifying test data on one of their products. Because local management was involved in the deception, a direct, safe hot line to top management was important.

The best place to deal with many improvement ideas is in an employee's own work team. Often, the team can immediately implement many of the suggestions, particularly if it has a budget to make some small purchases. If the group cannot implement a suggestion immediately, it may be able to work on the issue, develop it further, and respond to the individual later.

If the group cannot handle an idea, then certainly it is appropriate for the group to use electronic mail, videotapes, or other approaches to be sure that the idea reaches management. The Scanlon plan ensures that suggestions reach management by creating a group that processes and approves suggestions.

Attitudes and Opinions

Data about employee reactions to the way the organization is managed and how employees feel about their work situation have typically been gathered through attitude surveys, interviews, and focus groups. These are effective, time-honored methods of gathering data but are sometimes slow and labor intensive (Nadler, 1977). Data from the Fortune 1,000 companies suggest that 70 percent of them use attitude surveys, and the number seems to be increasing (Lawler, Ledford, and Mohrman, 1989). IBM is probably the leader in the use of attitude surveys; it regularly surveys all employees and has done so for over twenty years. A number of consulting firms sell questionnaires and data that allow companies to compare their scores on the questionnaires to those of other companies.

An interesting way to speed up the data collection process is to use electronic mail or even voice mail. IBM, for example, gathers some of its survey data by putting questions on an electronic network and letting employees respond. This method allows data to be gathered and reported back overnight and avoids the sticky issue of people denying the validity of the data because it is "too old."

An organization can also use an electronic network to create interactive discussions of how individuals feel by putting open-ended questions on the network and asking individuals to discuss or debate how the organization is doing in a particular area. This approach can provide people throughout the organization with a good sense of what is happening in the organization and how effectively certain systems or activities are being carried out.

In traditional top-down organizations, the results of attitude surveys often are only used by senior managers to help them get a feel for what is occurring at low levels in the organiza-tion. When used in this way, surveys do little toward creating a high-involvement organization; instead, they help traditional organizations maintain control. Survey results also can and often are used to help parts of the organizations analyze their operations and to facilitate problem solving at all levels in the organization. The *survey feedback approach* does just this by giving work teams their survey results and encouraging them to use the results in a discussion of how they can operate more effectively (Nadler, 1977). This apporach, which helps transform data gathering into a participative problem-solving process that is supportive of high-involvement management, has been used effectively by IBM and a number of other companies for decades.

Input to Decision Making

A few organizations have used their electronic mail network to gather employee input on key decisions. For example, when Sun Microsystems considered changing the location of its corporate headquarters, it allowed individuals to participate in the deci-sion by asking for their opinions on the electronic mail system. For several weeks, employees debated whether or not the head-quarters should be moved. Management considered the results of this debate when it made the final decision not to move the headquarters to a new location.

An organization can use many approaches to solicit em-ployee input to decisions. For example, employees who could be affected by possible changes can review and critique new pol-icies and strategies in meetings. Meetings or small focus groups are particularly important when the decisions will have a signifi-cant effect on how business is done or how employees are treated. Where appropriate, study groups or teams can develop recommendations about what the organization should do. Methods for running meetings exist that can allow a large number of employees to participate in important mission, strat-egy, and operational decisions (see, for example, Weisbord, 1987).

Moving Information Horizontally

The horizontal movement of information is one of the major features that distinguishes a high-involvement organization from a control-oriented one. Because of its flat hierarchy and emphasis upon coordination at low levels in the organization, a high-involvement organization needs to move large amounts of information horizontally, including operating information and ideas for improvement. Horizontal communication links need to be designed to substitute for the supervisors who act as links and channels in traditional hierarchical organizations.

As was already discussed in Chapters Four and Five, work teams are one method of dramatically improving the horizontal communication structure of an organization. They can, if properly designed, handle many of the ongoing coordination activities that are needed to make an organization effective. They can be particularly powerful if they are structured to completely serve external customers or produce products from beginning to end. However, in complex technologies, single work teams cannot do everything themselves; therefore, other mechanisms are needed to facilitate horizontal communication.

Electronic mail and other forms of technology can be very helpful in facilitating the horizontal movement of operating information and knowledge throughout an organization (Walton, 1989). A number of organizations use electronic mail to hold conferences on topics ranging from developing personnel policies to developing new pieces of technology and new products. Electronic communication mechanisms, in effect, substitute for face-to-face meetings and the kind of communication that can take place in these meetings. The obvious advantage of electronic communication over face-to-face meetings is that it saves on transportation costs and allows a wider range of individuals to participate in educational activities or policy development.

Live television feeds can also be used to facilitate coordination among groups doing different parts of a production process. At Compaq Computer, for example, it is impossible to structure teams that produce an entire product because of the manufacturing technology involved. Therefore, the company uses television feeds to tie together teams that are producing different parts of the final product. Thus, individuals can have interactive discussions with employees who are doing other parts of the production process and can see exactly what other teams are doing, how it might be improved, and how it affects what they are doing.

Electronic mail can also be used to facilitate horizontal problem solving. In a number of manufacturing facilities that I have worked with, electronic bulletin boards were created that allow individuals to ask questions of others throughout the corporation. Production employees in different plants are thus able to share their knowledge about how to fix a particular problem and how to operate equipment more effectively. I have seen this system work well at Procter & Gamble, where operators in one plant can communicate with their counterparts in other plants in order to share ideas for improving production and to solve maintenance problems. In a service situation, electronic mail can allow individuals to share sales ideas and service techniques. The key to an effective electronic network is setting it up to allow and to facilitate horizontal communication (Walton, 1989). Information systems that block employees' access to certain bulletin boards or data on a hierarchical basis get in the way of this kind of problem-solving communication.

The flow of horizontal communication should be organized around particular topics. The key topics and the communication method should be publicized throughout the organizations so that the individuals who need to communicate with each other know how and where to reach each other, can identify their common interests, and can learn from each other.

As with all other types of communication, face-to-face meetings are particularly effective in horizontal communication. If teams need to coordinate with each other but are not in the same physical location, many organizations take their employees from one location to another for face-to-face meetings. Xerox holds an annual worldwide meeting to facilitate horizontal communication and to recognize the efforts of problem-solving groups. At these meetings, teams present their ideas to others and celebrate their successes. The meetings take place at all major Xerox locations and are linked by a television network.

Team visits to customers and suppliers are particularly effective because they give team members the kind of feedback and familiarity that simply cannot be obtained through electronic communications or even videoconferencing. In fact, personal contact is a good first step in establishing videoconferencing or other electronic communication approaches. Video is also an effective way to show employees the impact of their particular product or service on the customer and how the customer uses the product or service. Lexus asks all its employees to phone at least one customer a week to see how he or she likes the car.

The division of Hughes Aircraft that makes control systems for Navy airplanes found that by taking its production teams to the "top gun" school in San Diego, it could give the employees a very positive perspective on how their technology was being used. The pilots whose lives depended upon the guidance system also gave the employees meaningful feedback about the importance of their activities. Much less dramatic, but perhaps equally important, is the work that I did with an automobile seat manufacturer. Employees from the seat manufacturing plant were sent to the Ford assembly plant they served in order to see how the seats were put into the cars and how they were handled. This meeting was the beginning of an ongoing electronic communication link between the assembly group and the employees that made the seats, which ultimately led to a number of improvements in seat design and in how the seats were packaged and delivered to the assembly plant.

To facilitate horizontal communication, organizations often need overlay structures. As was discussed earlier, an overlay structure consists of groups or teams that take responsibility for coordination activities (Galbraith, 1973). The groups may be temporary or permanent. A good example of an overlay team that facilitates horizontal communication is a product management team.

Overlay teams often are needed when the basic structure

of a company is organized around customers. Without these teams, horizontal communication about a particular product or service that goes to multiple customers may not occur. For example, in banking, the basic unit of a bank is the branch and its customer base. An overlay structure, however, is needed to manage the products that are offered through the branches. This overlay structure gathers information about how particular products are performing and how they can be improved and it accumulates findings from the different parts of the organization. Individuals may be assigned full time to an overlay team or product management team, or a task force of representatives from the different branches who are familiar with the product may meet regularly to assess the product and, if appropriate, to change and develop it. The work of the overlay group can be facilitated by electronic communication that gathers information from the different branches about how the product is performing.

Some companies have developed overlay groups that exist via electronic connections; that is, they do not meet in person nor are they all assigned full time to work on a particular project or product (Savage, 1990). They are linked, however, by the commitment to improve and coordinate activities around a particular product or process. Electronic communication allows them to exchange information, develop policies, and coordinate their activities. Digital calls this type of overlay group a *virtual* group. Often, these groups are self-managing in the sense that the members appoint their own leader and establish their own operational rules.

The idea of virtual groups has great potential in high-involvement organizations that have to cope with a rapidly changing environment. For example, work teams that are not in the same location and are not traditionally supervised can be linked electronically in order to coordinate their work. In rapidly changing business environments where organizations need to adapt quickly, this approach may be more realistic than moving individuals geographically every time new teams and projects are started, particularly if geographical moves involve great expense and hardship. Apple has developed a computing system that can help organizations create teams and horizontal relationships. The *Spider* system combines personal computers, videoconferencing, and a data base of employee records. The system makes it possible for individuals to call up skill and performance profiles of employees who work anywhere in the organization and ultimately could forge work groups that are independent of geography.

Work systems that electronically link employees who work at home with the office can potentially save organizations money spent on office space and transportation costs. However, for such telecommunication systems to work, an organization must develop an approach to managing that does not rely on traditional supervision and control since these methods cannot be used (Walton, 1989). Close electronic links and new and different levels of involvement are possible however. AT&T, for example, links many of the members of its sales force who operate from their homes by computers that use innovative software to move information and help employees keep in touch with each other.

The Informed Employee

The discussion so far has emphasized the importance of the upward, downward, and horizontal flow of information in organizations. It has also stressed that many communication channels and techniques are available to facilitate communication within organizations. Because the discussion has focused on mechanics, it may not have captured the overall organizational transformation that is possible when information begins to flow freely throughout an organization. The extensive use of communications technology and its ability to open up communication channels can help to fundamentally change an organization.

Creating new communication channels and putting more information into the hands of employees are not by themselves enough to transform an organization into a high-involvement organization. However, when employees also are given knowledge, the power to make decisions, and rewards that are dependent upon how they use their power and information, fundamental changes can result. An organization can change from one in which top-down control is the only way to operate to one in which control and the power to make decisions can move swiftly and effectively throughout the organization (Zuboff, 1988). Those people who are closest to the issue and who have on-line information about what needs to be done can make decisions about the issue, improving and speeding decision making in ways that will lead to faster development of products and response to customers.

The overall impact of new information flows in an organization can be to allow people throughout the organization to learn about their business and be involved in it in a way they never could before. They will be able to understand it, see its dynamics, and influence it from virtually any position in the organization. Individuals can have an unprecedented opportunity for learning from each other and for changing both products and processes to fit what they have learned through customer contact.

As employees learn to control and receive new kinds of information, their jobs are enriched whether they operate in teams or in an individually enriched job. Even those employees at the lowest level of an organization can have access to incredibly rich data bases that they can use to guide their decision making. Financial data can be provided which gives a sense of how the business is performing and what its competitive issues are. Many employees can end up with external customer relationships so that they experience the marketplace and the business environment in a way that is not possible with internal customers. In essence, all employees, not only those in high-level management positions, can be informed and, therefore, are able to make even relatively complex decisions.

The potential exists to break down the barriers between those individuals who do the work and those who control the work and have information about it. Everyone, in effect, can be at least partially in a decision-making and management role. With hierarchical information flows and little ability to generate ongoing operational data at the lowest level of an organization, this simply is impossible.

The industrial robot is a good example of how technology

can change the nature of work and decision making (Walton, 1989). It not only eliminates the need for manual labor but also takes away highly repetitive tasks from human operators. It can produce extensive amounts of information about how the production process is operating, and this information, in turn, can be given to employees who are monitoring the process and who can make corrections in the process. Employees suddenly can get detailed information about the operation of a particular part of the production process that was never available before. This, in turn, can allow employees to make decisions and perform in ways that simply would not be possible if they were doing the production work instead of the robot.

The increasing availability of new information and communication technology is one of the key ingredients that makes a high-involvement management approach possible. This capability, more than any other, makes it possible for individuals to become self-managing, to be involved in the business, and to control processes and operations that previously could only be controlled by high-level managers.

Chapter Ten

Establish
High-Involvement
Management
Practices

The human resources management strategies, policies, and practices used by any organization have an important impact on its success. However, they are particularly critical for a high-involvement organization. They must be consistent with the overall strategy and philosophy of the organization, and they must support the creation of a work force that can operate effectively with high levels of information, knowledge, power, and performance-based rewards. In short, they must support the creation of a work force that is motivated and capable of understanding, managing, and being involved in the business of the organization. Before we talk about specific employee selection, training, career development, and job security policies and practices, it is important to consider how policies and practices are developed.

Process for Developing Human Resource Management
Policies and Practices

The process that is used to develop human resources management practices should be consistent with a high-involvement approach to management. Such a process will not only help to assure that the policies and practices are consistent with high-involvement management but will also contribute to them being accepted by the work force. In addition, it will help reinforce the organization's commitment to using participative decision-making processes.

Traditionally, in most organizations the human resources department has designed and developed the human resources policies and practices and senior management has made the final decisions. In a high-involvement organization, this approach is inappropriate. In large organizations, it may be impossible for everyone to participate directly in the development of most human resources practices. However, everyone can be given opportunities to provide input through surveys, group meetings, and focus groups. Employees can vote on the policies, which offers final assurance that they fit the work force and that everyone has had an input. Design of the policies and practices should be done by task forces that are representative of those employees who will be affected by them. This is the best way to assure that these individuals will have appropriate amounts of input into the development of the policies and practices and that they will accept the policies and practices. In this approach, senior management can either reserve the right to approve the recommendations made by the task force or agree in advance to accept them if they fall within specified parameters.

Senior managers commonly fear that if employees participate in developing policies concerning hours of work, benefits, and a host of other human resources issues, that they will be too lenient or generous. In fact, research shows that when employees are involved in developing these policies, they often set higher standards than would be set by senior management (Lawler, 1981, 1990b). If employees are involved in the business, they understand the importance of these policies and are as committed as anyone else in the organization to seeing that the policies will help the organization be effective. Thus, employee groups often design high standards and demanding policies.

A good example of the type of gains that an organization can realize by using employees to set policies comes from America West Airlines. This nonunion carrier used a representative sample of pilots to set and develop the rules concerning flight schedules for pilots. In most airlines, these rules are extensive and are subject to union contracts. The policies that were ultimately developed by the pilots led to a productivity gain of approximately 25 percent over the schedules that are used by other airlines. The policies were readily accepted by the pilots because they were developed by other pilots and, of course, because of the types of financial and other high-involvement management practices that are part of the management approach at the company.

Time after time in my work with organizations, I have used task forces to develop policies and practices for reward systems. For example, task forces have developed compensation strategies, gainsharing plans, skill-based pay plans, absenteeism policies, and layoff policies. In virtually every situation, employees have worked hard and were capable of understanding the organizational and business issues involved in developing these policies. At times, the groups have needed education and direction, but once they were trained and given the appropriate business information, they functioned effectively and produced an outstanding product.

The extra start-up time that is involved in bringing task force members up to speed on human resources issues is time well spent. It not only leads to the development of better policies and practices but also ultimately leads to quicker implementation and better acceptance of the policies and practices because they have more credibility with the work force. And because employees have developed the policies and practices, they are in an excellent position to lead the communication effort by talking to other employees and becoming part of the training process.

Selection of Employees

The high-involvement approach to management requires that individuals be selected based on their ability to grow and develop as a member of the organization and, of course, to be a contributor to and supporter of the culture and management style of the organization. This is a far different situation than the one in traditional organizations, in which the key question in selecting an employee is whether or not the individual can do the work involved in a particular job. This is a much narrower consideration than whether or not an individual can be a long-term contributing member of a high-involvement organization. Not surprisingly, the former question can be answered more easily and at a lower cost than the latter. For example, an organization can use a variety of testing procedures to determine whether individuals can perform specific jobs (see, for example, Ghiselli and Brown, 1955; Schneider and Schmitt, 1986).

Because of the type of work structures that are created in high-involvement organizations, individuals are not selected so much to do a job as they are selected to join the organization. Thus, the selection process has four objectives. First, the selection process needs to allow the individual to make an informed decision about whether or not he or she wants to join the organization (Wanous, 1980). The emphasis here is on the organization because individuals should not be thinking of themselves as taking a particular job but as joining an organization that has a particular culture and way of operating (Bowen, Ledford, and Nathan, 1991). Second, the process needs to create a sense of commitment to the organization on the part of the individual (Rynes and Barber, 1990). Third, it needs to develop a commitment on the part of the organization to seeing that the individual will succeed (Lawler, 1986). Fourth, it needs to ensure that the individuals who enter the organization have the abilities and values to be effective (Dunnette, 1966). Accomplishing these four major objectives is not easy, but the research on employee selection and organizational entry provides a number of ideas about how they can be accomplished.

A realistic preview of what the work situation is like has been shown to be a powerful way to help individuals make an informed choice about joining the organization and to help them be committed to the organization (Premack and Wanous, 1985). Giving individuals as much valid information as possible about what will be expected of them once they join an organization often leads people who might otherwise have joined the organization to decide that it simply is not appropriate for them, thus saving both them and the organization the costs of a misfit. Also, once individuals join, they tend to be more committed to the organization and to succeeding than if they joined based on a misunderstanding of what was expected. Inevitably, the expectations that they did not know about when they decided to join are difficult for them to accept as valid, and they may be dissatisfied and either quit or have low commitment.

The challenge in any situation is to create a truly realistic preview of what membership in an organization will be like. Perhaps the best approach is to simulate the actual work activities that the individual will be expected to perform. A common practice is to have the individual do the actual work for several days or, in some cases, weeks. After he or she has done the work — usually at a temporary pay rate — a final decision is made by the organization and by the individual. This approach has a great deal to recommend it but may not capture all of the performance demands that are present in a high-involvement organization. It is hard, for example, to set up self-managing work groups in a few weeks. However, a few weeks of working with a particular piece of equipment or being in a particular work environment can give the individual a sense of what the tasks are like.

It can be helpful to put applicants through activities that give them a sense of the kind of group activities that take place in a high-involvement organization. This can also help the organization gather information about how applicants will respond in a group setting. For example, if work teams exist in the organization, team members should interview applicants. The work teams thus have a chance to influence who is hired and who their new members will be. Because they influence the hiring decision, they are committed to seeing that the individuals who are finally hired are successful.

As has already been indicated, individuals need certain kinds of values as well as certain kinds of abilities to be effective in a high-involvement organization. Organizations can check potential employees' basic math, verbal, and learning skills through written tests (Dunnette, 1966). However, tests are not enough by themselves to indicate whether an individual will flourish in a high-involvement organization. If the organization is team based, it is also important that individuals have social skills and, in fact, enjoy social interaction. Data about social skills can be gained from group interviews and team interviews, and some written tests can begin to get at the personality issues that are involved in being an effective team member (Nathan, Ledford, Bowen, and Cummings, 1989; Wellins, Byham, and Wilson, 1991).

There is one additional reason why the selection process for a high-involvement organization should be an extensive and thorough one. A great deal of research from the psychological literature shows that when individuals do finally succeed in entering an organization after an extensive selection process they are extremely committed to succeeding in the organization and they feel they are special and the organization is special (Wanous, 1980). In a sense, a rigorous and extensive selection process is basic to having an organizational culture of excellence and high commitment. Who can feel special about joining an organization that either randomly admits people or quickly passes them through a screening process? Interestingly, many of the Japanese organizations that started operations in the United States have recognized this psychological factor. They screen their potential employees extensively, using weeks of selection activities, before they decide whom to hire (MacDuffie, 1988). In some cases, they send their new employees to Japan for their initial training in order to assure that they learn to do things the "right way." In at least one organization that I studied, this practice created a climate of elitism and strong commitment to the organization.

One company, Motorola, has used videotaped simulations of actual work situations to test the orientation that individuals have toward group and organizational behavior. The applicants watch the videotape and then answer questions about what they would do in that work situation. These situations involve typical work team issues such as a problem with product quality or a dispute between two employees. Motorola has determined which answers fit best with the type of work culture that they wish to create. A Motorola plant in Scotland has developed a screening process for all new hires that is able to predict applicant success in a high-involvement setting based on their background and experience.

An organization can do a number of small things to communicate to individuals that working in a high-involvement organization is different. For example, in some plants, all applicants are asked to submit resumes instead of filling out traditional job applications. This communicates to applicants that the organization is different and wishes to hire people who think of themselves as professionals with careers. New employees also can be given a list of responsibilities associated with working in the organization rather than the typical list of personnel policies and procedures. This list can include such things as being a good team member, taking responsibility for quality, and making a commitment to continuous learning and improvement. It is often helpful to have individuals sign a contract that specifies their willingness to adhere to the core principles of the management style of the organization. This can assure that the individual understands what is expected and, if needed, can provide a defensible basis for dismissal of the individual.

The applicants themselves should play an active role in the hiring process. It is important for members of the organization to continually ask job applicants whether they want to do the kind of work that is offered. Applicants should be encouraged to ask questions about the organization and they should be given time to decide whether they want to join. Informal discussions with employees should be built into the selection process. Some individuals will realize that they are not right for a high-involvement work situation and decide to withdraw their application. This two-way process can help assure that both sides are committed to the individual's being a successful new member of the organization.

Selection of employees for high-involvement organizations can be very expensive because many people usually apply for each position and because a long, intensive selection process is used. In new plants, start-up costs of over $10,000 per hire are typical. Money spent on employee selection is usually money well spent, however, because it can produce big savings if it reduces turnover and leads to a work force that can operate in a high-involvement manner. Also, the selection process is the first training employees get, and it plays an important role in shaping their long-term relationship with the organization. The money spent on selection is not just a necessary start-up cost that has no long-term impact on the employees who are hired. It is the starting point of a potentially long-term relationship, a relationship that is partially shaped by what happens during the selection process.

Employee Training and Development

High-involvement organizations need a highly trained and skilled work force to be successful. Employees throughout these organizations must have extensive technical, business, and organizational knowledge. Every employee, for example, needs to have basic problem-solving skills, an understanding of business economics, interpersonal skills, and, of course, the quantitative and analytical skills that will enable him or her to participate in critical decision making (Commission on the Skills of the American Workforce, 1990). Employees also need self-discipline, organizing skills, and planning skills to be able to manage themselves. In addition, if the organization is built around work teams, they need the ability to be effective team members and leaders.

In any training program, an employee must receive a basic understanding of quality and how it can be built into a product or service. The training needs to include the concepts of statistical process control and theories of variation as well as the costs associated with poor quality. It should include the various problem-solving technologies and process-improvement models that are part of a total quality approach. These concepts are important; employees need to know them in order to take responsibility for the management of quality. This knowledge is just another kind of expertise, like financial expertise, that needs to be transferred to the work force in general so that all employees can make decisions in their day-today work that reflect their knowledge of quality and financial considerations.

A strong commitment to training and developing all employees is necessary for an organization to flatten its hierarchy and eliminate layers of supervision. It is also a necessary precondition for many of the cost savings that are essential to high-involvement management. Simply removing managers and support staff without transferring the knowledge from these functions to other employees is not only unwise, it is potentially disastrous for an organization.

Unfortunately, organizations cannot count on finding a large number of people in the work force who already have the necessary skills to operate in a high-involvement organization. Indeed, as many studies of the American work force have indicated, basic skills are often missing so that even traditionally managed organizations may not be able to obtain employees with sufficient skills (see, for example, Johnston, 1991). Thus, high-involvement organizations may have to invest heavily in training and developing their employees. The use of skill-based pay can help motivate individuals to learn additional skills, and careful selection can help guarantee that an organization has employees who are willing and able to learn. The bottom line, however, is that an organization must make substantial investments in developing individuals once they join the organization.

Most organizations in the United States do a poor job of investing in human resources development (Lawler, Ledford, and Mohrman, 1989). They spend too small a percentage of their revenue on training (often less than 1 percent) and their employees spend too few hours in training sessions (Commission on the Skills of the American Workforce, 1990). Xerox, Motorola, and IBM are among the few companies that have realized that lack of training for employees represents a serious problem for an organization's long-term competitiveness. Motorola is now committed to providing forty hours of training per year per employee for its over 100,000 employees (Wiggenhorn, 1990). Similar policies and practices are in place at IBM. Xerox spends almost 3 percent of its total revenue on training. Of course, in high-technology organizations such as IBM and Xerox, training is particularly important and is not just remedial education because technology changes so quickly.

Most organizations probably should have policies that require employees to participate in a certain amount of training. In a sense, requiring training is a "push" approach to training, while the preferred strategy is a "pull" approach in which managers realize the value of training and "pull" it into their particular work areas. Ultimately, the pull approach is far superior to an approach that rather bureaucratically requires a certain number of hours of training per year. Nevertheless, a mandatory training policy may be a necessary step toward building an organization that has a cultural commitment to training and developing all employees. Unfortunately, in the absence of such a bureaucratic policy, many managers are willing to sacrifice training in order to increase short-term productivity and profitability.

As was noted earlier, a skill-based pay system can help to facilitate the movement of knowledge to all levels in the organization. This pay system creates a pull effect among the employees because training becomes doubly desirable to them; not only do employees get the satisfaction of learning, but they also get financial rewards for learning. Therefore, employees put pressure on their supervisors and managers for additional training. Ultimately, this pressure might be able to replace policies that require that employees have a certain number of hours of training or that managers spend a certain percentage of their total budget on training.

One other feature of the approach to training and development in the United States needs to change dramatically. Consistent with the traditional top-down model, most U.S. businesses continue to spend the majority of their training and development dollars on managers and professional employees. A report on the skills of the U.S. work force said that most companies rely on an outdated system in which a small, educated and highly trained group of managers directs the activity of another three quarters of our workers with minimal skills (Commission on the Skills of the American Workforce, 1990).

The report adds that of the $30 billion that business spends on employee training, only 7 percent reaches frontline employees. This division of training money makes sense in an organization that expects so much of managers and so little of others. But it does not make sense in a high-involvement organization, which expects a great deal from all employees and which needs to spread knowledge broadly throughout the organization. Training dollars should be spent on individuals who are directly adding value to the products or services the organization has to offer. If they are not, these employees will be unable to add the kind of value to products and services that can make businesses competitive in a global economy.

Career Development

The long-term career development of individuals is critical to the success of high-involvement organizations. Because high-involvement organizations are structured to be flatter and to have fewer managers than traditional organizations, individuals' career paths need to be quite different from those in traditional hierarchical organizations. Indeed, those individuals who have a linear career orientation — that is, an orientation that measures success by the number and speed of a person's upward moves — do not belong in high-involvement organizations. Not many upward moves are available to individuals in high-involvement organizations; unless the organization is growing very rapidly, upward mobility is likely to be a very rare event.

The lack of upward mobility does not, however, have to limit individuals' career development progress. It is important for high-involvement organizations to structure careers that are both horizontal and vertical. One organization calls its approach the "ninety degree" career track. In this organization, individuals must make at least one sideways career move in order to make an upward move. This is a possible way to think about career moves, but in many organizations, individuals need to make two or three horizontal moves before they make a vertical move.

For an organzation to be capable of good horizontal coordination without the use of an extensive hierarchy, its employees must develop horizontal skills. It is very hard for organizations to coordinate their activities without a hierarchy if all or most employees have a single-function career. All too often, employees simply do not understand what is going on in other departments and other areas, so when they must coordinate activities with their peers in other areas, all parties are talking from substantial ignorance. An organization can partially solve this problem by encouraging horizontal moves so that individuals will have a broad understanding of the business.

Horizontal movement of employees can also help to develop effective general managers and senior leaders for the organization. In large corporations, individuals usually get to the top by going straight up a particular function. They may know a great deal about managing finances, for example, but relatively little about what goes on in other areas of the organization or what it takes to be a successful manager in these other areas. Thus, they tend to be poor general managers because they simply do not have the broad understanding that is necessary to be successful. Horizontal career moves help to solve this problem because they encourage individuals to learn about multiple functions and how these functions are integrated.

Traditional organizations usually need only a few general managers because separate functions are not combined to produce a business unit except at high levels of the organization. As was noted in Chapter Three, the best organizational design for a high-involvement organization is one in which the structure is oriented toward products or customers and many small business units or mini-enterprises. Thus, a high-involvement organization needs more general managers than a traditional organization, even though it has fewer managers overall. It is not acceptable for a high-involvement organization to have only a few individuals with the kind of work experience that qualifies them to manage a business unit and get involved in all aspects of the business.

To encourage employees to make horizontal career moves, organizations need to structure their reward systems, specifically their pay system, to make horizontal moves financially rewarding. As was discussed in Chapter Seven, they can accomplish this by using skill-based pay systems that reward horizontal moves as well as promotions. As individuals make horizontal moves within a level of management, the organization can give them substantial pay increases to reflect the additional skills that they develop because of the horizontal move. The same approach also allows for rewards to be given to those individuals who develop their skills in depth.

A high-involvement organization may also need individuals to further their career by developing in-depth knowledge of their areas, particularly when organizational strategy involves developing a high level of competence in certain areas. Thus, it is important for these organizations to provide individuals with a rewarding career in which they gain more and more knowledge about a discipline or topic. Skill-based pay can be used to reward expertise, as can titles. An emphasis on titles generally does not fit in with a high-involvement approach, but if titles are used to designate expertise in a particular subject matter, they may be appropriate. Motorola, for example, makes its technical experts vice presidents (there are over three hundred in the company). Titles do not necessarily support or indicate job size and hierarchy at Motorola; instead, they say something about the person.

The traditional practice of having a secret "fast track" system to develop employees is not appropriate in a high-involvement organization. These systems are usually controlled by a corporate staff group that uses an "invisible," or "heavy hand," approach to developing key individuals. The group develops a short list of fast track managers and then sees that these individuals make the correct career moves to assure their development. Often, this list is secret, and individuals simply have to accept on faith that their career is being well managed.

In the top-down organization, employees often feel that there are a few crown princes or princesses in the organization and that the development process is not a fair and open one. Managers may also make the wrong assumptions about how individuals want to develop and progress in their career. Individuals are rarely asked what they want; instead it is assumed that everyone wants to move up the organizational hierarchy. With the kind of diversity that exists in today's workplaces, this usually is an erroneous assumption (Jamieson and O'Mara, 1991).

Individuals in high-involvement organizations are in charge of their career and thus they need to participate in managing it. The organization needs to train individuals in how to manage their career and provide opportunities for individuals to express their interests and ambitions and to receive feedback and advice.

The practice of posting job openings is very consistent with the idea of individuals taking responsibility for their career and development. It also helps to bring the promotion process into the public domain and provides good opportunities for organizations to give feedback to individuals about their skills, abilities, and job prospects.

Many organizations post lower-level job openings but do not post high-level job openings. Posting low-level openings is a step in the right direction, but dealing differently with the high-level openings reinforces the organizations hierarchical culture. The practice of posting all openings and first considering all internal candidates for the openings is consistent with a high-involvement approach to management. This does not mean that in a high-involvement organization all promotions have to be made from within, but it does mean that internal candidates should have the opportunity to express their interests and desires to obtain whatever positions are open in the organization.

In a high-involvement organization, it is critical that individuals receive substantial feedback about why they did not get a job. If a work team, for example, selects a new member, the team needs to meet with the unsuccessful internal candidates and give them feedback. Similarly, if an individual manager or group of managers makes a promotion decision, they need to give feedback to the unsuccessful candidates. They particularly need to stress what an individual can do to develop himself or herself to improve his or her chances of getting a similar job the next time an opening appears. Sometimes, it is appropriate for managers or work groups to suggest that individuals use assessment centers or other approaches to identify strengths and weaknesses. Where practical (it usually should be), specific training and development experiences should be recommended to the individuals.

The right time to begin introducing individuals to the career orientation that they need to accept if they are going to work successfully in a high-involvement organization is during the selection process. The selection process must acquaint applicants with the idea that careers are not validated by upward mobility but rather by the employee's growth in skills and increased understanding of key elements of the business. Individuals who cannot accept this idea are best eliminated during the selection process, not after they have joined the organization.

Stability of Employment

High-involvement organizations need to do everything possible to guarantee that they maintain a stable work force. As has already been pointed out, it is important that membership in a high-involvement organization be difficult to achieve and cherished when accomplished. It is also critical that once individuals join a high-involvement organization their membership be considered permanent. The reasons for this are many, and I will discuss a few key ones.

Individuals in high-involvement organizations are asked to suggest ideas and work in ways that will reduce the number of employees needed to do the work. If individuals are concerned about losing their job or if they are concerned that some of their fellow workers will lose their jobs, they may be unwilling to suggest improvements.

High-involvement organizations make a considerable investment in employees and a considerable investment in the work relationships among employees. Effective teams, for example, take a year or more to develop because individuals need to develop skills and they need to learn to work together. Therefore, it makes sense for the organizations to retain the assets that these relationships and skills represent. Laying off someone or reducing the work force, in effect, liquidates important assets, assets that may have taken years to develop.

Individuals in high-involvement organizations are asked to make substantial, even extraordinary, commitments to the organization. They are expected to tailor their careers and aspirations in many ways to the particular characteristics of the organization. It is hard to ask people for this commitment and unreasonable to expect it of them if in fact the organization is unwilling to commit to seeing that they remain as employees.

The value statements of most high-involvement organizations stress that employees are the organization's most important asset. It is critical that this philosophy be actually translated into behavior and practice in the organization. The best way to do this is to practice employment stability.

Just how strong a commitment to employment stability a particular organization can reasonably make is dependent upon its business situation. In some organizations, it may be realistic to make the kind of commitment that has been made by IBM, a commitment to no involuntary layoffs. In other situations, such a commitment may simply be unrealistic. In highly cyclical businesses or in the face of severe economic downturns, even those organizations that are committed to employment stability may have to lay off employees.

Any organization's approach to employment stability should include a well-thought-out strategy for reducing costs if the need arises (Work in America Institute, 1984). One way of thinking about reducing costs is to plan "rings of defense" against layoffs. At the core of the rings are the full-time employees, who are to be protected by the outer rings of defense. The first ring of defense can be to have in place pay-for-performance plans, such as profit sharing, that automatically reduce the organization's labor cost when money is not available.

A number of additional rings of defense are possible. For example, extensive use of temporary and part-time employees can help assure employment stability in seasonal and very cyclical businesses. Another relatively painless approach to reducing labor costs is to see if any individuals want to take a leave of absence. Often a small number of volunteers will take a leave simply because they are at a life stage or have personal issues that make taking some time off without pay highly attractive to them.

Sometimes, reducing salaries across the board, as Hewlett-Packard and other organizations have done, is a good way to cut labor costs and retain employees. It may be appropriate for managers to take larger reductions in pay than those taken by nonmanagerial employees. This approach makes sense in traditional organizations because, in fact, managers are the ones who have the major responsibility for the fate of the organization. But in high-involvement organizations, a more appropriate approach is to ask everyone to take a similar reduction in pay and to combine this with a short work week. This approach sends the message that everyone shares responsibility for the success and failure of the organization.

An organization can also reduce labor costs by offering employees cash payments to resign or early retirement packages. These incentives make sense only if relatively permanent reductions in the number of employees (such as the ones IBM, Digital, and a host of major corporations have gone through) are needed. Again, these incentives should be accepted by employees voluntarily, if possible. They should be the approaches of last resort, however, since often the best employees take advantage of them, they are expensive, and they change the composition of the organization so that many skills and relationships need to be rebuilt.

I have seen a number of organizations whose business levels have fallen appreciably continue to employ everyone, even though the work clearly is not there for them to do at a particular time (for example, Delta Airlines, the Toyota plants in the United States, and Digital). Often the employees are trained during this period or asked to do cleaning and maintenance work. Although this is an expensive approach, in my experience it has very positive effects: it communicates to employees that they are important and that the organization does have a real and meaningful commitment to them. Over and over again, employees tell stories about how their organization kept people working during a problem period. These stories help validate employees' feelings that they can count on the commitments the organization has made to them. They also strengthen employee commitment to the organization and help create a very positive culture.

I would like to make one final point about maintaining employment stability. In any organization, individuals can develop personal problems that interfere with their work. These include family crises, personal health problems, and various forms of substance abuse. In a traditional organization, it might make sense to simply fire these individuals and look for new employees who are less troublesome. In a high-involvement organization, however, a substantial investment has been made in each and every employee. Therefore, the organization should do everything possible to assure that all employees remain valued members of the organization, including offering all employees various forms of counseling and assistance.

Some organizations provide low-interest loans and other assistance programs to help individuals maintain their status as effective employees. Pacific Bell has developed an exceptional program to help employees who develop the acquired immune deficiency syndrome (AIDS) (Kirp, 1989). Providing such assistance programs is a very enlightened and humanitarian approach to management and also may be a very good business practice. Hiring, training, and developing employees is an extremely expensive activity for any organization. If a current employee needs help to remain effective on the job, providing that help, whether it is child care, a drug rehabilitation program, or a short-term loan, may in fact be more cost effective than hiring a new employee.

Justice and Due Process

In any organization, some individuals have to be denied pay raises, disciplined, or fired. In addition, inequities and unfair policies and practices are almost inevitable in complex organizations. Supervisors make mistakes, work teams make mistakes, and organizational policy committees and task forces make mistakes. Individuals sometimes are affected by policies in ways that were never imagined when the policies were created, and managers sometimes simply make decisions that look good to them but that are in fact unfair and discriminatory.

In the United States, employees who feel unfairly treated can and do go outside of their organization for help. They can get a lawyer or government agency to support them and can take the organization to court. In high-involvement organizations, individuals should feel that going to court to resolve a problem is the last resort. They should have many ways to pursue their grievances within the organization. A number of organizations have developed aggressive approaches to assuring that their policies and managers are in fact fair and reasonable. Polaroid and IBM are particularly good examples.

It is easiest to design fair policies and practices if the design process includes input from many individuals. When task forces that represent the total organization are used to design policies and practices, more than just the views of one limited part of the organization are considered. As a reuslt, problems are often identified and resolved before a policy is developed and implemented.

An organization also needs to have forums in which employees can discuss the fairness and reasonableness of various policies and practices. Electronic mail systems can allow any individual to ask questions directly of the chief executive officer. Focus groups and other policy discussion groups can allow individuals to voice their concerns about particular policies and practices. Attitude surveys can ask employees about specific policies to see how the work force in general accepts the policies. Needless to say, it is also critical that supervisors encourage individuals who work for them to raise concerns, and these individuals should never be punished or slighted simply because they have challenged existing policies and practices.

Concerns that individuals have about the fairness of their individual treatment are more difficult to deal with than general policy and practice issues. Often employees are concerned about how their work team treated them or how a particular manager treated them. Individuals who feel that they have been treated unfairly must have a safe and credible avenue of review and appeal open to them. At Polaroid, for example, peer groups hear certain cases and decide them. The use of peer groups is a particularly good practice because it involves employees in resolving grievances and it has credibility in the eyes of individuals whose cases are being heard.

An approach that has worked well for a number of organizations is to allow individuals to work their way up the hierarchy until they are satisfied with the resolution of their particular case. In some organizations, this may take the individual all the way to the office of the chief executive officer. Admittedly, few individual complaints go that far, but it is important that individuals have this option. Such an approach clearly communicates that the organization is very concerned about fairness and that the chief executive officer has the time to deal with human resources issues.

Individuals who raise grievances must be protected from any retribution. Organizations that are clearly committed to internal fairness usually have a rule stating that any supervisor or anyone else for that matter who punishes an individual for raising an issue is subject to immediate dismissal. Although this may seem harsh, it is a very important policy. Without this policy, it is possible that individuals who raise tough issues will be punished and the culture of the organization will be one in which individuals do not feel free to raise their concerns. If the internal channels for resolving problems are closed, individuals will quite naturally go to outside channels such as the courts to seek resolution of their particular concerns. Court cases are not only expensive for an organization but they also have a negative impact on the organization's internal culture.

It sometimes can be useful for an organization to have the human resources department act as the initial contact for employees with complaints or grievances. People in the department can try to solve the problems without holding formal hearings or presenting the problems to high-level managers. In essence, they act as ombudsmen and, in some cases, resolve issues in a simple and low-visibility way. In most large organizations, it makes sense to have this relatively inexpensive and simple avenue to resolve problems, open to all individuals. It should not be the only channel that is open, however. If an individual cannot resolve his or her problem through this low-key approach, he or she must be able to use more formal channels and present the problem to higher levels of the organization's hierarchy.

Discipline Practices

Although a high-involvement organization must create a climate of fairness and openness, it should not be soft on discipline issues. If employees perceive an organization to be soft on discipline, the organization may end up as a "country club" with out-of-control employees — a fatal situation for a high-involvement organization. The starting point in any high-involvement organization has to be people who are trustworthy and capable of handling responsibility. Employees should have the freedom that goes with trust. However, if individuals fail to behave in a way that the organization expects, and it is inevitable that some will fail, it is critical that the organization take immediate strong action.

In many respects, a high-involvement organization is less able to afford leniency in dealing with discipline problems than a traditional organization. A traditional organization has controls and disciplinary methods in place that allow it to deal with individuals who are problem employees. High-involvement organizations simply are not designed to catch and punish troublesome employees. Thus, they must be particularly careful in dealing with these employees, and in most cases, should remove them from the organization. Dishonesty, theft, and clear breaking of organizational policies on ethics should be dealt with in the strongest possible manner.

A good example of a high-involvement organization dealing with theft is provided by an organization that I studied. Two employees stole a few gallons of gasoline to use in their personal truck. When their teammates and managers found out about the theft, they debated how to deal with the individuals. One group argued that the two should be given a warning and treated com-

passionately because high-involvement organizations are supposed to be concerned about people and committed to employment stability. Another group argued that these employees had
violated the most important principle of a high-involvement
organization: individuals must be trustworthy. They had failed
to live up to the trust that had been put in them; thus, the only
thing to do was to end their employment with the organization.

The organization fired these individuals, even though it
was their first offense. I think this was the correct decision
because high-involvement organizations simply cannot tolerate
individuals who have demonstrated their unwillingness and
inability to handle the freedom and trust that is inherent in this
management approach. They don't have many of the traditional
bureaucratic controls in place; thus they are not as likely to catch
a dishonest employee. In this situation it simply is too risky to
have someone who has already been proven to be untrustworthy.
In short, the rules and controls in high-involvement organizations may be fewer and more general than in traditional organizations, but when major rules are violated punishment needs to
be sure, swift, and large.

Individual Choices and Organizational Flexibility

High-involvement organizations should be designed to give all
employees a great deal of choice about when and where they
work and how they are rewarded for two reasons. The first stems
from the well-documented increasing diversity of the work force
in the United States and other developed countries (Johnston,
1987, 1991). The personal situations of employees differ significantly, and thus the standard organizational model that assumes
that everyone will be able to work at the same time, for the same
length of time, and at the same place simply does not fit well
anymore.

A diverse work force also has important implications for
how individuals are rewarded. In a homogeneous work force,
individuals tend to want the same type of rewards. If all or most
employees desire the same benefits, perquisites, and other rewards, an organization can hand out these rewards in a relatively

standardized way. The situation changes dramatically, however, when employees differ widely in age, family situation, and values.

The second reason for giving individuals considerable choice and flexibility about their work situation comes from the underlying values of high-involvement management. The policies of most organizations, particularly in the area of benefits and rewards, have a strong paternalistic flavor to them. Inherent in most approaches is the assumption that the organization knows what is best for individuals, and, thus, the organization prescribes certain benefit levels for all employees.

Most policies about hours of work and location of work are designed to enable organizations to control employees by having them all work at the same place at the same time so the supervisor can effectively see what they are doing and how well they are doing it. A high-involvement organization acts on the assumption that control will come more from intrinsic motivation and from other members of an individual's work group rather than from a supervisor. Thus, in such an organization, it is not critical that the work setting be one in which direct supervision by management is easy. Indeed, systems that are designed to enhance the ease of direct supervision are inconsistent with an approach to management that emphasizes involvement, self-control, and trust of individuals.

Hours and Location of Work

Many organizations are moving toward considerable flexibility in hours of work and in location of work (Jamieson and O'Mara, 1991). Increasingly, individuals are working highly flexible hours as well as working at home and using electronic communication systems ("telecommuting") to connect them to the organization. High levels of flexibility about hours of work and location of work are congruent with the high-involvement approach, with one important exception. If the organization is committed to teamwork, the amount of flexibility that is available has to be limited.

For most interdependent teams to work effectively in a

traditional manufacturing or service setting, individuals simply have to all be at a workplace at the same time so they can coordinate their work. Team structures, therefore, make it difficult for individuals to do large amounts of work at home. In this respect, team structures may be a little bit less flexible than traditional individual work structures, and this needs to be kept in mind before a team structure is created. Teams are not as easy to use with a highly diverse work force that has large differences in family situations and life-style preferences as are individual approaches to job design. For a diverse group of employees, an individual enrichment approach to work design that reduces the need for coordination may, in fact, be the most appropriate design.

Some teams can achieve flexibility by combining telecommuting with team days in which individuals meet at a common workplace to interact and make decisions. As was mentioned in the previous chapter, with intellectual work such as computer software development it may be possible to handle some of the interdependency and team issues through the use of electronic networks. In some cases, software can be used to facilitate team interaction and decision making.

In some situtions, I have seen teams adapt to the particular needs of individuals. For example, teams that are responsible for all the production that is needed in a particular area have proven to be quite good at assigning individuals to various hours of work and work situations. They can take into account family responsibilities and time constraints and, in essence, schedule work hours around family situations and the amount of production that is needed at a particular time. This type of flexibility requires moving away from a traditional concept of a team that is responsible for a work shift to an approach in which a single team is responsible for all the production across the entire work day or week. This change can be a reasonable way to adapt to the needs of teams and individuals while at the same time ensuring the kind of production or service flow that the organization needs.

Benefit and Perquisite Choices

In the last ten years, the way employee benefits can be and are delivered by U.S. corporations has changed significantly. An organization can give individuals considerable amounts of choice concerning the benefits and rewards that they receive (Bloom and Trahan, 1986; Gifford and Seltz, 1988). Flexible, or cafeteria, benefit plans give individuals an allocation of dollars and allow them to use those dollars to choose whatever benefits they wish to have. Because giving employees choices about benefits is consistent with individual differences and with trusting individuals to make informed and knowledgeable decisions, these plans are a natural fit with high-involvement management.

Unfortunately, many organizations with flexible benefit plans have a paternalistic attitude and give individuals only limited choices. For example, employees are not allowed to take all cash and to forgo vacations, medical insurance, and other standard benefits. Instead they are given the option to choose among different kinds of medical plans and perhaps the option to choose beneifts that involve extra coverage, like legal services and dental plans. In high-involvement organizations— particularly with the increasing diversity of the work force— a strong case can be made for allowing much more choice than this. Allowing employees to have many choices communicates the organization's trust in them and keeps the organization from being paternalistic. The organization thus becomes "diversity friendly" by recognizing the increasing prevalence of dual-career families and other situations that create radical differences in the kind of benefits that individuals prefer.

In addition to being consistent with a high-involvement management style, a flexible approach to benefits represents a good way for an organization to spend money. A considerable amount of research shows that the typical individual simply does not value most benefits at 100 percent of their cost (Bloom and Trahan, 1986; Lawler, 1990b). The organization is spending money to attract, retain, and satisfy employees but is getting poor value for the dollars spent. To reverse this undesirable situation, an organization must be sure that the rewards individuals receive have a value that is at least equal to their cost. Otherwise it makes no sense for the organization to buy them — it should simply give employees cash. If individuals choose the benefits that they want, this guarantees that they will only receive those benefits that are attractive relative to their cost.

It may also make sense to allow employees to choose certain perquisites. If certain parking spaces, offices, or furnishings in an organization are more desirable than others, one alternative is to give individuals the chance to choose these perquisites from a flexible perquisite package. This would assure that the people who want the perquisites and special items that often go with high-level jobs can get them. However, they are not allocated on the basis of hierarchy or seniority but on the basis of willingness to give up other rewards. Thus, these items become nonhierarchical features of the organization and are allocated only to those people who truly value them.

Egalitarian Policies and Practices

Traditional organizations are well known for their very hierarchical approaches to human resources management. People at different levels in these organizations are treated very differently in a wide range of areas, not just in the obvious areas such as the kind of training programs that are available. High-level managers typically get different benefit programs, better parking spaces, bigger offices, better office furniture, a special lunchroom, country club memberships, and special financial counseling. In a vast number of small and big ways, they are treated both differently and better by the organization than other employees are treated.

Some different treatment of employees at different levels in the organization is necessary. For example, the law in many countries requires that employees at the lowest level be paid for overtime work. In addition, labor laws having to do with union-organizing efforts regulate the treatment of some employees. With these exceptions, however, no legal or social mandate requires that people at different levels in the organization be treated differently.

An egalitarian approach to the treatment of employees is consistent with a high-involvement approach to management for a number of reasons. For instance, high-involvement management stresses that all employees are valued members of the organization. Indicating through numerous policies, practices, and symbols that some employees are valued much more highly than others violates this principle.

In traditional organizations, the symbols of office such as titles and office size indicate to all individuals where the power is, who should make the decisions, and whose order is to be obeyed. Indeed, it is often said that decisions are not made by individuals but by offices, and, therefore, orders should not be looked upon as coming from a person but from a rank in the organization.

In a high-involvement organization, the emphasis is upon individuals making decisions and influencing the way the organization operates. The ideal is to have decision making move around the organization according to the ability of individuals to make decisions and influence events. Decisions should not necessarily be made by someone simply because that person has a high rank in the organization. They should be made by an individual who has more knowledge and expertise or is better positioned to make the decision than other employees. This approach assures quick, high-quality decisions that allow the organization to adapt to changes in the market. Symbols of office and hierarchy interfere with this type of decision making because they signal levels in the hierarchy rather than signaling who has the knowledge and can best make the decision.

Some of the Japanese plants in the United States are leaders in eliminating hierarchical perquisites. At Honda, for example, all employees wear uniforms, eat in the same lunchroom, and share the same exercise facilities and no one has an office. Kodak struck a blow for egalitarianism when it created a "parachute" program to protect employees in the case of a takeover by another company. In most companies, "golden parachute" plans cover only the top executives and often guarantee very large amounts of money. Kodak's "tin parachute" plan covers all employees and treats them all the same with respect to severance benefits. Putting perquisites into a flexible benefit plan is another way to make them nonhierarchical, but so far no organization has adopted this practice.

One of the issues that is always raised when the idea of an egalitarian organization is suggested is how the absence of special treatment will affect the attraction and retention of high-level employees. One concern is the attraction of individuals from the outside, and the second is the desire of people inside the organization to move up the hierarchy.

Let us look first at the issue of attracting individuals from outside the organization. It probably is quite correct that organizations that have few hierarchical perquisites and benefits will have trouble attracting certain individuals from the outside. In particular, they will have trouble attracting managers for whom status symbols and hierarchical perks are an important aid in doing their job and who, in many cases, choose to be managers because they enjoy these kinds of rewards. The fact that this type of manager will not come to work in a high-involvement organization is more of a positive than a negative. The absence of hierarchical perquisites and symbols should be emphasized in recruiting as an important part of the self-selection process for individuals who are considering joining a high-involvement organization.

The issues of individuals not wanting a promotion because there are few perquisites associated with it is essentially the same as that of not attracting individuals from the outside. Admittedly, some individuals may not want to be managers if they do not get a reserved parking space, bigger office, financial counseling, first-class air travel, and so on. I think a strong argument can be made, however, that if these are important reasons why an individual wants to be a manager, then he or she probably should not be a manager. In a high-involvement organization, it is critical that people become managers because they enjoy managerial work and have the kind of leadership skills that are associated with a managerial position.

One other point needs to be made about an egalitarian approach to rewards. Although perquisites should be allocated with an egalitarian approach in mind, cash compensation does not have to be or for that matter should it be. It would be nice if managers were simply paid the same as all other employees so that individuals would gravitate into those positions strictly because they like the work and are good at it rather than for the money. Under these conditions, I have a feeling more managers would take the jobs for the "right reason" and we might have more effective managers. However, the market value of some employees in the United States and in most parts of the world is higher than it is for other employees. Position in the hierarchy is an important determinant of market value. This market value has to be reflected in the kind of compensation levels that are offered to individuals who take senior management positions, otherwise it may be impossible for an organization to attract and retain highly talented managers.

Should the pay differences in a high-involvement organization from top to bottom be as great as they are in most traditionally managed organizations? I think the differences should be somewhat smaller because decision making is more broadly shared and more is expected of people at the bottom. Therefore, large amounts of separation are inappropriate in most high-involvement organizations (Foulkes, 1991).

Ben and Jerry's Ice Cream is committed to a five or six to one pay ratio from top to bottom. This means that the highest-paid employee makes only five or six times as much as the lowest-paid one. Although I like the value statement this policy makes, I have trouble seeing this ratio as a practical approach in most organizations. Most large organizations in the United States have a ratio in excess of eighty to one (Foulkes, 1991). A more reasonable ratio is the one that Herman Miller, the very successful furniture manufacturer, has adopted. It is committed to a ratio of twenty-two to one. In most cases, this ratio gives enough of a difference from top to bottom to attract the kind of managers that will fit a high-involvement approach to management. It also fits in well with the ratio that exists in most developed countries in Asia and Europe.

Chapter Eleven

Support Positive Managerial Behavior

The behavior of managers is a critical determinant of the effectiveness of any organization, particularly a high-involvement organization. In a sense, traditional organizations make life easy for managers; by supporting them with numerous policies, practices, and procedures, the organizations help them direct and control employee behavior in ways that are simply not possible in high-involvement organizations. In addition, traditional organizations contain a generous supply of managers so that close supervision and tight control is not only possible, it is virtually mandated by the organizational structure. A high-involvement organization has not only fewer managers but also fewer traditional structures to support the type of control that is usually desired in a hierarchical organization.

Although the manager's role is perhaps a more challenging one in a high-involvement organization, it is not an impossible role to carry out. It requires some different behaviors and a different concept of how managers can exercise power and influence the behavior of others than are found in a traditional organization (Kanter, 1989a). Good managers start with a passion for managing. They must be obsessed with constantly improving their performance as managers, not just their performance as accountants, engineers, or finance professionals. They need to understand the leadership features of managerial work better than they understand technical business issues.

A number of recent articles and books have emphasized that organizations need more leadership from their managers and less behavior that is control oriented (see, for example, Burns, 1978; Bennis and Nanus, 1985; Bennis, 1989; Kotter, 1990). This observation is undoubtedly true for all organizations but particularly true for high-involvement organizations. Leadership can be a substitute in a number of ways for the traditional practices and controls that exist in hierarchical bureaucratic organizations (Lawler, 1988b). However, stating that high-involvement organizations need more leadership from their managers does not tell us what effective leadership is or how managers can demonstrate this behavior in the work setting. A number of phrases have been coined to capture the difference between managerial behavior and leadership. One of my favorites is "Managers do things right; leaders do the right thing." Of course, this statement and others like it do not define the behavior involved in leadership or clearly distinguish it from managerial behavior, they simply give a flavor of what the behavior is like.

Bennis and Nanus (1985) in their book on leadership go a step further (see also Bennis, 1989). They talk about leaders managing people's attention through vision, creating meaning through communication, and developing trust. A slightly different perspective is offered by Kotter (1990). He talks about leadership as establishing direction for the organization, aligning people with the organization's interest, and motivating and inspiring behavior. In many ways, the message from Kotter and the message from Bennis and Nanus are similar. Leadership involves the "high road," the more philosophical and the more inspirational parts of a manager's activities in an organization. These researchers point out that most modern organizations are underled and overmanaged. As a result, employees tend to be programmed toward doing things right and not focused enough on figuring out and doing the right things. The potential exists, in their view, for organizations to control and direct behavior through leadership instead of with traditional bureaucratic structures.

History is full of what some people have called *magic*

leaders and *transformational leaders*, who inspire and align the behavior of their followers through their own actions rather than through job descriptions, hierarchies, and accounting systems (Nadler, 1989; Tichy and Devanna, 1986). Strong leadership can be seen as a cost-effective way to direct and influence the behavior of the members of an organization because it rarely requires a corporate staff and a substantial amount of overhead.

Although leadership ability is an important part of what managers need to be effective, it is not all they need. Indeed, even the most inspiring leaders often need to use some managerial behaviors to make an organization effective. In high-involvement organizations, magical, inspirational leaders still need to pay, hire, and fire people and perform a host of other managerial activities. Some of these activities can be carried out by individuals who are not in managerial jobs, but managers still need to see that the tasks are performed well. Thus, this chapter will discuss the overall pattern of behavior that is needed from managers in high-involvement organizations. The discussion will first focus on managers throughout the organization and then will focus on the particular role of the top managers in a high-involvement organization.

The theme throughout this chapter is that for high-involvement organizations to be effective, managers at all levels need to behave in ways that provide leadership but also assure that the basic managerial functions in an organization are performed well. My belief is that managers who combine strong leadership with effective managerial behavior are critical to the success of a high-involvement organization. Thus, the development, training, and socialization of managers is extremely important. Without effective managers, the goal of creating organizations that are faster, more productive, and perform in high-quality ways will never become a reality. The organizational designs, policies, and practices that have been discussed in the previous chapters depend upon managers that effectively combine leadership and managerial behavior.

Effective Managerial Behavior

Effective managers in high-involvement organizations must deliver information, knowledge, power, and rewards to employees in their work area. Unless they are committed to doing this, their employees are not likely to experience high-involvement management. In other words the "negative power" of managers is great—much of the writing on employee involvement focuses on it (for example, Walton and Schlesinger, 1979). However, we should not overlook the positive contributions managers can make to the development of a high-involvement organization (see, for example, Kanter, 1989a; Lawler and Mohrman, 1989).

Information

Managers must regularly and honestly share with employees valid data about the organization's and the work unit's past performance and future plans. Without some sense of where the organization is going, it is hard for employees to identify with and contribute to its success and business agenda. In a number of respects, the easiest thing for managers to do is to move business information downward in the organization. Providing that the managers receive information about production, product quality, service levels, and business plans, they only need to be willing to share this information with others. It is particularly important that plans for new equipment, new work processes, and new schedules be shared with employees. This is the kind of information that directly affects employees' lives and is their closest link to the future direction of the organization. Senior managers typically take the lead in developing the vision and direction for an organization, but all managers throughout the organization need to communicate this vision to employees and see that they understand it.

Information can be shared in regular state-of-the-business meetings that are held for all employees or in small regular meetings of work groups. An interesting way to bring information to a work area is to invite individuals from other parts of the organization to the area, particularly staff groups and senior management, to share information about the future direction of the organization. The visit of a staff member or high-level manager to their area also communicates to employees the importance that their manager places on keeping them informed.

These visits also can familiarize the visiting parties with the concerns and activities of the work group. Such visits are a bit risky for a manager because they may expose problems in his or her work area; nevertheless, the risk is small and the approach can be an effective way of communicating to employees the direction the organization is taking.

Managers can also do a great deal to influence the horizontal flow of information. Regular visits by groups and individuals from other parts of the organization can be helpful, as can the short term or temporary rotation of employees. Advanced Telecommunications Corporation, for example, holds a monthly "open house" where a specific department gives the rest of the company a briefing on what it does and how the other departments can help them. Employees at remote locations participate with a videoconferencing hook-up. Overall, by arranging a mix of meetings and other communication activities, managers at all levels can contribute to informing employees and thus play a role in leading the organization.

Perhaps the most important communication links that a manager can build are with customers and suppliers. The work on teams establishes this point as do the writings of Juran, Deming, and others who are part of the total quality movement. As has been discussed previously, it is critical that the members of a work group or unit have a sense that they are serving internal or external customers and that they get feedback and reactions directly from the customers. All too often, individuals performing work or offering a service get information about their customers through their supervisor or through others who are removed from the work group. The feedback then tends to be diluted and important customer demands may seem arbitrary and capricious. Statements by supervisors simply do not have the same impact as communication directly from the customer who says "I need it tomorrow," "Service is poor," "The product failed for these reasons," or "It is an outstanding product, the best one I have ever owned." Employees also should be given the responsibility for dealing directly with suppliers because this contact helps individuals influence the behavior of their suppliers and in the process develops a sense of responsibility for the quality of their part of the work process.

In addition to dealing with downward communication, horizontal communication, and customer-supplier communication, the manager should facilitate the upward flow of communication. Each manager must be sure that the employees in his or her work area are heard by people at higher levels in the organization. A good way for supervisors to start this upward flow of information is to regularly and systematically ask the people working for them how well they are performing as managers. This practice establishes the idea that feedback and the upward flow of information are important, and research suggests that it also leads employees to see managers as effective (Ashford and Tsui, 1991). To establish trust and overcome employee discomfort with face-to-face feedback, a manager may want to collect feedback through an attitude survey. The manager can then share and discuss the results of the survey in a group meeting.

The upward flow of information, of course, needs to extend beyond the boundaries of a particular work unit. Managers need to carry suggestions and feedback on organizational directions and changes outside their particular work area and be sure that they are processed and acted upon by upper management. This type of communication is particularly important because it allows employees to make significant changes in their work area and to have an impact on organizational performance. Managers often fail to follow up on employee suggestions. Letting subordinates know the final fate of any ideas they submit shows that the organization took the ideas seriously and provides important feedback—just the kind of feedback that produces learning and intrinsic rewards and encourages further upward communication. Through such a follow-up, a manager can also communicate business directions and educate employees on the economics of the business.

Knowledge

Managers usually are in a position to add to the knowledge and expertise of the employees in their work area. Employees in a high-involvement organization must have knowledge of how the organization operates and how a particular work area operates. It is almost as critical that they understand and act on the kind of financial and other information that is provided by the organization's information system. In the absence of this knowledge, it is difficult for employees to be meaningful participants in any decision-making processes. It is also difficult for them to have an understanding of the business and feel responsible for the results that it produces.

In most cases, there is nothing to stop a manager from familiarizing employees with all work done in the unit and even training employees broadly in the operation of the total work unit through peer cross-training and formal educational experiences. Regular exchange of information among employees about the projects they are working on, the procedures they use, and the problems they encounter can be accomplished in routine meetings or special quarterly updates. The important point is that employees know the overall operation of the work area so that they can understand and influence its performance.

Managers should also help employees understand the larger context in which their work area operates and can do this by providing formal training by staff personnel or by others who understand the operations of the organization. They can also swap employees with other areas or other companies for temporary periods of time so that the employees can see what happens to the product or service before it gets to them and after it leaves their work area. It can be particularly helpful for employees if they can experience what it is like to be a customer of and a supplier to their work area.

Managers also need to support formal training programs and classroom education for their employees. These off-the-job learning experiences can help employees develop the understanding of business economics and the technical skills that they need to operate the organization and participate meaningfully in decisions that affect their work area. The attitude that managers have toward training is often important in establishing a positive organizational attitude toward employee development. If managers regard training as a "bother" and "extra cost," they will send all the wrong messages to employees with respect to the organization's commitment to employee development and the importance of learning. The manager who is committed to training and development brings to life statements like "Our employees are our most important assets." The manager that blocks training and treats it as an inconvenience makes a mockery of these statements.

Power

The key to moving power downward in an organization is a manager who is willing to allow employees to influence a number of the decisions that affect their day-to-day work life. As I argued in Chapter Three, sharing power must be preceded by, or done in concert with, sharing knowledge and information, for power without knowledge and information is dangerous. However, once a manager has made progress in seeing that employees have knowledge about how the organization operates and information about the organization, he or she should address the issue of power.

The relative effectiveness of autocratic versus democratic, or participative, decision making has been the subject of research and theory for decades (Bass, 1981; 1990). Literally, thousands of studies have tried to determine the advantages and disadvantages of each approach to decision making, and a number of studies have attempted to determine the conditions under which each approach is optimal (Vroom and Yetton, 1973; Vroom and Jago, 1989). It is beyond the scope of this chapter to review the extensive literature that exists on this topic. However, I would like to make some important points about decision-making approaches.

The choice of a decision-making approach is not a dichotomous one. Rather than think of decision making as being either autocratic or democratic, it is best to think of a continuum. At one end of the continuum is pure top-down decision making, in which an individual in authority simply makes a decision and announces it to others. At the other end of the continuum is totally democratic decision making, in which

all individuals who will be affected by a decision debate it until
they reach a consensus on a decision. In between these two ends
of the continuum are various levels of participative and autocratic decision making. For example, in *consultative decision making*, the manager or leader gets inputs from those who are going
to be affected by the decision but ultimately makes the decision
himself or herself. In *representative decision making*, a task force or
small group convenes to make the decision for the rest of the
organization. This group may make its decision through consensus or a simple majority vote.

As a general rule, the more participative the decision-
making process, the higher the acceptance of the decision by
those people who are affected by it and the higher their satisfaction (Bass, 1990). Also, the more participative the process, the
longer the time to make the decision and, in many but not all
cases, the higher the quality of the decision (Bass, 1990).

Because the participative approach to decision making
has some disadvantages, a number of theorists have argued that
the correct approach is to choose the decision-making style that
bests fits the situation (for example, Vroom and Yetton, 1973).
The key elements in deciding which decision-making style to use
are the degree to which acceptance of the decision is important,
the degree to which general knowledge and information about
the decision are spread throughout the organization, the degree
to which the work force is motivated to make a good decision,
and the degree to which quick decision making is important
(Vroom and Yetton, 1973).

Even in a high-involvement organization, it is unlikely
that all decisions can or should be made in a highly participative
manner. In some cases, time is short so the decision needs to be
made by an individual, without widespread involvement. Although a decision may need to be made quickly by an individual, this does not always mean it has to be made by a manager. Sometimes, other employees have more information and
knowledge than managers, so they should make the decisions. In
other situations the knowledge and expertise is not present so a
participative decision process cannot operate quickly enough

or effectively enough. These situations should be relatively rare, however.

High-involvement organizations are designed and managed in a number of ways that support most decisions being made in a participative manner or being delegated to low-level employees. Unlike the work force in the traditional organization, where individuals do not receive information, the work force in a high-involvement organization is not only ready to participate in most decisions but also expects to participate.

Also relevant to participative decision making is the degree to which those involved in the decision-making process can be counted on to rise above their narrow self-interest and arrive at the decision that is best for the organization as a whole. Again, the design of a high-involvement organization should help assure that most individuals will be committed to the success of the organization. Personnel policies ensuring stability of employment and reward system such as gainsharing, profit sharing, and stock ownership create a world in which what is good for the organization is also good for the individual.

High-involvement organizations lack the traditional kinds of controls that are used to implement autocratic decisions in highly bureaucratic organizations. Because they use rewards and punishments to implement decisions, traditional organizations perhaps do not have to worry as much about individuals being committed to the decision; they can rely on the bureaucracy to implement the decision. In high-involvement organizations, commitment to the decisions that are made is critical because bureaucratic measures, controls, and rewards are not used to coerce people to support the implementation of decisions.

Participative decision making is consistent with the core values and principles in the high-involvement organzation. If many decisions are made in a traditional top-down way, the whole credibility and integrity of the organization's approach to management will be suspect. But what about those cases in which decisions simply have to be made in a top-down way? For example, perhaps the securities and exchange laws or the complexity of the issue simply makes it impossible for employees to participate in making the decision. In such cases, it is appropriate for upper-level managers to make the decision. But, it is also important that the senior executives explain why a top-down decision-making approach will be used or was used in a certain situation. It is critical that, over time, employees understand the type of situations that require the organization to use a top-down decision-making approach. Managers need to make it clear to employees that this approach is the exception rather than the rule. Traditional management differs from high-involvement management in the importance of justifying autocratic decision making: top-down management does not require an explanation, high-involvement or participative management does.

Managers can and should allow employees to make a number of decisions concerning their work methods and work procedures. In a high-involvement organization that has moved knowledge and information downward, no one should know how to do a job better than the person performing it. If managers refuse to let employees make decisions or second-guess and override their decisions, the managers will negate the employees' feelings of self-control. These are necessary in order for employees to be involved in and committed to the success of their organization. If the organization has quality circles or problem-solving groups, managers must support the groups, provide time for them to meet, be receptive to their recommendations, and provide resources for them to implement suggestions. If the managers fail to do these things, the groups are unlikely to be successful.

The literature on goal setting points out that goals can be powerful motivators of performance and can be effectively set by work groups and individuals (Locke and Latham, 1984). Goals that are set through employee participation are "owned" by everyone in the work unit and typically are seen as achievable by all employees in the unit. Employees often see goals set by management as imposed upon them and, therefore, are not committed to the goals. Again the key is the manager. He or she must give employees enough information and knowledge so that they can set meaningful goals and must create opportunities for employees to participate in the goal-setting process. In many cases, managers can also get employees involved in planning activities that focus on future directions for the organization. With sufficient information and knowledge, employees can help develop new products and plan for the introduction of new technology and new equipment. In some cases they also can participate in setting the strategic direction for the organization (Weisbord, 1987).

Ralph Stayer, the president of Johnsonville Foods, has presented an interesting case of participative decision making in his company (Stayer, 1990). I cite this case because it involves a decision that most traditional organizations would have made in a top-down manner. The decision to be made was whether or not to acquire a new manufacturing facility, and time was of the essence. Stayer and his senior management group decided to let individuals throughout the organization get involved in the decision. As he notes, until this time, the senior management team had always made the strategic decisions. They called the entire plant together and presented the problems. Through meetings of small and representative groups, employees worked hard trying to decide whether taking on the additional operations was feasible and desirable. Within two weeks, the organization had decided to take on the additional operations and had a way to make the acquisition viable. According to Stayer, had the decision been left to senior management, they probably would have turned down the acquisition. The result of the acquisition exceeded the best projections. Because people were committed to making the new operation work, quality and cost performance reached new, unprecedented levels. Admittedly, this is just one case, but it shows that by using creative decision-making processes, organizations can make strategic decisions quickly and in ways that involve a relatively large number of individuals in the process.

The personnel decisions a company makes are particularly important since they contribute strongly to employee's trust and motivation. In many high-involvement organizations, employees decide who will join particular work units and who gets and does not get a pay increase. Sharing this kind of power is an important part of the high-involvement approach because it gives employees control over a vital part of what makes their work area effective. If managers do not share power in this area, they can legitimately be accused of not letting employees participate in "hard decisions."

As a first step, the manager can solicit input about job applicants so that it is clear that no one is hired into a work group without the participation of the employees in that group. A second step can be performance appraisals done by peers and peer input into reward decisions. Involving employees in decisions about evaluations and rewards can be difficult. Nevertheless, it is important for managers to solicit input from peers when employees are being evaluated. Employees often have the best information about their peers, particularly in a team environment (Kane and Lawler, 1978). And in all involvement-oriented environments, they need to have input because it is consistent with the idea of employees influencing critical decisions (Lawler, 1990b).

Employees need to influence personnel decisions, not have total authority for them. It is critical that the manager review the decision-making process and be sure that it is a fair and reasonable one. If it is not, then the manager must challenge it. Making such a challenge can be difficult in a participative culture but is at the core of what distinguishes an effective participative manager from one who abdicates control.

Employees need to be involved in the evaluation of their manager for a number of reasons, perhaps the most important of which is that they have the best information on how they are being managed. It also is a necessity if managers are to be held accountable for how they manage. It is critical that managers use data from their subordinates in their own learning. They need to listen to the data, explore the data with others, and where appropriate, change their behavior. They must avoid defensiveness and above all else avoid punishing individuals who give them feedback they do not like. They do not always have to change, but they should always listen.

Rewards

When work units are successful, managers should be sure that everyone involved is acknowledged and that celebrations and other forms of recognition occur. This recognition can be something as small as pizza for everyone; a day of casual attire; a chance to go home early; a meeting in which a senior manager acknowledges the employees' good work; or a special party, dinner, or weekend excursion. The important point is that performance in the work area be recognized as the product of everyone and that the rewards and recognition that come from good performance be shared broadly in the work unit.

Managers often have the greatest control over rewards other than pay and promotion such as recognition, learning, and friendship. Social rewards and recognition clearly are important. They can come from the boss as well as from the peer group. A skilled high-involvement manager needs to develop the ability to give social rewards to groups and individuals who perform particularly well. The personal credibility and integrity of the manager is vital in social rewards because employees do not value social recognition unless it is given by individuals who are respected and whose opinion they value.

A manager's praise is more likely to be valued if he or she only gives it when the group feels it is deserved, and gives it in a way that expresses emotion. Personalizing rewards can also help—a ticket to a baseball game, for example, may not be valued by one employee but might be valued highly by another. Sometimes a picture, symbol, or memento can be highly valued. One way for a manager to be sure that the rewards given are valued is to ask the employees whether they are given appropriately, at a meaningful time, and in a meaningful way. The ability of the manager to give recognition, in short, is partly an earned ability and one that can be lost if the manager uses it unreasonably, too frequently, or inappropriately.

Training can be an important reward and can be broadly and vigorously used by a manager to help acknowledge excellent performance and promote employee involvement in decision making. Improvements in the work itself can also be used as a reward. As managers sense individuals gaining more information and knowledge, they can give more decision-making authority to them. This moves power and the ability to influence decisions downward in a way that rewards learning and improves organizational performance.

Extrinsic rewards, like pay and promotion, often are difficult for an individual manager to completely control since they are part of an organization's overall personnel system. However, as suggested earlier, if an organization's pay policies, benefits, career paths, and promotion systems are designed to support employee involvement, managers should have the chance to influence a variety of rewards, including pay increases and career moves. The decisions about these rewards need to be made in ways that are consistent with high-involvement management. Even in organizations that base pay on job evaluations, managers sometimes can reward employees for doing more. They can argue that because of the way the work has been restructured in their work unit, jobs need to be reevaluated. This reevaluation can lead to higher pay levels, and individuals ultimately can be rewarded for taking on additional power and responsibility.

If managers can do little to change the pay and promotion systems of an organization, they still may be able to make the existing system clear to people in their work area. In traditional organizations, mystery and secrecy often surround the pay and promotion systems, which helps to reinforce the power of managers because they are the ones who control not only the rewards but also the information about how to achieve the rewards. Letting individuals know how the system operates can make the system seem more fair and may give individuals a chance to influence their rewards through their own behavior. At the least, it makes it clear to them what is possible and what is not possible in the context of the existing reward system. To help explain and clarify how the reward system operates, managers can, for example, invite an appropriate member of the human resources staff to their work units to explain how the pay system works, how the promotion system works, and what individuals can do to influence their own career situation.

Most managers have the opportunity to involve their subordinates in performance appraisal and career planning (Mohrman, Resnick-West, and Lawler, 1989). They can plan work schedules, set performance goals, and agree on performance measures with their subordinates. They can invite individuals to present their views in the appraisal process before any evaluative discussion of performance begins. If a manager and an individual have a serious disagreement on how well the individual performs, the manager can take the responsibility for getting a third party to listen to the different viewpoints so that the situation is resolved in a fair way. Overall, managers can see that the performance appraisal process is a two-way experience in which employees have an understanding of how rewards are determined and can influence how their performance is appraised.

To handle promotion decisions in a participative way, managers can get employee input on who should be promoted. They can help educate individuals about the career opportunities that exist and support relevant training, and, if appropriate, they can involve individuals from other parts of the organization in these discussions. They can make the whole career planning process much less mysterious and much more open to input and influence by individuals in their work area.

Practices of High-Involvement Managers

The following is a list of practices that managers can implement to manage with a high-involvement or participative management style (Lawler and Mohrman, 1989).

- Appraise the performance of all subordinates annually
- Allow substantial subordinate input into performance appraisal
- Counsel all employees about their career at least every two years

- Allow substantial subordinate input into the career development plan
- Gather data from subordinates and include it in all appraisals of managers
- Be open to suggestions about work methods and procedures
- Ask subordinates if they agree that openness to new ideas and methods exists
- Install methods or suggestions that come from subordinates
- Hold frequent state-of-the-business meetings
- Educate employees on how success is measured in the business and the economics of the business
- Cross-train employees and expose them to work that is done in other areas
- Meet regularly with employees in the work area to exchange information
- Share success and recognition with all members of a work unit
- Explain the reward system
- Make sure employees receive feedback from their customers
- Provide employees with opportunities to give feedback to suppliers
- Encourage employees to make decisions about how to do their work
- Train employees in how their work fits into the larger organization

No one of these practices constitutes a final or complete test for being an effective high-involvement manager, but taken together, they give a good picture of this type of manager. The manager who follows these practices can move information, power, knowledge, and rewards downward in the organization and can go a long way toward establishing a high-involvement workplace. Many of these practices can be installed in a relatively traditional work situation. In high-involvement organizations they should be easy to do and must be done.

Management Behavior at the Top

Most discussions of employee involvement do not give a clear view of what high-level managers should do and what their role is. Demonstrating critical leadership behaviors certainly is a part of what senior managers need to do but only one part. They must also perform other management activities in a particular way if a high-involvement organization is to be effective. At the present time, knowledge about what constitutes effective behavior for senior managers is limited because so few senior managers have worked in high-involvement organizations. Nevertheless, some effective behaviors can be presented, based on knowledge about leadership and the experience of Motorola, Xerox, Herman Miller, SAS, and other organizations whose senior managers have worked to implement high-involvement management.

Direction Setting

It is the unique responsibility of senior managers to set the overall direction for the organization (Burns, 1978; DePree, 1987). This responsibility has little to do with how an organization operates but much to do with what an organization is trying to accomplish and in what direction it is heading (Hamel and Prahalad, 1989). Setting the direction involves decisions about which mountain the organization is going to try to climb or, even more broadly, the decision that the organization is in the business of mountain climbing rather than in the business of underwater exploration.

The best corporate statements of strategic intent tell people the right things to do in their jobs; how to behave toward one another; and how to behave toward customers, suppliers, and others (Prahalad and Hamel, 1990). Establishing such statements is clearly a difficult process and is one in which leadership skills as well as managerial skills are very important. In a high-involvement organization, senior managers need to lead the decision-making process in this area and ensure that there is a consensus in the organization about the direction that the business is heading (Nadler, 1989). This does not mean, however, that the decision about direction has to be made in a unilateral, top-down manner. It does not have to be made, for example, by a few senior executives going off to a retreat and coming back with a statement of objectives or purpose for the business. Nor does it have to be made by a single executive who has an inspiration about the business and its direction.

Senior managers can, and in most cases should, seek input from employees throughout the organization about the company's direction and should test the ideas throughout the organization once they have been proposed. This is an ideal time for the organization to use task forces and study groups as was done at Johnsonville Foods in the example mentioned earlier.

Once the strategic direction of an organization has been set, senior managers have the responsibility to keep it in the forefront of the employees' consciousness. It is their job to see that everyone in the company understands the objectives of the organization and embraces them as the guiding focus of the organization. There are no prescribed formulas for doing this, but in some organizations, certain kinds of meetings, symbolic activities, and publications have helped (Peters, 1978). For example, senior executives meeting with all new employees to tell them what the goals of the organization are and employees meeting with customers and suppliers to discuss quality are potentially important symbolic acts. Television advertising and other forms of media attention can help capture and communicate the organization's strategic direction. Ford has adverstised its emphasis on quality and SAS has advertised its emphasis on customer service. Both have included employees in their advertising and have mentioned employee involvement.

As part of the focus on strategic direction, senior managers need to develop feedback mechanisms that help make everyone aware of the organization's progress toward competitive goals and the goals of the strategic agenda. One process that can be particularly useful is *competitive benchmarking*, or a comparison of the company's performance to that of competitors. Xerox has used this process very skillfully to identify what the organization is striving to achieve and to give employees ongoing feedback about how well it is doing. Eaton Corporation has used internal benchmarking to assure that different parts of the organization are making progress toward its goal of being an involvement-oriented organization. Teams of managers visit plant locations, interview employees, and give the local management team feedback on how it is doing at implementing the corporate vision.

Participative Behavior

Much of the writing on participative management highlights the importance of senior managers modeling the kind of behavior that they expect to see demonstrated throughout the organization (see, for example, Likert, 1961; Argyris, 1962, 1964). Modeling correct behavior helps provide people at all levels of the organization with an example and helps establish a climate and culture in which this behavior is seen as acceptable and even demanded (Bennis, 1989; DePree, 1987). It is hard to argue with this point of view, but we need to go one step further and talk about some of the kinds of participative behavior that are appropriate at the senior levels of management.

One of the most visible things that senior managers do is hold meetings and convene groups. How these meetings and groups are run can be an important symbol of the type of information exchange and decision-making processes that exist at the senior management level (Nadler, 1989). For example, in a traditional organization, staff meetings frequently are sessions in which individuals make long formal reports on what is occurring in their area, the purpose being basic information exchange. Little discussion typically takes place except for a few questions, and the meetings are run by the most senior executive present in a rather top-down "efficient" manner.

Organizations, such as Xerox, that have moved to more participative management styles, have made a significant effort to alter the type of activities that take place in staff meetings. For example, they have tried to incorporate many of the principles of good participative decision making into their meetings. They have trained their executives in group processes and decision making. Instead of focusing meetings on information exchange, they have used them for making decisions and have tried to change the highly formal methods of presentation by using flipcharts, having discussions, and encouraging individuals to voice disagreements.

One intriguing possibility that was mentioned earlier is the idea of executive teams. A great deal is known about how to structure and manage production teams in an organization but virtually no research discusses work teams at the senior management level — perhaps because they simply do not fit the kind of work that needs to be done at this level. But before we conclude that teams are inappropriate at the senior management level, some experimentation would seem to be worthwhile.

Some organizations have adopted structures that include an office of the president that has three or four members and operates as a limited work team (for example, General Electric and Motorola). As was mentioned in Chapter Five, it may not be too difficult for an organization to create a somewhat larger group that in fact covers the major operations of the organization. Clearly, with the level of technical specialization that is required in some areas of senior management, some individuals must take primary responsibility for specific areas, but a more flexible deployment of people may be possible. For example, individuals who have come to senior management through careers that have involved their working in multiple functions should be able to operate in more than one functional area. Thus, in a senior management group these individuals could take responsibility for projects instead of for functional areas. Such an arrangement could lead to executives taking supervisory responsibility for more than one function and sharing responsibility for managing some functions.

One of the major advantages of a team approach could be to create a senior management group that is familiar with the total functioning of the organization and that is a much better decision-making body when it makes decisions that affect several functions. The management group should also make better decisions about issues that involve several lines of business and core organizational competencies.

Often, the decision-making process at the top is critical in determining whether people throughout the organization see the organization as seriously committed to participative management. If the most important organizational decisions are made in a traditional top-down manner, the employees are likely to get the impression that employee involvement is okay for trivial decisions but not for the most important decisions. Senior managers, therefore, need to take a careful look at how critical decisions are made. For example, in many organizations, all employees should be given an opportunity to influence such things as the capital expenditure and budgetary decisions for their particular work unit or work area.

As discussed earlier in this chapter, even in a high-involvement organization, it is unlikely that all decisions should or can be made in a highly participative manner. Indeed, one of the most important kinds of decisions that senior managers need to make is which type of decision-making style to use in a particular situation (Vroom and Yetton, 1973).

Feedback and Communication

Critical to the high-involvement approach to management is the willingness of managers to seek information about how effective they are in their decision-making and leadership behaviors (Argyris and Schön, 1978). It is hard for any manager to ask for feedback because of the risk involved, and it is often difficult for subordinates to give valid feedback because they, too, perceive a risk. Senior managers can encourage this kind of feedback throughout an organization by asking their subordinates about the way these individuals react to their leadership. The senior managers are thus modeling the kind of behaviors that are needed throughout the organization.

Senior managers are in a particularly good position to share organizational results and talk about overall operating profits, goals, and performance. Because an important part of high-involvement management is the sharing of information about financial results, it is critical that senior managers communicate this information throughout the organization. In most organizations, multiple communication methods are appropriate and need to be carried out on a regular basis; indeed, it is hard to imagine too much downward communication about operating performance and results.

Support of Training

Because an important part of every participatively managed organization is the knowledge base of the employees, senior managers need to be particularly concerned about the kind of training that is available in their organization. They need to do more than just assure that the organization offers individuals good training opportunities. They also need to look at their own behavior and ask whether they are modeling the kind of learning behavior that they expect to see demonstrated by people throughout the organization.

A good way for managers to be sure that they are in fact supporting the kind of training that is needed in their organization is for them to participate in the training. They should be the first ones to go through any training programs that focus on leadership style, decision-making processes, performance management, and the development of participative management behaviors. They should also participate in the training programs which involve their direct subordinates. When possible, they should play a role in conducting the training sessions. This kind of "cascading" process can be extremely valuable in reinforcing the importance of managerial behaviors throughout the organization.

Xerox is one organization that has done an excellent job of developing training approaches that give managers a key part in developing and supporting participative behaviors from the top to the bottom of the organization. When they introduced employee involvement, they started at the top of the organization and had each management level train the next level down. At General Electric, senior executives attend management training programs at all levels of the organization in order to reinforce the type of culture they want and to get a sense of how the organization is operating. I have done training sessions at TRW, Hughes, and other companies in which the chief executive officer has been an active participant. These sessions are always received better than sessions when the CEO is absent or simply says a few introductory words and leaves.

Federal Express, Hyatt, and United Parcel Service have for decades used a system in which senior managers actually do nonmanagement jobs. In Federal Express, for example, senior executives are expected to do a nonmanagement service job in the organization on a regular basis. This gives executives a good opportunity to see how the organization is working at a different level and gives them contact with customers.

In many ways, actually having supervisors perform different jobs is vastly superior to having them wander around the organization trying to sense how people are feeling by watching them and having casual conversations with them (Peters and Waterman, 1982). The latter approach can be superficial and, in some ways, is a condescending interruption of important work. By actually getting out and doing work, the manager demonstrates to employees that everyone in the organization is willing to participate in the basic work of an organization and receives an intensive and realistic experience of how the organization acutally operates. These managers do not have to imagine or ask what it is like to do the work; they experience it!

High-Impact Behaviors

Nadler (1989) has pointed out that mundane behavior by executives as well as "grand gestures" can be important in shaping organizational behavior. He lists the following as behaviors that can have a great impact:

- Scheduling of time and calendar management
- Shaping of physical settings
- Control over agendas of events or meetings
- Use of events such as lunches and meetings
- Summarization—interpretation of what occured in meetings
- Use of humor, stories, and myths
- Use of small symbolic actions, including rewards and punishments

To this list I would add:
- Asking the right questions in meetings and tours of company facilities
- Rejection of status symbols and signs of hierarchical difference
- Where possible, performance of customer service jobs on a regular basis

These are all things that an executive can do to signify what is important and what type of behavior is expected in the organization. Used skillfully, these behaviors can strongly support the effective practice of high-involvement management.

Monitoring of Decision-Making Processes

In high-involvement organizations, senior managers often have to accept responsibility for decisions that they do not directly influence or make. Accepting this responsibility involves trusting the individuals and the decision-making processes at levels below them in the organization. Indeed, one of the "stressful" things for managers about operating in a participative organization is being held accountable for decisions made by others. However, even though managers may not personally make all decisions, they do have an opportunity to influence how all decisions are made in a participative organization just as they do in a traditional one. They have this influence because they are responsible for monitoring the kind of decision-making processes that exist in the organization—it is one of their most important tasks. They must be virtually obsessed with improving decision-making processes and must systematically gather data about how effectively these processes operate at levels below them and how the processes can be made better.

There are a number of techniques or approaches that senior managers can use to learn about how the organization is operating. In addition to the normal financial and quality data which are available to senior managers, they can use formal opinion surveys and sensing sessions throughout the organization. Senior managers also need to be accessible to individuals throughout the organization through both formal and informal channels. Access can occur through hot lines, a formal appeal process, electronic mail, written questions, an open-door policy, and other methods. Senior managers can eat lunch with employees on a regular basis in order to create casual contact. Even arranging the office space in such a way that people throughout the organization have casual and informal contact can help (for example, avoiding an executive office floor).

For some decisions, senior managers need to go beyond just listening to the recommendations that come from the organization. They need to personally check on how the decision was made and to ask the various decision makers how they feel about the decision-making process. Senior managers need to be sure that individuals are given the opportunity to participate in making decisions where their expertise is relevant. These managers are in the best position to test the decision-making processes to be sure that they are operating effectively. Only then can they or should they trust and fully commit themselves to the decisions that are made by employees below them in the organization.

Decisions About Pay and Promotion

Senior managers often can have the greatest influence on whether high-involvement management is practiced throughout the organization through their decisions about promotion and pay. Organizations that promote managers who practice participative management tend to develop participative managers throughout the organization. Organizations that preach the importance of participative management and then disregard it in promotion and pay decisions do not elicit participative behaviors from managers. Donald Petersen, former chief executive officer of Ford, makes this point in his book on the change process he used at Ford (Petersen and Hillkirk, 1991).

If senior managers want to strongly encourage participative management, they need to ask questions and demand that data be gathered about how managers behave throughout the organization. These data, obtained from subordinates and by observing the behavior of managers, must be an important part of decisions about pay and promotion. And managers throughout the organization must realize that their behavior as managers has an important influence on their career moves and on their pay increases.

In several ways, one of the most important things that senior managers can do is identify and reward the kind of organizational performance that contributes to the organization's strategic direction. The rewards need not be of material or financial value, they can simply be symbolic. The attention of a senior manager itself is often very rewarding to employees. Senior managers need to become role models for the kind of reward behavior they expect from managers below them in the organization.

Results of Executive Effectiveness

We are now ready to look at a few key indicators that tell senior managers whether or not they have been effective in creating a high-involvement organization. Perhaps the key communication change that an executive should see is much more upward communication, both positive and negative. This communication should range from direct feedback about their own behavior to informal communication from people throughout the organization about how things are going. In the effective high-involvement organization, the senior managers should feel that they are in touch with what is going on throughout the organization, particularly with respect to how decisions are made and the overall operation of the organization.

Executives should also notice an increase in the degree to which people at all levels can talk about the condition of the business, its cost, its performance, and its customers. They should be able to ask people throughout the organization how the business is performing and get informed answers. Furthermore, they should notice a high level of ownership over business results; that is, individuals should feel responsible for how their particular work unit is operating and, indeed, how the total organization is operating. Often ownership of the business shows in the language of individuals—they say "we" when they talk about the organization, not "they."

In a high-involvement organization individuals should recognize and reward each other for effective performance. Managers alone should not have to be responsible for fomally recognizing and acknowledging good performance. Peers should recognize peers and subordinates should recognize bosses for good performance. This type of interaction only occurs when people are committed to the effectiveness of the organization and feel a shared sense of responsibility for the operation of the organization.

Senior managers should also be able to observe that employees have a strong and accurate sense of the right thing to do in a particular situation and, of course, the willingness to do it (Carlzon, 1987). Employees should not, for example, talk about what their job description calls for or "what they are not responsible for." In effective high-involvement organizations, individuals worry about what needs to be done in order to make the organization effective. Of course, they also need to make good decisions about what is the right thing to do.

If senior managers perform their work effectively, certain behaviors should be easy to observe throughout the organization. Individuals at all levels should take responsibility for the organization's effectiveness and make a strong commitment to the organization's long-term performance. In the absence of effective behavior by senior managers, this type of organization-wide commitment is hard, if not impossible, to generate. In a very direct sense, the effectiveness of senior managers is ultimately visible in the behavior of the organization.

Chapter Twelve

Involve Unions
in the
Organization

U nion-management relationships in the United States and most of Europe have, by tradition and design, been adversarial. This adversarial relationship represents a way of moving power to the rank and file employees in an organization. Collective bargaining is designed to allow employees to influence such areas as pay, job structures, discipline, and working conditions. The adversarial relationship is limited, however, in what areas it allows employees to influence. For example, it rarely gives them a chance to influence an organization's capital investment, business strategy, and marketing decisions.

The adversarial approach also does little to move information throughout an organization or to improve the skills and knowledge of nonmanagement employees. In fact, it often inhibits the downward flow of information because management becomes concerned about sharing information that will harm its bargaining position. Although the adversarial approach moves rewards downward, it does not usually create systems in which rewards are directly tied to the success of the organization or to the skills of the employees. It does little to move organizations toward employee involvement, and, in some respects, it reinforces and institutionalizes bureaucratic top-down management practices by putting them into contracts.

Perhaps the most damaging criticism of the adversarial

approach is that it is inefficient. Adversarial relationships involve great amounts of time and effort, extra staff members, and an extensive bureaucracy. They represent an enormous parallel structure since they require a union hierarchy as well as an organizational hierarchy of labor relations specialists. When labor and management cannot resolve their differences through the adversarial process, employees go on strike. Differences that cannot be amicably resolved often end up as formal grievances, which are time consuming and expensive.

For decades, researchers and theorists have suggested that a more cooperative union-management relationship would be advantageous to both parties (Walton and McKersie, 1965). Cooperation offers the hope of wider and more efficient employee involvement in organizations as well as more effective organizational performance — in short, a win-win situation (Lawler and Mohrman, 1987b).

Decline of Unions

Many organizations have decided that they can no longer afford an adversarial union-management relationship. What is less obvious, but equally true, is that many unions can no longer afford an adversarial relationship either. The union movement in the United States is in trouble (Hoerr, 1991). As recently as the 1950s, over 30 percent of the work force belonged to unions. Data from the U.S. Bureau of Labor Statistics show that union membership had fallen from 23 percent of the work force in 1980 to 17 percent in 1990 (12 percent in the private sector), the lowest level in recent history. This percentage decline represents a decrease of over three million dues-paying union members. Interestingly, comparable declines have not occurred in other industrialized nations (Hoerr, 1991).

The reasons commonly cited for the decline in union membership are many and varied: automation, layoffs in unionized industries such as automobile and steel manufacturing, the increasing success of employers' antiunion efforts, the sharp growth of service industries, the changing legal situation with respect to union organizing and employee rights, and the changing expectations of the new work force. The environment that unions have historically operated in has changed dramatically, and, as a result, their very existence is threatened because the role that they used to fill is not viable in the present environment. Their survival, therefore, depends on their finding a new role.

For decades, unions have presented themselves as organizations that can offer their members certain tangible benefits that the members cannot get without being in a union. These benefits are primarily better wages and working conditions, job security, and due process appeals. Unions have been effective in accomplishing many of their objectives. The wages of unionized employees have been estimated to be as much as 33 percent higher than those of nonunion employees, and unions should be credited with dramatically improving working conditions and safety in the United States (Walton and McKersie, 1965). The protection that unions offer their members against arbitrary actions by management is also well documented; grievance procedures and contracts protect employees from unfair salary changes, layoffs, and discipline.

Indeed, many of the gains that unions have achieved for their members have spread to the work force in general through legislation supported by unions. In addition, companies, in order to avoid unionization, have given their employees working conditions that are comparable to those in unionized companies. In short, the union movement has established many of the standards of employment that are generally accepted in our society today.

If unions have been highly successful, why are they in a state of serious decline? Essentially, unions have been so successful that they have made themselves unnecessary; that is, they have accomplished their objectives so well that many people now believe they are no longer needed. Evidence of this is provided by the difficulty unions have had in organizing new high-involvement plants and Japanese-owned plants in the United States (see Lawler, 1978, 1990a, 1991, and Chapter Thirteen). Virtually no high-involvement plants have been organized despite numerous efforts. The United Auto Workers (UAW)

Union has tried to organize employees at Nissan, Honda, and Toyota by emphasizing such traditional union issues as safety and work pace, but has had no success.

Some people may believe that unions should go out of business because they are no longer necessary; however, they are still needed for two reasons. First, a considerable amount of work still must be done with respect to the traditional issues that unions have addressed. Far too many people in the United States are killed and maimed on the job by avoidable accidents, and too many managements still engage in unfair and unreasonable practices. The economic situation of many employees needs to be improved, and the existence of unions probably motivates many managers, even those in nonunion settings, to do the right thing.

Second, we are at a time in history when the organization of work, the nature of large organizations, and the structure of the economy are fundamentally changing. Organized labor needs to be an important institutional voice for the work force during this time of change. In the absence of a viable union movment, the managers of our large organizations may not be sufficiently concerned about the human and organizational issues that companies must address to be competitive and ethical (Hoerr, 1991). Thus, a vibrant viable union movement in the United States is desirable, but there is no denying that a declining market for traditional unionism could lead to the demise of unions in the United States even though it is important to have them.

The leadership of some major U.S. unions has recognized the declining market for traditional unionism, and changes are taking place in the union movement (Herrick, 1990). A study by the AFL-CIO addresses the issue of the future of unionism in the United States and points to the need for a significant change in the union movement (AFL-CIO, 1985). However, the study also points out that unions often find themselves behind the pace of change. The study states that "it is not enough merely to search for more effective ways of doing what we've always done: we must expand our notions of what workers can do through unions." But what can employees do through unions that is new and different? What are the new services or products that unions can offer people that will prevent unions from becoming obsolete? One answer is quality-of-work-life (QWL) programs that bring unions and managements together in a joint problem-solving approach.

QWL Programs

In the early 1970s, two events were catalysts for the introduction of cooperative union-management projects in hundreds of workplaces. First, the UAW signed a contract with General Motors that called for QWL programs in that corporation. Second, a program begun by the Institute for Social Research at the University of Michigan called for starting union-management QWL projects around the country (Lawler and Ozley, 1979; Seashore, 1981). Both of these efforts launched many cooperative programs that were intended to improve all aspects of work life, not just productivity.

Virtually every major union has become involved in at least one QWL project: the UAW, the United Steel Workers of America, and the Communication Workers of America have been particularly active. Most major corporations with unions, including Corning, General Motors, Ford, Shell, Xerox, AT&T, and most steel companies, have also become involved. The U.S. Department of Labor lists over a hundred cooperative union-management projects, and in response to the growth of these projects, the department has instituted a Bureau of Labor-Management Cooperation to support and encourage the projects.

As one of the original advocates of QWL programs, I am pleased by the number of union-management QWL programs, but I am concerned that the original QWL model is too often seen as the ultimate approach to union-management relations. Despite its success, it has important limitations. We need to increasingly focus on a second-generation QWL model of union-management relations. But before considering what a second-generation model might look like, I will present in some detail the basic QWL model. Most QWL projects follow a well-developed and well-established model (Herrick, 1990; Lawler, 1986). Of course, each project ultimately defines its own structures, traditions, and approaches, but this is usually done within the context of a general model that includes the features that I will describe next.

Committee Structure

A committee structure is at the core of most QWL projects. These committees form the cooperative bridge between the union and the organization and are, in essence, a parallel structure that sits between the union and the organization. In a large corporation, one committee is usually created at the highest level of the union and the organization. For example, in both Ford and General Motors, a corporate-level committee includes corporate officers and senior union officials. Committees are also created at other major levels in the company, down to and including the plant level. The plant-level committee typically creates additional groups and participative activities in the plant.

The joint committees are responsible for providing the direction and impetus for the QWL program and are the key structural vehicle on which the entire program rests. The hierarchical nature of these committees reflects the hierarchies in both unions and work organizations. As with any hierarchical structure, different tasks are allocated to different levels in the organization. The top level provides general direction and support, and the lower levels identify and carry out specific activities.

Agreements

The union and management typically sign a letter of agreement stating, among other things, that no individuals will lose their job or pay as a result of the project and that the project will not deal with collective bargaining issues. The latter point is particularly important since it is often a very sensitive one for the union. Unions often are concerned that QWL projects will undermine

collective bargaining arrangements. Instead of undermining
them, the QWL program is supposed to complement them by
allowing the union to influence various decisions that are not
able to influence through collective bargaining. Letters of agreement also often talk about the kind of committee structure to be
created by the QWL program, state that the program is volun-
tary, and set some general objectives for the program.

Objectives

QWL programs typically have three kinds of objectives—union
objectives, management objectives, and joint objectives. Although most objectives are not specified as being primarily
sought by the union or by management, both parties enter into
QWL projects because they wish to accomplish specific things.
For example, the union may wish to strengthen its position and
popularity with the work force, increase its membership by
making the company more successful, and provide a better work
environment for its membership by increasing its influence in
areas where it normally does not have much influence. Management may wish to reduce the adversarial union-management
relationship, improve the collective bargaining process, and, of
course, improve organizational performance through improvements in productivity and quality.

The objectives of the program are usually stated in a letter
of agreement and are widely disseminated to the participants.
Often they are summarized into a few general ideas, such as
improving product quality and the quality of work life or increasing employee involvement. In the QWL program at General Motors, the emphasis is on quality of work life as a method
of improving product quality. Ford calls its program *Employee
Involvement* and focuses on improved product quality. The 1980
basic agreement between the United Steel Workers of America
and the major steel companies calls for employee participation
teams to discuss and decide on means to improve performance,
employee morale and dignity, and conditions of work.

Training Programs

The initial step in QWL programs is a general training program for all participants. The work force at a plant, for example, is introduced to the general concept and objectives of a QWL program. All participants learn cooperative problem-solving skills and are given information about the business and the company. This initial training indicates the company's and the union's commitment to the project and represents the beginning of information sharing and skill building. Depending on the structure of the program, this training may take anywhere from a few hours to several days.

Change Areas

QWL programs typically start with higher level committees picking a plant or location that they feel is particularly attractive as a starting point. In some cases, projects start at a plant without any top-level union or company involvement. This typically occurs where a company has a variety of unions and can deal with each location on a separate basis.

The QWL committees identify specific changes to be made by the program. There may be only one committee at a location or many, depending on the structure of the program. Usually, one or two QWL committees are created at each level in the organizational hierarchy. The number of committees often expands to create a structure similar to those that exist in quality circle programs. Numerous shop-floor problem-solving groups as well as some joint task forces are created to look at particular issues.

The type and number of joint problem-solving groups is the key design feature in any QWL project and determines the issues the program addresses. If numerous groups are created at the shop-floor level, then the program typically looks like a quality circle program; jointly sponsored groups focus on improving work methods as well as working conditions. Training in work methods and procedures is a common activity. Simi-

larly, groups often get involved in improving physical surround-
ings, safety, and general working conditions. This is hardly
surprising since in many plants safety has been a joint union-
management concern for decades.

Sometimes, QWL committees deal with gainsharing and
may even look at contractual issues such as hours of work and
work schedules. These are difficult areas for QWL programs
because they are contractual and, as such, not within the mandate of most QWL projects. As a result, QWL projects have
rarely produced significant changes in collective bargaining
issues.

Third-Party Facilitator

Most QWL projects depend heavily on a third-party facilitator
who helps define objectives, provides training, and facilitates
group processes. At General Motors, the facilitators are typically
employed by the company, but, in most cases, the facilitators are
private consultants who specialize in QWL programs. Before
the mid 1970s, few of these experts were available in the United
States. However, the number has grown tremendously and there
are now numerous facilitators and consultants as well as local
union-management centers and support groups that can recommend facilitators and provide training. Some state governments
have QWL centers that provide technical assistance.

Impact of QWL Programs on Involvement

The impact of QWL projects on information, knowledge,
power, and rewards is limited because these programs are parallel structures to unions and companies. They usually do
not affect all the systems in an organization and therefore
do not create a high-involvement approach to organizing and
managing people. Nevertheless, they do have an impact. QWL
projects often produce changes that affect everyone in an
organization. The union should receive much of the credit for
this because it is the first to raise issues of equality of treatment.

Information

One of the objectives of most QWL programs is to share plans and business information more widely in the organization, and the major impact of a QWL program is often in the area of information sharing. In many but not all cases, the creation of committee structures and task forces opens an array of communication channels, particularly when task forces deal with such business issues as the purchase of new machinery, problems with suppliers, costs, causes of poor-quality products, and bids and proposals for new business. As a result of the improved communications, people often come to understand the business better and to particpate more effectively in problem-solving activities.

Knowledge

QWL projects typically increase the skills and knowledge of a significant number of employees, especially the people who end up on the QWL committees. Committee members often receive interpersonal and group-skill training as well as training in decision making. Other members of the organization usually receive less training. As was mentioned earlier, a plantwide organizational training program in which everyone partici-pates typically introduces the program. Additional training may be provided to members of the work force as a result of the specific recommendations of the QWL committees. It is common, for example, for the committees to recommend specific training in quality control, work methods and procedures, su-pervisory behavior, and the like.

Power

The effects on power are somewhat subtle but, nevertheless, significant. First, it is important to remember that QWL commit-tees are usually prohibited from discussing bargaining issues — not that they do not sometimes discuss them. Second, these committees typically have no formal power to decide things.

They merely make recommendations to the existing power structure about the kinds of changes that are desirable. Their power is very much a function of the quality of the recommendations that they make and their ability to persuade the existing power structure of the value of their ideas. If the members of the QWL committee are representatives of the key power groups in the organization, the committee's recommendations probably will be implemented.

Most consultants who set up QWL programs emphasize the importance of having the major power groups well represented in the QWL committee structure. For example, at the corporate level and at the local plant, the key management people should be involved, and at the plant level, the local union leadership should be represented. To be successful the "powerless" QWL committee must have direct links to the individuals who can make decisions. It is probably fair to say that the major power of QWL programs rests in their bringing together key individuals from the union and management to discuss issues that are not traditionally addressed by them.

Because QWL committtees involve high-level managers and union officials, QWL programs typically have more effect on the sharing of power with employees than do quality circle programs. The union officials can follow up on ideas to see that they are implemented; no comparable group exists in most quality circle programs. However, QWL programs do little to directly shift power to union members in the organization. In effect, they are a move to a very limited form of representative democracy, with the union officials in the role of spokespersons for the work force.

Rewards

QWL programs emphasize rewards of recognition and do little to affect financial rewards, largely because they are not allowed to deal with contractual issues. A few programs have started gainsharing plans, often set up outside of the formal collective bargaining agreement. Some QWL programs also have devel-

oped changes in pay and promotion practices that have ultimately been incorporated into contracts.

Results of QWL Programs

The literature on QWL programs is full of reports about the
success of these programs (Simmons and Mares, 1983). Some
programs, such as those at the General Motors at Tarrytown,
New York, plant (Guest, 1979), and several Ford plants (Copenhaver and Guest, 1982), have become major examples of how
unions and management can relate together in new and positive
ways. On the other hand, a number of programs have failed and
have been abandoned (Lawler, 1986). At present, only a small
number of programs have been systematically studied to determine their impact, and there are no accurate data on the success
rate of QWL programs. Unquestionably, the programs that have
been studied the most are those that were part of the original
University of Michigan QWL project (see, for example, Goodman, 1979; Hanlon, Nadler, and Gladstein, 1985; Macy, 1982;
Nurick, 1985; Macy, Peterson, and Norton, 1989; Moch and
Bartunek, 1990). They were subject to extensive measurement,
and, therefore, we have fairly good data on their success rate
(Lawler and Ledford, 1982). As I will review next, they did have
some positive results.

Employee Satisfaction

QWL programs rather consistently improve employee well-
being and satisfaction (Lawler and Ledford, 1982). They usually
reach this important goal because of the kinds of activities the
projects sponsor. Problem-solving groups involve a number of
people, and at least initially, as noted in the discussion of quality
circles, membership in the groups has a positive impact and
people are eager to join the groups. Membership in task forces
and problem-solving groups can be particularly satisfying when
the groups take on and solve major organizational issues such as
developing bids for new business, solving major quality problems, and making important purchasing decisions. An attitude

survey at Ford in locations with a QWL program, for example, found employees were more satisfied as a result of their being involved in the thinking side of their work.

QWL committees often recommend changes in the workplace that employees want. In particular, they support changes in the physical environment: parking lots, cafeterias, restrooms, and time clocks. The committees focus on working conditions for two reasons. First, many managers, union leaders, and employees believe that employee satisfaction leads to productivity; therefore, project leaders try to find ways of making the organization a more satisfying place to work. Second, it is often easier to create a more pleasant work environment than it is to change management styles, job design, patterns of coordination and communication, and reward systems. Suggestions for improving physical working conditions are easy to generate since making the suggestions requires no special expertise and such problems are usually highly visible—anyone can see the need for a bigger parking lot. On the other hand, problems with the way the work is performed are usually complex and difficult to solve.

If changes are implemented in job design, work methods, and work coordination, employees often are more satisfied. As was noted earlier, people find it satisfying to work in an effective organization where jobs are interesting and challenging. Sometimes the grievance procedures become smoother and the adversarial relationship is also reduced because of QWL projects.

Organizational Effectiveness

The few case histories that have studied the long-term effects of QWL programs on productivity or organizational effectiveness show mixed results (Lawler, 1986). Data from those QWL programs that have been carefully documented indicate that productivity improvements can be obtained. Two of the eight original programs sponsored by the University of Michigan showed clear impacts on productivity (Lawler and Ledford, 1982). In some of the organizations involved in the University of Michigan project, productivity was difficult or impossible to measure, so no conclusions could be reached. In other cases, there were no improvements in productivity simply because the QWL programs did not directly focus on improving productivity and quality through changing communication patterns, employee skills, work methods, or employee motivation.

For several reasons, simply improving employee satisfaction through better working conditions does not improve productivity. First, the simplistic belief that employee satisfaction leads to improved productivity is wrong (Lawler, 1973). Thus, even though improvements in the workplace increase employee satisfaction, increases in productivity and organizational effectiveness may not occur. Some long-term gains in productivity may be expected because of lower turnover, fewer strikes, fewer grievances, and less absenteeism, but companies measure financial performance and productivity in the short-term. Thus, increases in employee satisfaction may not have a detectable impact on the bottom line.

Second, implementing changes in the work environment often takes longer than anyone expects. Major construction projects can take months or even years, and changes in the work environment often require several levels of financial approval, thus making management appear slow and unsympathetic. During long delays in making changes, employees and managers may come to view the QWL program as a failure, and it may be abandoned before it even has a chance to improve productivity.

Third, the cost of improvements in the work environment may exceed the benefits in productivity because even if a better work environment does translate into higher productivity and other organizational benefits, the benefits may be small. The cost of building a new cafeteria or air conditioning a work area, for example, are rarely if ever recouped in a way that is documentable. As a result, managers may come to see a QWL program as costly or futile, with no benefits to the organization, and thus may lose interest in it.

This does not mean, however, that working conditions should be ignored. It may be necessary to improve working conditions in order to win credibility for a new program. Employees may not trust management's motivation unless improvements are made, particularly if a work environment is dangerous or extremely uncomfortable. Furthermore, certain improvements in the work environment have potential benefits for both productivity and employee satisfaction because they may reduce grievances, absenteeism, and turnover. In addition, an organization has a social responsibility to provide good working conditions as well as safety and health improvements. Therefore, an organization ought to consider making the workplace pleasant as an end in itself rather than as a means to improving productivity.

Many QWL programs that have not been systematically studied claim to have achieved significant improvements in product quality as a result of the programs (see, for example, Herrick, 1990; Simmons and Mares, 1983). Since product quality contributes directly to productivity and to financial performance, improvements in product quality can satisfy management and financially justify the continuation of a QWL program. Ford claims that its QWL program has substantially improved product quality. One report on the company's program at the Sharonville, Ohio plant states that customer complaints dropped by 70 percent because of a QWL program. Attitude surveys of employees at Sharonville support the argument for improved quality. Before the QWL program was instituted, 54 percent of the employees rated quality as excellent, but afterward, this figure rose to 72 percent.

It is not surprising that improved quality is a common outcome of QWL programs because it is a goal both union and management share. Productivity increases, on the other hand, may be seen by unions as speedups and as something management alone wants. In addition, when people feel responsible for something, as was mentioned earlier, they want to do a high-quality job; thus, they are willing to improve work methods and pay more attention to quality (Lawler, 1973).

The degree to which a QWL program can improve organizational effectiveness perhaps is limited most by the fact that the collective bargaining contract itself cannot be directly affected by the program. Contracts can prevent elimination of work rules that stop employees from doing their own maintenance, for example, and can prevent people being cross-trained and functioning in self-managing teams. Thus, some obvious approaches to improved productivity may be ruled out.

No reduction in support or supervisory staff is likely because of QWL programs. Nothing in the QWL process requires an examination of the overhead structure of the organization or its management, control, and decision-making processes. These are areas in which an organization may be able to make tremendous improvements in its effectiveness, but they are typically left untouched.

QWL projects are expensive to operate, thus to get a payoff in net productivity and organizational effectiveness, they have to produce significant gains or savings. Accurate cost estimates for QWL programs are almost completely nonexistent. A study by Goodman (1979) of a coal mining project is a rare exception. Another exception is an estimate of a cost of $1.6 million for the training program at the General Motors Tarrytown, New York, plant (Guest, 1979).

In addition to the high cost of training, QWL programs have high operating costs because they are a parallel structure to the existing organizations and thus require extra people and involve considerable time for meetings, training, and other support activities. Increased training costs are likely to occur in any effort to increase employee involvement, but high overhead costs are not. The initial overhead costs of many change programs decrease as the programs mature while those of parallel participation programs can remain high throughout the life of the program.

Union-Management Relationships

Numerous studies report that QWL programs improve the basic relationship between the union and management (Guest, 1979; Herrick, 1990). Even though QWL programs are formally kept separate from collective bargaining, the adversarial process has to be influenced by the ideas, improvements, and changes that result from the QWL program. Some evidence of this exists in the claims of quicker and more efficient bargaining and fewer strikes at those locations that have had QWL programs (Herrick, 1990).

QWL projects may indirectly influence the kinds of provisions that are put in contracts, as has been the case at General Motors, where the contracts with the UAW that cover new plants and GM's new car company, Saturn, include QWL-type provisions. For example, pay for skills is included as a feature in these new plants specifically as a result of QWL activities. And job descriptions are more flexible and manning levels are quite different in these new plants.

QWL projects often have an impact on the structure and leadership style of the unions involved in them. In a number of cases, support for QWL programs has become an issue in union politics. Union leaders who support QWL programs generally gain in popularity and power because they are seen as leading the union in a positive direction. Of course, traditional union leaders may not enter into QWL projects because they see them as threats to their power base — particularly when they have built their power on an adversarial relationship and grievances, both of which are often reduced in the QWL process (see Parker and Slaughter, 1988). In several cases, this threat to their power base has led unions to withdraw from QWL projects.

Future of QWL Programs

QWL programs are a positive way for unions and management to relate to each other, and they are particularly likely to improve the general working conditions and the well-being of employees. They are less likely to improve productivity and operating effectiveness. Nevertheless, a number of organizations have used them to improve product quality and have reduced grievances, strikes, absenteeism, and turnover. With the exception of the Scanlon plan and some other forms of gainsharing, QWL projects represent the only well-established way for unions and management to create a more participative work culture and organization. Thus, even though the results at this point are mixed and these projects are expensive, they represent a good starting point for labor-management cooperation.

Perhaps the best way to think of QWL programs is as the first step in a long-term transition. They represent the "crawling" stage that ultimately must progress to the "walking" stage and the "running" stage if unionized organizations are to substantially improve their effectiveness. I think of them as at the crawling stage because of their limited impact on the movement of knowledge, information, power, and rewards to employees. Their impact will always be limited as long as they operate separately from collective bargaining and fail to address many business issues.

When I worked with others on the development of the original QWL model, I never thought of it as a permanent parallel structure. Instead, I thought of it as a way to change the organization's normal way of relating to its union and to get the union to substantially change its view of its role in the organization. The model has shown some ability to do this, but too often it has become institutionalized and has not led to a higher level of employee involvement in which unions have a dramatically different role, a role that supports high-involvement management.

New Role for Unions

Unions can serve their members and society best if they progress beyond their cooperative role in QWL programs to a role in which they assure employee involvement in the business of the organization (Lawler and Mohrman, 1987b). Unions need to become representatives of the work force in business decision making and assure that the inputs and views of the work force are effectively represented. To fulfill this role, unions need to become concerned about the effectiveness of organizations and at times to act as partners with management in order to assure the success of the organization.

Even with unions in a new role, contracts and collective bargaining certainly still need to exist, but they too must change. The union-management contract should be only a few pages outlining general philosophy and the organization's culture. It needs to set up decision-making processes that allow the details of work methods, procedures, and pay to be handled in an ongoing way through a regular participative structure in the organization.

Instead of giving details of all the actual reward system practices that will be put in place, the contract needs to state core principles about how the pay system will operate and leave it to the members in the participative process to decide the specifics of the reward system. The contract should bind the parties to general principles and guidelines rather than establishing a time-bound legal template and a "judicial" appeals process to handle violations. It should specify participative processes for determining the reward and work systems, introducing changes, and addressing problems that arise. Just this type of open contract has been negotiated by Shell for several of its chemical plants in Canada. Corning has a similarly flexible contract with its union and is converting all of its twenty-eight U.S. factories to team-based operations.

Unions need to take on a much more important role in corporate policy and organizational effectiveness than they do in the traditional adversarial relationship. As the elected representatives of the work force, union officials are natural spokespersons for the employee perspective. A union seat or seats on the board of directors of an organization is consistent with this role.

Unions represent an organized vehicle for building employee commitment to having an effective organization as well as assuring that employee knowledge and expertise are well utilized by the organization. Unions should be active participants in designing and structuring reward systems. They should support such practices as skill-based pay, employee ownership, and profit sharing because they align company and employee interests in having workers who are well trained and business units that perform effectively. Unions must also monitor the operation of the reward systems and assure their fairness and effectiveness.

Unions also should be quite active in the design of work methods and job structures, and they inevitably will need to act as partners with management in the selection of new pieces of technology and in the work design process. Union involvement in work design, pay, and other decisions should have a dramatic and positive impact on the quality of employees' work life and should strengthen the unions because they are providing something employees want.

The single most important role that unions can fill may be that of a check and balance on management. It is all too easy for management to slip in and out of participative management practices as the environment and management personnel change. In the absence of a union, management can pick and choose the issues on which participation is permitted and may solicit no employee input on issues such as the introduction of technology, which are of central concern to the work force. A union that is firmly committed to employee involvement can be an important safeguard that ensures employee input into key decisions. It can fill a corporate governance role that badly needs to be filled given the globalization of large corporations and the complex issues involved in holding global corporations accountable for their actions (Reich, 1991).

Unions may also need to challenge managers when the managers make decisions that affect their own pay, perquisites, and time. The growth of executive compensation levels in the 1980s is a clear example of what can happen when managers' power is not balanced by other interests. When management makes inappropriate self-serving decisions, unions should be in a position to challenge them. For example, the board of directors of Chrysler decided to approve the use of the company employee-relocation program to buy two of Lee Iacocca's homes that he was having trouble selling. Since Iacocca had not moved, the action appeared inappropriate and was challenged by board member Owen Bieber, president of the UAW. Unfortunately, this incident did not move Chrysler toward better union relations and high-involvement management. The board still approved the purchases and Bieber is leaving the board. He will not be replaced by another union official; nevertheless, he did exactly what more union leaders need to do.

Unions should take the position that employees' job security is best provided by increasing the skills of employees and the effectiveness of the organization. Unions can play a critical role in increasing both skills and effectiveness. As already mentioned, they can help see that the organization is effective. They can also help to assure that employees are trained and developed in ways that will give them the personal security that comes from having transferable skills and the ability to cope with a turbulent economic environment. This, of course, is a quite different kind of job security than the one that typically comes with seniority-based union contracts.

Some QWL programs have moved beyond the parallel structure approach. In these programs, union representatives are members of all plant committees and the union president is a member of the top management team and actively participates in all meetings. At the moment, however, no union-management relationships incorporate all the elements of a high-involvement union-management relationship. Perhaps the closest example is the joint effort of GM and the UAW at Saturn. The union and management have jointly made policy decisions and participated in structuring the work environment. Joint union-management groups have selected technology and advertising agencies and made a wide range of start-up and operating decisions. This joint effort may be a much needed prototype of a high-involvement union-management relationship in the United States.

Moving toward a high-involvement approach represents a vast change in orientation for the union movement, and it calls for dramatically different behaviors on the part of many union leaders and managers. Union leaders need different skills when they assume roles in business decision making. To start with, union leaders need to understand the business; help solve problems involving its important issues; and, of course, remain in touch with the needs, desires, and views of union members. Managers need to learn how to include union leaders in discussions and to facilitate decision making on issues that involve legitimate differences of opinion.

It is not surprising that many union leaders are opposed to union-management cooperation. The joint effort at Saturn is highly controversial within the UAW (Parker and Slaughter,

1988). One UAW official has noted that "inherent in this agreement is the demise of the UAW and the trade union movement as we now know it." Perhaps so, but such joint efforts do not necessarily signal the end of the UAW or the union movement; quite to the contrary, they may signal a new beginning, a beginning that is based on providing members with new information, knowledge, power, and rewards.

The macroeconomic trends affecting the United States suggest that the adversarial model of union-management relationships is doomed because of the restructuring of work and organizations in the society. The current economic challenges facing organizations are far too complex to be easily addressed by advocacy for single stakeholders and wasteful adversarial struggles. New approaches are needed that create win-win relationships between labor and management. Unions must learn how to create these relationships to be able to offer employees a reason for being a union member. If they do not make such a change, unions are likely to continue to lose members and to become increasingly irrelevant.

PART FOUR

Creating

High-Involvement

Organizations

Chapter Thirteen

Develop
High-Involvement
Business Units

I n the late 1960s, a few American companies began building a
new kind of manufacturing facility. These new plants emphasized a high level of participative management and utilized a
number of new management practices. They represent the first
step toward a true high-involvement business unit. Procter &
Gamble was the first company to build one of these plants, but
within a few years, Mead, TRW, Sherwin Williams, Cummins
Engine, General Foods, and a host of other companies built
similar plants. The building of these plants was a critical development in the evolution of high-involvement management. The
plants represent one of the first systematic installations of participative management by large U.S. corporations. They showed
that participative management could be used in manufacturing
plants and that it could offer competitive advantages.

Ideas that were seen as radical and revolutionary when
these new plants were built are now standard operating procedures in many large organizations. In a very real sense these
new plants helped overthrow the traditional management para-
digm about how manufacturing facilities should be managed
and replaced it with a new one. This *new plant approach*, as I call it,
has led to a number of significant developments. First, many new
plants have been started with a participative management
model (Lawler, 1990a). Second, many nonmanufacturing situations have used the participative management model that was

pioneered in these new plants. Third, many participative management practices have been used in other situations because
they were proven to be valuable in the new plants.

Characteristics of the New Plant Approach

Elsewhere, I have outlined the specific employee involvement
practices that make up the new plant approach (see Lawler,
1978, 1986, 1990a, 1991). A review of them will help to establish what the approach looks like and point out the degree to
which the approach constitutes a high-involvement approach to
management.

Selection of Employees

The selection process in the new plant approach is similar to the
approach recommended in Chapter Ten for high-involvement
organizations. It places a great deal of emphasis on acquainting
applicants with the nature of the jobs they are expected to fill
and the nature of the management style that will be used in the
organization. This emphasis allows people to decide whether
or not they want to work in a participative environment. A
great deal of the selection process is handled by production
employees. They interview and interact with the job applicants
and ultimately make the decision as to who will join the
organization.

The selection process is often a long one, with applicants
asked to do the actual work of the organization for a period of
time before they are hired. They are also often asked to join the
organization a considerable time before the start-up of a new
plant so that they can be involved in determining personnel
policies and establishing various procedures and work methods.
And they are typically sent to an existing plant so that they can
get a good sense of how the technology operates.

Physical Layout

The new plants are notable for the degree to which they have an
egalitarian physical workplace. Employees and managers tend

to park in the same parking lots, enter through the same doors and eat in the same cafeterias, and, in some cases, the managers have minimal offices or no offices. The physical layout of many new plants is designed to facilitate teamwork around particular products or services. For example, rather than having assembly lines, the plants often have manufacturing cells that build entire products.

Job Design

In the new plant approach, employees perform jobs that are challenging, involve doing a whole piece of work, and allow them to control how the work is carried out. Typically, this means that relatively self-managing work teams are responsible for the production of a whole product. They are self-managing in the sense that they make decisions about who performs which tasks on a given day; set their own production goals; and are often responsible for quality control, purchasing, and the control of absenteeism and employee behavior. Team members are expected to learn how to do all of the tasks that fall within the work area of the group.

Reward System

Most plants that adopt the new plant approach evaluate the skills of each individual and pay each person based on the number and kind of skills they have. Typically, everyone starts at the same salary, and as people learn more, they are paid more. All employees are considered salaried employees and no time clocks are used. Job security also is typically offered to all employees.

Organizational Structure

One of the most striking features of the new plants is their structure. These plants are characterized by very flat hierarchies and extremely wide spans of control. Typically, the traditional foreman's role is eliminated completely and multiple work teams report to an area manager. Most plants have only two levels of supervision, although some of the large plants may have three levels. A flat structure is important because it helps assure that work teams will have the autonomy to manage themselves. It also, of course, leads to considerable cost savings because it eliminates a number of highly paid managerial jobs. The new plant approach is also characterized by relatively lean staff groups. Work team members are given responsibility for areas such as quality control, employee selection, inventory management, and production scheduling that typically are done by staff specialists in traditional organizations.

Training

All the new plants place a heavy emphasis on training, career planning, and personal growth. This emphasis is usually backed up with extensive in-plant training programs and strong encouragement for employees to take part in training outside of work. A strong commitment to training and development of the work force is a cornerstone of the management practices in the new plant approach and is supported by the skill-based pay system.

Spread of the New Plant Approach

No definitive data exists on just how many companies have built plants using the new plant approach, but a good estimate is that the number of plants has grown to over five hundred. Procter & Gamble appears to be the organization that uses this approach most frequently. Since the late 1960s, every new plant Procter & Gamble has built has been based on this approach, giving the company a total of over fifteen new facilities that use it.

Some industries seem to be particularly high adopters of the new plant approach, especially chemical, food, and paper manufacturers. These industries need high levels of coordination among employees in order to operate the production process effectively. Because these industries are capital intensive, it also is critical that the plants be kept running and that they run efficiently. Efficient operation takes employee coordination, knowledge, and expertise; simply working "harder" and "faster" is not enough. Thus, companies in these industries can gain a competitive advantage by having employees who can solve problems, coordinate their behavior, and manage the production process themselves. And because these industries are capital intensive, labor costs are not a critical part of their cost structure.

The approach has also been applied in some service situations. In the airline industry, for example, SAS uses much of the thinking that underlies the new plant approach. Financial service companies also increasingly have been adopting it. For example, AT&T has used the approach in its financial service units (AT&T Capitol and American Transtech), as has American Express (IDS). A number of insurance companies have adopted the approach in units that do claims processing (for example, Lincoln National and Aid Association for Lutherans).

Converting old plants to the new plant approach has proven to be a difficult challenge. Indeed, few conversions were tried until the 1980s, and most organizations that have tried converting plants report slow going. One of the most important reasons why old plants are difficult to convert to the new plant approach is the deeply entrenched control-oriented cultures that are in place in the old plants. Another reason is that the managers and employees of the old plants were selected and socialized to work in a nonparticipative environment. Furthermore, the physical layout of the facilities often prevents the use of teams. Nevertheless, Amoco, Corning, Digital, Mead, Procter & Gamble, Rockwell, General Mills, TRW, Eaton, and a number of other companies have successfully converted a number of their old facilities.

Not surprisingly, the organizations that have been most successful in converting their old facilities are often the ones that were the early adopters of the new plant approach. They have seen firsthand the advantages of this approach and, therefore, feel a particular urgency to transfer it to their old locations. They also have greater knowledge of how to make it work than other companies. Thus, they have a competitive advantage in undertaking the difficult task of converting old plants to the new approach. Procter & Gamble is a leader in the conversion of old plants. For a number of years the company had successful participative new plants but no conversions of their old plants. In the 1980s, the company set out to systematically change all of its existing facilities to the new plant approach. When I asked why the company did this, Procter & Gamble managers typically responded that the company wants to get the same performance from the old plants that it gets from the new ones.

Increasingly, when they start a new facility, whether it be a production or service facility, organizations are deciding to use the new plant approach. The approach has gone from being a revolutionary set of ideas to being standard operating procedure in many organizations. In addition, many of the practices that are part of it have been developed and are much more mature technologies than when the first new plants were built. The new plant approach is supported by an extensive network of consultants and networks of adopters who meet regularly to exchange information and further develop the approach.

Toward High-Involvement Business Units

It is appropriate at this time to look back at the new plant approach and ask how it has stood the test of time. Are there weaknesses in it that have appeared as these plants have matured? Are there things that could have been done better or that need remedial attention? During the years since I first studied a new Gaines dog food plant in the early 1970s, I have had the opportunity to visit and study a number of plants that have used the new plant approach. My overall reaction to these visits has been one of great admiration. Virtually every plant has thrived and continues to be managed in a very participative way. Even the Gaines plant in Topeka, Kansas, often cited as an example of a "problem" participative plant, still is operating effectively and in a participative manner. Stories of the problems in this successful plant have been grossly exaggerated and generally are inaccurate. Despite the fact that the plant has changed plant managers and been sold several times, it remains an impressive participatively managed organization.

Although the plants I have visited have been and continue to be successful, they are not without problems and they are not the best models of employee involvement. I think they fall short of what can be done. The new plant approach was developed over twenty years ago; since then a great deal has changed and we know a lot more about how to design and manage organizations. Significant new management technologies have been developed, particularly in the areas of quality management and the utilization of information technology. In addition, the business environment has changed in many respects. Many markets have become global, and, as a result, organizations face higher performance standards for quality, speed, and costs.

The new plant approach focuses heavily on being sure that individuals have control over and information about their piece of the production process. It might best be called a *productivity involvement approach* or *plant-operations involvement approach* to management. Getting individuals involved in the business of the organization represents a significant step beyond this type of involvement. It requires the adoption of the same practices (for example, work teams, salaried work force, and skill-based pay) that are part of the new plant approach, but it requires going beyond them. Many of the other practices that were considered in earlier chapters that move information, knowledge, power, and rewards downward in an organization need to be adopted. Individuals at all levels of an organization need to receive new information, develop additional skills, be rewarded differently, and ultimately have the power to influence many parts of the business process.

When I wrote my first article about the new plant approach, I was able to report that some plants already existed that followed the model (Lawler, 1978). The same is not true with respect to the high-involvement approach that I will outline next. I know of no existing plant or business unit that fits the model perfectly; however, a number of organizations are clearly moving in this direction, including Corning, Mead, TRW, and Hewlett-Packard. If, as seems likely, this model can offer gains in the areas of overhead, quality, flexibility, and responsiveness to the business environment, then its widespread use is not far off.

Let us turn to a more detailed consideration of the features that need to be built into a manufacturing or service organization to create a high-involvement business unit in which individuals at all levels are involved in the business of the unit.

Organizational Structure

The new plant approach includes a flat organizational structure and the extensive use of self-managing teams. This basic design approach is appropriate for a high-involvement business unit as well. As discussed in previous chapters, it is particularly important that teams have the responsibility for producing a whole product or completely serving an identifiable customer base. Thus, in the manufacturing world, a team needs to be given responsibility for producing an entire product and needs to be given the responsibility for dealing directly with both customers and suppliers. Teams need to be responsible for all the value-added activities that occur with respect to a particular product. In service organizations, teams need to be given responsibility for performing all activities with respect to a particular customer. For example, work teams which are processing and managing mortgages for an individual, or handling their credit card business, need to be given responsibility for the entire service process with respect to the particular customer.

As stressed in Chapter Five, teams should have external customer-supplier relationships if possible because they provide the most realistic business experience for team members. They keep the team in contact with the competitive business environment and the kind of demands that the organization faces from its external markets and suppliers.

Often, staff support members, such as engineers and accountants, need to be members of a team so that the team can handle a full scope of business issues and in effect operate as a mini-enterprise. When teams can operate in this way, control and motivation are being provided by the external environment or market and little control by internal management is needed.

The physical layout of the facility needs to be designed to facilitate the teams' ability to produce an entire product or serve a customer completely. Equipment needs to be positioned so that employees who are on the same teams are located together. Staff support individuals need to be located in the production areas they support. Walls and other blocks to communication need to be minimized or eliminated as do symbols that indicate differences in power and status.

Some work designs present interesting examples of organizations giving teams responsibility for taking a product from suppliers to completion. For example, some Digital plants allow team members to deal directly with suppliers and give them direct contact with customers for the electronic products that the teams make. Team members have business cards and a toll-free telephone number appears on the products. Customers can call team members directly if they have a question or problem with the product that the team has produced. The teams are also encouraged to visit customers and to invite their suppliers into the plant to work with them in assuring high-quality supplies.

The new manufacturing facility of Volvo at Udevalla, Sweden, carries the team model further than any other manufacturing facility of which I am aware. This is the plant mentioned earlier in which teams build entire cars. The customer places an order directly with a manufacturing team, and the team informs the customer of the manufacturing schedule for the customer's car and invites the customer to be on hand when the car is built. Once the car is built, the team delivers it to the customer. After delivery, the team is given data that allow it to maintain an ongoing performance record for the car. A team can also communicate with the customer through information technology that ties it to the dealership and to the customer.

This approach ties a team that builds an entire car to a customer over a sustained period of time and allows the team to get ongoing feedback about the quality of the cars it produces and to respond to customers' questions and issues. It is still too early to determine if this approach is an economically viable alternative to the assembly line approach used so skillfully by the Japanese automobile companies, but without question it is an interesting effort at involving production employees in the business (Womack, Jones, and Roos, 1990).

Total Team Environment

The new plant approach stresses the use of teams at the production level, but does not create teams in other parts of the plant. Managers, office personnel, and staff support individuals have different jobs than in a traditional plant because they have to deal with teams, but they are not in a team structure. This inconsistency has created some problems and, in some respects, has limited the effectiveness of the new plant approach because staff support groups do not have the same kind of flexibility and performance gains that are characteristic of the production area.

The obvious solution to these problems is to create a "total team environment." Several organizations have done this by placing as many support people as possible in production teams and creating management teams and staff support teams. These teams meet regularly to allocate their time and effort and, like production teams, do a considerable amount of self-managing. They usually are not as flexible as the production teams since it is harder for individuals to learn other jobs in many staff and managerial roles. Nevertheless, with some cross-training they still can be flexible and do a substantial amount of self-management.

The use of team structures throughout the organization should contribute to an even flatter hierarchy than is characteristic of the new plant approach. The hierarchy in plants using a team approach in the production area is usually quite flat with wide spans of control, but there is always a limit to just how flat it can be because of the need to have a supervisor for at least every three or four work teams. Using a team supervision approach so that individuals in managerial jobs can help each other out and cover the varied work demand that is inherent in supervising a number of teams can help to flatten the hierarchy further.

Integration of Functions

The new plant approach typically has been applied to locations that do only manufacturing. Thus, employees in the manufacturing area have had little input or contact with individuals in product development, sales, customer service, and customer relations. This lack of contact means that in most organizations individuals are not involved in all areas of the business and do not have external customer contacts. This can be changed by better integration of other functions with the manufacturing process. As was mentioned earlier, the use of concurrent engineering by an increasing number of organizations represents just such a positive step. Hewlett-Packard and others who use this approach give their manufacturing employees an active role in product design in order to assure that new products can be quickly manufactured and brought to market.

When product development is located at manufacturing sites, it is easier to involve individuals in the manufacturing areas in product design and product development. Production employees may not know a lot about who the customers are for a product, but they do know a great deal about if and how a product can be manufactured. It is important to capture this expertise in the process of product development. Similarly, if the marketing and sales function is located in the manufacturing area, individuals in the manufacturing area can have an opportunity to deal with customers more directly and to have inputs to the marketing and sales process.

Locating product development, manufacturing, and marketing and sales together is not the only way to involve individuals in all phases of the business process. Task forces can involve individuals in all parts of the development, manufacture, and marketing of a product. Information technology can also be used to allow individuals in the manufacturing area to have input into product design, sales, and marketing activities (Davis and Davidson, 1991). Digital has used a computer network to give manufacturing employees the opportunity to comment on new product designs and, in some cases, to answer marketing and sales questions about the products and services they produce (Savage, 1990).

Reward System

Two important and visible features of the new plant approach are the extensive use of skill-based pay and the commitment to job security. Both of these features are consistent with an involvement approach that pushes information, knowledge, power, and rewards downward. However, in the new plant approach, a skill-based system is applied only to individuals who are in self-managing work teams, which in effect means it applies only to production employees. With the use of teams throughout the organization, it is appropriate to extend skill-based pay to all employees in the organization: staff, managerial, and clerical teams should have skill-based pay just as do production teams. Few organizations have extended skill-based pay to these employees, although Polaroid stands out as a notable exception. Skill-based pay has the potential to create a more flexible and knowledgeable work force, and it is highly congruent with a team-based management approach that stresses learning and continuous improvement.

Reward systems that are based upon organizational performance are nonexistent in the new plant approach. This is an enormous void, and one that needs to be filled for employees to achieve a high level of business involvement. Individuals need to be accountable for the performance of their business, and the best way to do this is to make their pay at least partially dependent upon the success of the organization through gainsharing plans, profit-sharing plans, and employee ownership. The discussion of these plans in Chapter Eight pointed out that a number of critical factors need to be considered in deciding just which approach or set of approaches fits a particular situation. The more parts of the business an individual unit or location can be held accountable for, the more important it is to use an approach which bases bonuses on the success of the business. As was suggested earlier, more than one pay-for-performance approach is likely to be appropriate in an organization. The key is to make an important part of each employee's compensation variable based on the controllable performance of his or her work unit. It may not be appropriate to use a gainsharing or other variable pay plan when a plant is just opening.

It is often difficult to design a good gainsharing plan in the beginning because it is hard to know what to measure and even harder to know what the performance standard should be.

However, an organization can make a commitment to the development of a gainsharing or profit-sharing plan and can begin the development of the plan within several years after the start-up of the new location or business.

In the new plant approach, teams make the decisions about who receives pay increases. There is no reason to change this feature of the reward system. In fact, with the greater use of teams, it is important to extend this decision-making power to white-collar and managerial teams. These teams may have a harder time making such decisions than do production teams. The quantification of performance and skill acquisition is more difficult in white-collar and managerial areas than it is in production areas. Nevertheless, this important feature needs to be built into these work teams as well because without it they cannot control a part of their environment that influences performance.

Technology to Improve Communication

When the new plant approach was developed, computers were used very little by organizations and computer networks were not used at all. The kinds of decisions that work team members could be involved in were limited by the lack of computers because it was difficult to deliver many kinds of information to employees in a timely fashion. With the advent of cheap computing and sophisticated information system networks, the situation has changed dramatically. It is now possible for all employees to have almost immediate access to personal computers or terminals that are linked to corporatewide information systems. Some companies, including IBM, Digital, and Sun Microsystems, are close to achieving this type of system. Their employees have immediate access to a great deal of information about the business, local operations, and operations in other plants. Thus, they can be involved in a wide range of decisions and get feedback in areas where it was not practical before.

As was stressed in Chapter Nine, a high-involvement approach to management needs to take advantage of information technology so that individuals have access to a great deal of data about what is occurring in other areas of the company and how their product or service is performing, how it is seen by customers, and how much it is costing to produce. Access to this information can increase tremendously the amount of feedback employees receive as well as change their decision-making processes so that they can consider more than just quality and production numbers. It can allow them to confront the economic tradeoffs that are involved in their performance and thus enable them to be involved in the business.

If arranged correctly, information technology can also help with problem solving and education. For example, it can allow employees to communicate with each other when they have a technical problem and avoid the entire process of going up and down the hierarchy to find out who has expertise in a particular area and what the correct solution is for a problem. A considerable amount of education and training can be done electronically. Since training is critical in high-involvement management, it makes sense to use electronic means to teach individuals what they need to know in order to understand and participate in their business.

Television can be used to help link employees who are involved in different aspects of the production or service process. Videotapes can show employees what other employees outside their work area are doing, or as has been done in some plants, individuals earlier in the production process can be linked to those later in the production process by closed-circuit video cameras. These systems improve communication and understanding of employees throughout the production process. They help individuals conceptualize what is going on elsewhere in the production process so that they can suggest improvements.

Information technology also can help managers deal with the large number of individuals for which they are responsible. At Cypress Semiconductor, for example, every team and individual maintains a list of ten to fifteen goals, with due dates, start dates, and relevent measurement data. This information is put on the company's computer network so a manager can relatively quickly review these data to see what is occurring throughout the organization and can intervene when performance problems occur and where effort is misdirected. This system also helps to make the organization's structure flexible since it can, in effect, be changed simply by individuals or teams taking on new activities and new goals for themselves.

Technology to Improve Quality

When the new plant approach was first implemented in the late 1960s, very little was known in the United States about the type of quality programs that were being used in Japan. The situation has changed dramatically since then. Virtually every major corporation has a total quality management system that is based on the work of Juran, Deming, and Crosby. These so-called quality gurus have had a strong impact on the way quality is conceived of in the United States. They stress the importance of employee involvement in producing high-quality products and offer a number of specific management tools to improve the quality of products. In many respects, their concept of employee involvement is much more limited than the one used in the new plant approach, but this does not mean that the tools for improving product quality that they have to offer are inappropriate. Indeed, organizations using the new plant approach need to adopt most of these tools because they can help work teams and plants do a better job of managing themselves and understanding their production or service process.

Statistical process control, cost-of-qualtiy measurement, self-inspection, and some of the problem-solving approaches that are part of the technology for improving quality fit well with a high-involvement approach. When they are installed in a high-involvement business unit, they can substantially improve the ability of teams to understand their work process and become more self-managing. The focus on continuous improvement that is found in the total quality approach should be combined with a focus on competitive benchmarking. Together, these two features can help reinforce the need to constantly look for better ways to operate in a world in which performance standards for most products and services are always going up.

Work teams can make continuous improvements if they are given the appropriate information and support, but separate structures may also be required to address organization-wide improvements. As was stressed in the earlier discussion of improvement teams, an organization may need to create task forces or design teams that assess the organization and look at its competitive position. These groups need to use attitude surveys and competitive benchmarking to see how well the organization is operating and then to involve people within the organization in the improvement process.

It is hard to say exactly how often an extensive organizational renewal or assessment process should be undertaken, but I estimate that it should be done at least every two years, with competitive benchmarking being done at least annually. Customers and suppliers can be invited to contribute to the process. Similarly, outside experts in critical areas can be brought in to help describe the newest management technologies and the newest manufacturing technologies.

Chapter Fourteen

Manage the Change
Toward
High-Involvement

I f it's so great, why doesn't everyone do it already?" When I talk about high-involvement management, I hear this question repeatedly. Implicit in the question is the assumption that people in general, and those in organizations in particular, typically behave in the way that is most effective. But people do not always make well-informed rational choices. In addition, if one looks at the obstacles to changing a traditional organization to one that practices high-involvement management, it is rather surprising that any organization makes the change.

I have already discussed why organizations should change to high-involvement management. It offers potential improvements in speed, cost, and quality—key performance indicators for almost any organization. In addition, it is more consistent with the national values of the United States and many other countries than is top-down autocratic management.

A number of organizational realities make it very difficult for existing organizations to change to high-involvement management. The whole thrust of this book has been to argue that high-involvement management is not a fine tuning of the traditional bureaucratic management style but rather a complete change in the way an organization operates. All of the internal systems, operating procedures, and structures of most organizations need to be changed in order for them to move to high-involvement management. In short, a massive change is needed, one that may take not just years but in some cases decades to complete (Mohrman and others, 1989).

Sometimes, an organization that wishes to practice high-involvement management must adopt management technologies that are not fully developed. For example, skill-based pay and gainsharing, although not new, are certainly not as well developed as are such traditional compensation practices as the point factor approach to job evaluation and merit pay systems. Thus, not only does any organization that wants to move to high-involvement management have to make a major change in how it administers rewards, it also must abandon proven methods and move to ones that can best be described as in the developmental stage.

Adopting a strategy that is still being developed requires an organization to do some development of its own and spend time monitoring the environment and learning what other organizations are doing (Mohrman and Cummings, 1989). In this way, an organization can maintain state-of-the-art systems as technologies develop. Keeping up with developing technologies is expensive, and the cost may deter an organization from changing its management system.

Creation Versus Resurrection

In many respects, the easiest place to start to practice high-involvement management is in a new company. Employees are typically highly involved in an organization when it is just beginning. The challenge is to keep them involved and to avoid the bureaucratic structures and encumbrances that create indifferent employees who neither care about nor understand the business of their organization. Organizations like Compaq Computer and Sun Microsystems have shown that even with fast growth it is possible to keep individuals involved in and caring about the business.

Clearly, it is easier to start a new organization unit with a high-involvement approach to management than it is to move one from a traditional to a high-involvement approach, as has been shown in the case of new plants and other new organizational units. However, even with a new unit, some cost is involved in protecting the new entity from the existing systems in the organization so that it can behave differently (Beer, Eisenstat, and Spector, 1990a, 1990b). But this challenge is small compared to the challenge that an organization faces when it wishes to make the transformation from traditional management to high-involvement management.

Maybe we should simply forget about trying to change the large bureaucratic organizations that populate the business environment and assume that they will go the way of the dinosaur and other species whose time has simply come and gone. Evolution eliminates those species that simply are not effective in the current environment (McKelvey, 1980). Clearly, in some businesses, the time has passed when a traditional bureaucratic organization can be effective enough to survive. Many of the large bureaucratic organizations in North America are failing to successfully adapt to the new world.

The Fortune 500 companies accounted for a smaller and smaller percentage of the total production of goods and services in the United States during the 1980s and this trend probably will continue. Many of the large organizations in Europe (such as Phillips Electronics) also are in trouble and need to dramatically increase their operating effectiveness. General Motors, Ford, AT&T, and IBM are significantly smaller than they were just a few years ago, despite the fact that the markets in which they compete continue to grow. They simply have lost market share, sometimes to foreign competitors and sometimes to new organizations in the United States that are more flexible and innovative in the way they manage.

Despite the difficulties that many large bureaucratic organizations have had during the last decade, I am optimistic that at least some of them can change and survive. Some of these organizations have gone through major reorientations and changes that have made them much more effective (Beer, Eisenstat, and Spector, 1990a). For most organizations, the key question is not whether they will succeed by doing business as usual or go out of business, it is how they will try to change. Business as usual is not a viable option. Organizations considering change appear to be choosing one of two approaches to management: the high-involvement approach or the total quality approach. While these approaches overlap in many important ways, they also differ in some important ways. Recent research shows that about three-fourths of the Fortune 1000 companies are emphasizing total quality management while the other one-fourth of the companies are emphasizing high-involvement management (Lawler, Mohrman, and Ledford, 1992).

Total Quality Versus High-Involvement

In several respects, it is not surprising that total quality management is more popular than the high-involvement approach. Total quality management is a powerful tool, one that has been used extremely effectively by many Japanese organizations to gain a competitive edge (Womack, Jones, and Roos, 1990). It requires less organizational change than does high-involvement management and, as a result, is less threatening. Many of the statements about involvement in the writings on total quality management say that employees should be involved as part of total quality process (Deming, 1986). Although the total quality approach stresses employee involvement, the type of involvement it stresses is limited to allowing employees to make suggestions and control certain elements of the production process and the quality-control process. It does not suggest that organizations be restructured and redesigned to emphasize employees having the information, knowledge, power, and rewards that will give them a business experience. Instead, employees are given information, knowledge, and power to improve certain elements of the organization's work processes.

When an organization installs the total quality approach, it usually creates new training programs and parallel groups, changes managerial behavior, and develops new information systems. Admittedly, these are significant changes, but these changes are not as great as the ones required to move an organization to the high-involvement approach. In many cases an organization using the total quality approach can remain within a hierarchical model and keep its structure organized around functions. This approach does not require or advocate self-managing teams that have responsibility for significant pieces of the business, nor does it require or advocate financial rewards that tie into the success of the overall organization and business units.

Because it does not put as much information, knowledge, and power in the hands of employees, total quality management is understandably very popular and comfortable for most organizations that have been traditionally managed. It is particularly comfortable for senior managers because it does not require them to make radical changes in their sense of being in control over operations; in fact, it may give them a greater sense of control.

A total quality program may either be the right first step toward creating a high-involvement organization or it may be as far as an organization should go in employee involvement. If, in fact, a more hierarchical management approach fits the business an organization is in, total quality management can lead to just the kinds of improvements in organizational performance that are needed. However, if the business is one in which the organization does complex work, faces a turbulent environment, has to react quickly, and must continuously improve its costs and quality, then high-involvement management would seem to be the best choice.

Although total quality fits with some parts of the American culture, it fits particularly well with the core of the Japanese culture. The lack of fit with the American culture raises the question of whether the United States can ever achieve parity with the Japanese in practicing total quality management. Indeed, even if the United States could hope to achieve parity, it is unlikely that it could achieve a competitive advantage with this management approach.

The high-involvement approach to management, however, represents a way of achieving competitive advantage that is Western in origin and values. It operates without the hierarchical approval processes, written suggestions, and bureaucratic trappings that go along with total quality management.

Self-managing mini-enterprises and business units that directly face external customers fit well with the values of entrepreneurism and democracy. The high-involvement approach has a potential for energizing employees in a way that the rigidity, discipline, and hierarchical structures of total quality management do not. Not every situation is right for the high-involvement approach and not every management is capable of using it, but where it is right it offers gains that can go beyond those of the total quality approach. These gains are perhaps uniquely available to organizations that exist in a culture with a strong emphasis on entrepreneurial behavior, democratic values, individual decision making, and teamwork.

High-involvement management represents a potential competitive advantage for the United States and for much of Europe, but it probably cannot be copied effectively by the Japanese because it does not fit their values well. High-involvement management potentially can lead to a microcosm in the workplace of what is best about Western cultures: control through environmental demands, control through competition, and a strong focus on self-determination, individual rights, and human development. It represents a giant step beyond the bureaucratic model of organizing that has been the basis for large-scale organizations for centuries. Where it fits the strategy of an organization, it can offer a substantial competitive advantage.

Creating Change

What must happen for large organizations to change to high-involvement management? I would like to approach this question by looking at what needs to be done by managers, employees, union leaders, board members, and the government.

Managers

The group that has the most to lose and the most to gain from major organizational changes is senior management, particularly if an existing organization changes from traditional management to high-involvement management. I believe the major reason why more U.S. organizations have not changed to high-involvement management is the failure of senior managers to provide leadership in this area.

Senior managers are often unwilling to lead the change to high-involvement management for several reasons. Major change in the way an organization is managed can take ten years to produce significant advantages and many senior managers are not in their jobs that long. Perhaps more important, senior managers often are very comfortable with the power, authority, and rewards that are associated with their positions and do not want to risk losing them. In addition, these managers have fine-tuned their skills over decades so that they will be effective in a traditional top-down organization.

A change to high-involvement management requires that senior managers learn new skills and that they give up some of the special perquisites and financial rewards that they receive. Indeed, given all the rewards, both psychological and financial, that are associated with being a senior manager in a large U.S. corporation, it is hard to imagine why these managers would ever lead a change effort that threatens their power, authority, and rewards. The only reason that they would take this leadership role, of course, is their desire to have a meaningful impact on their organization, an impact that will assure the organization's survival and effectiveness.

Unfortunately, U.S. business has not been blessed with a large number of senior managers who are willing to make a commitment to transforming their organizations (Tichy and Devanna, 1986). Most executives seem to have chosen to do business as usual, at least with respect to how the business is managed, and to reap the rewards that are associated with business as usual. It is important to note that those rewards have been more than ample by world-class standards, and, thus, it is hardly surprising that business as usual has been the norm rather than the exception (Foulkes, 1991).

A new generation of senior executives who see their role as one of building and developing an organization rather than one of managing assets is needed to change traditional organizations. Unfortunately, most managers do not get to senior management positions because they are interested in or knowledgeable about how to design and manage large organizations. Instead, they are in power because they are good at particular functional specialties. The functional specialty that leads to senior management positions varies depending upon the organization. It may be finance, marketing, or production. All too common, however, is the promotion to senior management positions of intelligent, ambitious individuals who are not well-developed managers.

A senior manager needs to be an expert in management, someone who is passionate about improving the organization's effectiveness and who provides leadership as well as better management systems. Some existing staff groups can provide expertise in particular functional specialties, but no one else can provide leadership and manage large-scale organizational changes. This type of leadership can only come from the senior managers or the senior management team. Senior managers are the ones who must focus on how the organization is designed and managed and who must constantly monitor its effectiveness. They must understand a great deal about organizational effectiveness and performance and, in their own ways, be organizational theorists. Certainly, senior managers must understand the various functional specialties that exist within the organization, but they must also be the chief architects and designers of the organization and the way it is managed.

I have worked with hundreds of top executives and, unfortunately, it is rare to find one who is obsessed with making the organization more effective. All too often they are obsessed with getting the financing for a new project, marketing a new product, or making a new acquisition. These are all important tasks, but many of them can and should be done elsewhere in the organization. The one activity that can only be done by senior managers is the organizing, designing, and leading of the organization. Until organizations begin to value this function and develop senior managers to fill it, effective organizations will be the exception rather than the rule.

Currently, the senior management in most companies presents both the single greatest obstacle to the adoption of high-involvement management and the greatest opportunity for change. Chief executive officers like Jack Welch of General Electric, Robert Galvin of Motorola, and Paul Allaire of Xerox, clearly see their role as leading and determining how their organization is managed. The popularity of books on management and leadership points to the possibility that more and more managers will take a leadership role in determining how their organization is managed. Many of the next generation of managers have gone to business school. They grew up during an era in which democracy and participation were increasingly practiced in business, and they have seen that traditional bureaucratic organizations have their problems. Thus, they represent a chance for a significant break with the past.

For large-scale changes to take place in the way organizations are managed, it is vital that organizations become populated with managers who can and will lead transformations. I believe this is the single most important thing that needs to occur in order for more high-involvement organizations to be created.

Managers who are not at the senior level of management may well wonder if they can do anything to move their organization toward high-involvement management. If they have the support of senior management, lower-level managers can help implement and improve the new management systems that are installed. They also need to change their behavior.

Much has been written about the "negative power" of middle-level and low-level managers (Rosow and Zager, 1990; Walton and Schlesinger, 1979). They are often rightly described as major obstacles to change. Major changes may make them redundant or at least require them to learn new skills and behave differently. It is critical that organizations making major changes provide managers with the training and counseling services they need in order to change. They also need to guarantee the employment security of those who commit to changing.

In the absence of senior-level support, managers can do some things to foster organizational change, but their power is limited. As was discussed in Chapter Eleven, they can change their own behavior in ways that are more supportive of moving information, knowledge, power, and certain kinds of rewards to the employees who work for them. They may be able to restructure some work and produce small high-involvement units. As will be discussed later, changes of this type are particularly fragile since they can be undone by the next supervisor who comes along. Often, these changes are only made at the particular location and do not influence or change the rest of the organization. Nevertheless, these changes can be institutionalized and in some cases can be the basis for large-scale changes (Beer, Eisenstat, and Spector, 1990a, 1990b).

Employees

Just as high-involvement management requires managers to change their behaviors, it also requires employees to change their behaviors through taking responsibility for their actions, committing themselves to seeing that their organization is effective, and increasing and developing their skills. Clearly, not all employees want to make the kind of changes that are required for them to be successful in a high-involvement organization. In fact, employee resistance is one of the many obstacles that an organization has to overcome when it switches from a traditional to a high-involvement approach to management.

Often, employees have given up the idea of finding a work situation in which they can make a meaningful commitment and become involved. They have committed themselves to nonwork activities and may not be interested in changing their commitments. And some individuals simply are not capable of being responsible members of a high-involvement organization. In my experience, however, the problems with the employees is much smaller than the problem with the managers. Most employees see the chance to participate in a high-involvement organization as a positive opportunity and readily respond to the ideas and values that are basic to high-involvement management.

In some of the organizations I have worked with, employees have pointed out that it is much more stressful to work in a high-involvement setting. The responsibilities, the pressures of learning, and some of the interpersonal processes involved are new to many employees. As a general rule, employees do work through these issues and ultimately prefer a high-involvement approach. Although the employees do feel stress, they usually can manage it because they can do concrete things to reduce it and control it. The kind of stress that is particularly debilitating is stress that is caused by events that employees do not feel they can control and to which they cannot respond adequately (Kahn, 1981).

Union Leaders

In many traditional organizations, union leaders need to make enormous changes if organizations are to practice high-involvement management. As was discussed in Chapter Twelve, high-involvement management requires that union leaders be committed to seeing that the organization is effective and that employees are involved in making important decisions. It does not require that they totally abandon their adversarial role, but it does require that this role become only a part of their activities rather than their reason for being. The change in role that high-involvement management calls for clearly is one that many union leaders who have practiced traditional adversarial labor-management relationships have trouble making. Indeed, in my work with unions, I often find that new union leaders are more receptive to employee involvement than are veteran union leaders. They realize that the economic and social-political environment is a radically different one than the one that existed in the 1930s, when many unions gained their foothold in American businesses. They also have different skills and are not threatened by the loss of an adversarial relationship.

If major changes are going to take place in unionized organizations, a new generation of union leaders needs to emerge at the senior level of unions. This new generation needs to focus on what value a union can add to the organization and be confident of its ability to relate to management on business issues as well as on issues of employee rights and due process. Autoworkers, steelworkers, and communications workers have had senior union leaders with the kind of values, skills, and insights that have helped them move toward a new labor-management relationship (Hoerr, 1991). Unfortunately, union leaders with the kind of vision and skills that are required to transform an existing organization to a high-involvement one have been relatively rare. Because union leaders have not taken a proactive role in many situations, management has assumed that change is impossible and business as usual has been the norm in many unionized workplaces (Lawler, Ledford, and Mohrman, 1989).

I do not believe that most organizations can survive in global businesses if they have traditional labor-management relationships. These adversarial relationships are simply too expensive and too inefficient. Unions do not need to disappear, but traditional labor-management relationships do. The senior leaders in unions need to play an important role in transforming this relationship because managers cannot do it by themselves.

Board Members

Boards of U.S. companies usually are made up of senior managers from the company and some outside board members, many of whom are executives in other corporations. Boards need to be structured quite differently, however, if they are to be consistent with high-involvement management.

The degree to which a board is dominated by internal members versus external members is one issue. The argument for having outside board members who are more than tokens is particularly compelling in the case of high-involvement management. These outsiders should be powerful enough both in numbers and stature to check any tendencies on the part of executives to act arbitrarily or unilaterally on issues that directly affect employees and, of course, issues that are in the self-interest of senior managers, such as their level of pay. More than in traditional organizations, it is also important that these outsiders be experts in management. They need to have the ability to help the organization compare itself to the outside world in terms of its managerial effectiveness and to understand and assess how the organization is managed. They need to be able to go beyond the organization's financial performance and look at the business from the perspective of organizational behavior so that they can anticipate future problems and assure that the management is competent.

Perhaps the most important issue in high-involvement organizations is the presence on the board of employees. All employees have a significant stake in the success of the organization and, thus, should be represented on the board. Having employees on the board is also consistent with the general philosophy that information, knowledge, power, and rewards should move downward in the organization. In large organizations, this representation may be mostly symbolic. Nonmanagement employees, as a whole, cannot directly participate in the decisions of these boards, but, nevertheless, at least employees can be assured that someone is speaking for them. In short, the board can be a kind of representative democracy.

The idea of employees being on boards is far from a new one. A number of European companies have included employees on boards for years because it is mandated by law. Not surprisingly, this inclusion has not worked well when it has been done simply to fulfill a legal requirement. For it to work, employee board members need to be seen as a valuable resource and as representatives of an important group of stakeholders.

Chrysler added a union representative to its board when it was in financial trouble and needed union support for a financial restructuring. Employees are also board members in some ESOP companies (such as Wierton Steel) because employees own part or all of the company. However, including employees has not become an accepted practice in the United States; undoubtedly because it is inconsistent with the way most U.S. companies are managed.

Government

In some countries, the government has tried to actively legislate employee involvement. Perhaps the most aggressive action in this area has been in Sweden, but Germany, Norway, France, and other countries also have legislated various forms of worker participation in decision making. The United States has a considerable body of legislation protecting individual rights and enabling employees to join unions but little legislation that requires organizations to give employees a say in the way their organizations are run. For example, there is no legislation requiring that employees sit on boards of directors or even be able to comment on the major decisions that the organization makes. Indeed, employees do not even have to be informed of most important decisions that their organizations make. The plant-closing legislation that requires minimal notification of a plant shutdown is a notable exception to this and was seen as very controversial when it became law. Simply stated, there is little legislation which establishes that employees are important stakeholders in the organizations for which they work.

Some laws in the United States get in the way of employee involvement and participation. For example, some of the secrecy laws concerning financial disclosure prohibit the dissemination of certain kinds of information. The laws that cover overtime pay get in the way of treating all employees in an egalitarian way because they require organizations to identify two types of employees (exempt and nonexempt). And some of the laws that enable employees to join unions can make it difficult for companies to involve nonunion employees in decisions that affect their wages, hours of work, and working conditions (Lawler, 1986). Overall, however, even though some legal obstacles to employee participation exist in the United States, they certainly are not significant enough to prevent an organization from adopting high-involvement management.

There is one governmental program, the Malcolm Baldrige National Quality Award, that is designed to move organizations toward more employee involvement. This annual award recognizes those organizations that insititute practices that lead to high-quality products and services, including such practices as problem-solving groups. In addition, it encourages organizations to train their employees and to give them information related to quality. The award seems to have had a positive impact on management practices; at the very least, it has alerted U.S.

corporations to the need for change in the way they manage and in some organizations has produced real change.

Political commentators vary widely in what they think the role of the government should be in changing the way in which organizations are managed. At one extreme, some individuals argue that organizations are controlled too much by the government and that this control helps to create the competitiveness problem that exists in the United States. At the other extreme, some individuals would like to see organizations mandated to practice employee involvement because it is consistent with the national values of the country and potentially very effective (U.S. Department of Health, Education, and Welfare, 1973; Sashkin, 1984). I tend to fall somewhere in the middle of these two extremes. I do not feel that participative management can or should be legislated (Lawler, 1982). If employee participation is mandated through legislation, it could end up as a sham in which management manipulates employees to avoid giving them a role in important decisions. What governments do best is protect the rights of individuals to organize unions and receive due process with respect to conditions of employment and pay. They also can provide information, knowledge, and incentives that support change.

The U.S. government could offer more information, knowledge, and incentives to encourage the adoption of participative management. It has made a small but important step in this direction with the creation of the Baldrige award and with the dissemination of information on new approaches to management. But, it could do a great deal more, particularly in the area of research and development and dissemination of information on management practices. Little government funding currently exists for research on management practices, and, as a result, good data on the effectiveness of many management practices is not available.

Companies are unlikely to fund needed research on organizational effectiveness because it is not necessarily in their interest to invest in studying practices that already seem to work for them or, for that matter, practices that do not seem to work for them. Even if they do research, companies are not inclined to share information about what is effective for them. Indeed, if they view their approach as a competitive advantage, which many do, sharing information about the effectiveness of a practice weakens their competitive advantage. Just this type of thinking caused Procter & Gamble to close its new plants to visitors for almost twenty years. Thus, it is important that the government, as it has done in agriculture, be a powerful force in supporting research and disseminating information about the effectiveness of different management practices (Commission on the Skills of the American Workforce, 1990).

Throughout this book, I have emphasized that an educated, responsible work force is necessary for high-involvement management. The government needs to play an important role in preparing individuals to work in high-involvement organizations (Rosow and Zager, 1988). The public education system needs to provide organizations with individuals who have the basic skills to work in a high-involvement organization — it is unreasonable to expect organizations to do the entire education job themselves. Teaching employees basic skills is expensive, and it is often easier and cheaper for organizations to go to another country where either the wages are low so employees do not have to add a great deal of value to the product or individuals have the critical basic skills and do not need extensive training (Reich, 1991). Thus, if high-wage countries like the United States are going to compete successfully for value-added work, the government must educate a large portion of the society in the skills that are necessary to operate in high-involvement organizations (Commission on the Skills of the American Workforce, 1990).

The case can be made for the government encouraging companies to report to their shareholders on their managerial effectiveness. Currently, corporations are only required to report information about financial accounting data. This information gives one view of how effective the organization is, but it fails to tell investors and the public anything about how the organization is managed. Elsewhere, I have argued for broad social reporting on the part of corporations (Mirvis and Lawler, 1984). For example, an organization could be encouraged or required by the government to report on its human resources development practices and the condition of the organization as well as on the social costs that it creates for society. This report could include employee cost and attitude data as well as data concerning accident, turnover, and absenteeism rates.

At this point, the methods and measures that are needed for required reporting on the part of corporations are not well developed. Considerable work needs to be done. Organizations are unlikely to make such reports voluntarily. If, however, these means of reporting were developed, I think a strong case could be made for requiring it. This kind of information could be quite useful to shareholders in deciding where to invest their money and to employees in deciding where to work. It also could help society decide how to tax and deal with corporations. In the absence of this kind of information, it is difficult for employees, investors, and the public to make informed judgments about how a particular organization is being managed. At this point, I would not recommend that the government begin to require social reporting on the part of corporations but rather that the government become much more actively involved in research and development in this area. Governmental support is needed for the development of reporting formats and methods.

Overall I am hesitant to see the government go much beyond research, development, and education in their support of changes in management practice. Requiring certain management practices violates the idea of a free market with regard to management methods and is inconsistent with a free society that operates a market-based economy.

Change at the Organizational Level

Managing change at the organizational level is a complex and challenging undertaking. It is impossible to write a formula that all organizations can or should follow in order to transform their management approach from a traditional one to a high-involvement one. However, organizations can and should follow some general principles in managing this change process.

Leadership

Given what I have said so far in this chapter, it is hardly surprising that I feel senior managers must play an important role in any change effort. It is vital that senior managers be committed to and support any major organizational changes, particularly when the changes involve how an entire organization operates. When an organization is changing to a high-involvement style of management, senior managers face the challenge of directing or leading a nondirective change process; that is, they need to create a climate and a demand that pulls change out of the organization at the grass-roots level. Even in a traditional organization, senior managers have limited power to mandate corporate renewal from the top. They can create a climate in which renewal and change is supported and, indeed, even required, but they need to leave the actual details of the implementation and the design to individuals at the lower levels of the organization.

Ultimately, as was stressed in Chapter Eleven, senior managers have to change their own behavior and performance to be supportive of high-involvement management, but this does not have to be the starting place for the organizational change. Senior managers can, for a period of time, ask others in the organization to do something that they themselves are not doing. Ultimately though, senior managers need to change their own behavior to be consistent with the way they are asking the rest of the organization to behave. Of course, there is nothing wrong with senior managers leading the organizational change by modeling the new management approach that they wish the organization to take. Indeed, this may be the best way to start the change.

Research suggests that organizations do not change unless there is a clear business-based reason for change that involves organizational effectiveness (Beer, Eisenstat, and Spector 1990a; Mohrman and others, 1989). This is hardly surprising given the enormity of the effort required to make a major change in the way an organization is managed. Senior managers must clearly present the reason for change to the rest of the organization.

Some organizations have successfully changed on the basis of implementing new values and aligning themselves better with shared national or cultural values (DePree, 1987). However, in my experience, the organizations that have successfully changed based on values and doing what is "right" are few and far between. Most senior managers simply are not good at leading value-based change programs because they are not particularly good at articulating their values and using them as a motivating device. And sustaining and institutionalizing value-driven change is often difficult because values tend to get lost in the day-to-day pressures of meeting business demands.

What then is the best foundation upon which to build a program for change? I am convinced that it is organizational effectiveness and business necessity. Most of the successful organizational changes that I have seen were started because an organization needed to respond to a business issue. Business issues are the one thing that individuals from the top to the bottom of the organization can identify with and see as a common bonding agent. Incidentally, an organization does not always require a major crisis in order to accomplish a major change, although it is easiest to mobilize effort for change during a crisis. Motivation to change can be created without a crisis, however, if a leader can create a vision of a better world and provide strong support for the vision. The major changes made by General Electric during the 1980s, for example, were not driven by a crisis so much as by the leadership of Jack Welch. Xerox made organizational changes during a crisis, but it also had the strong leadership of David Kearns.

Senior managers, in most cases, are the people who must articulate how the change process relates to solving the business problem (Bennis, 1989). It is also up to senior managers to call attention to the business problem so that individuals throughout the organization see the need for change. As mentioned earlier, once the general direction has been set, the details of how the organization responds to the business problem can and should come from people throughout the organization.

How does an organization develop leaders that can manage the process of change? First, leadership needs to be an important criterion for promotion. All too often, organizations stress technical excellence in a function as the basis for promotion rather than leadership excellence and the ability to manage change. Leadership can be developed (McCall, 1988; Bennis, 1989). For managers to become effective senior leaders of change, they should have career tracks that move them across functions and, where possible, across different business units. These moves need to be based on learning opportunities rather than upward hierarchical movement. For example, new managers can be moved into well-managed units within the organization and can report to an individual who is a particularly effective leader and manager.

Organizations also need to assess managers on their leadership and managerial skills. General Electric and Xerox are two companies that are increasingly assessing managers on their ability to lead. Xerox for example, gathers attitude data from managers' subordinates and uses the data to determine who should be promoted. General Electric uses assessment teams to gather data from all levels in the organization to be sure the managers it promotes are capable of effectively leading the organization.

Strategies for Change

All too often organizations seem to assume that the way to produce a change in management style is to invest large amounts of money in changing manager's attitudes and skills. Training certainly is important, but decades of research have shown that changing managerial behavior requires much more than simply training managers in participative decision making and in the importance of focusing on human resources and listening to people (Campbell, Dunnette, Lawler, and Weick, 1970). Important structural changes need to be made in an organization in order to change the way it and its managers operate. This point takes us back to the beginning of this book where I said that meaningful change requires multiple systems to change in any complex organization. To change the way an organization behaves, the organization must change work structures, reward systems, decision-making processes, information systems, and human resources management practices. Thus, the most successful change programs are multifaceted (Argyris, 1970). They do not just offer training or change the reward system; they literally grab the organization by the neck and change multiple systems in a relatively short period of time.

Some of the most dramatic change programs are ones in which a total organization has been changed virtually overnight. This is obviously a high-risk strategy but one that may be appropriate if the organization needs to quickly change its effectiveness. A good example of this kind of change process is provided by those organizations that have, in essence, created a new organization by shutting down the old organization and beginning operations anew shortly thereafter. I have seen this approach used in a General Electric plant and in a Motorola plant.

In both of these cases, the old organization was literally completely abandoned along with all of its pay practices, organizational structures, traditional job designs, and, in some cases, even physical layout. Within a few weeks after the old ways were abandoned, the organization started operating with new systems in almost every area. Initially, of course, the changes caused a tremendous amount of chaos and disruption. Ultimately, however, the organization began to operate in new and better ways. This approach short-circuited what often is a decade-long change process. Admittedly, the costs of the changes were high in the short term, but in the long term, the organizations probably were substantially ahead of where they would have been if they had tried an evolutionary change in which parts were changed over several years.

The emphasis so far in this discussion has been on change that is led from the top. As was mentioned earlier, organizational change can also originate at the bottom of an organization. Changes started at the bottom can ultimately produce significant changes throughout the organization. For example, many of the most successful new plants are clear examples of bottom-up change. A single manager or a small group of managers at the lowest levels of the organization decided that it was time to manage differently in a particular unit of the organization. They started new plants that fit the new plant approach and served as insulators between their unit of the organization and the total organization. They had to serve as insulators because many of the practices that they needed to put in place were directly contrary to standard operating procedure in their organizations.

The same issues come up time and time again when a small unit or group of employees wishes to practice high-involvement management while the rest of the organization is managed in a traditional way. Under these conditions, it is extremely time consuming and labor intensive for the small group to begin high-involvement management. The group must be given exemptions from many standard systems so that it can operate in radically different ways. If they can gain these exemptions, local units often can successfully operate in a high-involvement manner.

Even if small units are successful in changing to high-involvement management, the total organization may not change. Indeed, bottom-up change often is not a particularly effective way to change total organizations. Instead of seeing the advantages of what units of the organization are doing and deciding to adopt the new practices, all too often, organizations encapsulate the divergent units. Many of the managers and others in the traditional organization resist adopting the changes, probably because they are threatened by what they see in units that have adopted different practices. Indeed, in some cases, change may be even more difficult to institute organizationwide after a single unit has been successful in making a change because other members of the organization have a chance to study the change and learn how to resist it. Also, they view the change as someone else's idea, so even if they successfully adopt it they may not get much credit.

It is not easy to decide whether or not to start a major change effort in a small unit or isolated part of an organization.

The chances of changes in small units influencing the total organization depend on senior management support for organizationwide change. Thus, before making a change in a small unit, those people involved must make a realistic assessment of the probability that they can win support for the change throughout the organization. If this support seems unlikely, they must consider how effectively they can insulate the unit.

If the organization is a highly decentralized one with dramatically different business units, insulating one unit may be possible and it can be "safe" to go ahead with a major organizational change in one unit or part of the organization. On the other hand, if the organization is an integrated one with a relatively strong culture, changing a small unit with little probability of producing organizational change typically is not a good idea. In fact, making the change could harm the careers of the individuals involved and harm the organization as well.

Learning Model of Change

For a number of reasons, the best organizational change programs approach making changes as a learning experience (Mohrman and Cummings, 1989). First, rarely does an organization get everything right the first time when making a change. Even with great planning and study, change programs are simply too complex to ever expect that all the right decisions will be made initially, particularly if the change has a bottom-up component to it. Because of the natural experimental environment that is created by a move to employee involvement, different parts of the organization may try different things. It is important that the knowledge about effectiveness that results from this experimentation be shared. What works for one part of the organization may in fact be important information for another part of the organization. An environment must be created in which this kind of learning can be transferred and accepted without a great deal of the "not invented here" resistance that is so common in large organizations.

Again, senior managers can play an important role in helping to create a learning environment by not punishing failure and by rewarding successful sharing of information. Also, they personally can help carry messages and information about what has worked in one part of the organization to another part of the organization. Senior managers can also help encourage parts of the organization to learn about how effective they are in the change process by assessing the effectiveness of the change process within the organization and outside it. There is always the great danger that any organization will fall in love with something it has invented and fail to recognize that better practices exist. Assessment needs to involve systematic data gathering with methods such as attitude surveys, time-to-market measures, cost-of-quality measures, and productivity measures. Again, senior managers need to take the lead in assuring that an organization is constantly asking how well its management system is doing and how its management practices compare with those of its competitors.

Beginning Change

Meaningful organizational change is extremely difficult to produce. Although attractive to many stakeholders, high-involvement management involves fundamental change in the way traditional organizations are managed. Most organizations cannot change overnight and will not show immediate positive results. Change in major corporations like General Electric, Xerox, and Motorola may take a decade — not a week, month, or even a year. To many people, this pace of change may be discouraging because the challenge seems so great. Other people may simply feel that it is better to start to change immediately rather than put off the long journey.

There is no one right place to start the change program. The key is to find the lever or levers that are most powerful in a particular situation and to begin the change sooner, rather than later. Once the change has begun, it is critical that it touch all the systems in the organization so that it balances information, knowledge, power, and rewards.

Organizations vary in their appetite for change. A critical first step in the change process is assessing the appetite of the organization for change. If it is in a crisis, an organization may be quite hungry for a change, and, thus, even radical changes may be possible. If radical changes are not possible, small changes may be. Even small changes may be meaningful if they lead to employees having more say in their workplace and developing new skills and abilities. Organizational performance depends on employees caring about the work they do, knowing how to do it, and doing the right things. Involving individuals in the business is the most effective way to produce an organization in which people know more, care more, and do the right things.

References

AFL-CIO. *The Changing Situation of Workers and Their Unions.* Washington, D.C.: AFL-CIO Committee on the Evolution of Work, 1985.

Argyris, C. *Personality and Organization.* New York: HarperCollins, 1957.

Argyris, C. *Interpersonal Competence and Organizational Effectiveness.* Belmont, Calif.: Dorsey Press, 1962.

Argyris, C. *Integrating the Individual and the Organization.* New York: Wiley, 1964.

Argyris, C. *Intervention Theory and Method.* Reading, Mass.: Addison-Wesley, 1970.

Argyris, C., and Schön, D. *Organizational Learning: A Theory of Action Perspective.* Reading, Mass.: Addison-Wesley, 1978.

Ashford, S. J., and Tsui, A. S. "Self-Regulation for Managerial Effectiveness: The Role of Action Feedback Seeking." *Academy of Management Journal,* 1991, *3*(4), 251–280.

Avishai, B., and Taylor, W. "Customers Drive a Technology-Driven Company: An Interview with George Fisher." *Harvard Business Review,* 1989, *67*(6), 107–114.

Barney, J. "Organizational Culture: Can It Be a Source of Sustained Competitive Advantage?" *Academy of Management Review,* 1986, *11,* 656–665.

Bass, B. M. *Bass & Stodghill's Handbook of Leadership.* New York: Free Press, 1981.

Bass, B. M. *Bass & Stodghill's Handbook of Leadership: Theory, Research and Managerial Applications.* New York: Free Press, 1990.

Beekun, R. I. "Assessing the Effectiveness of Socio-Technical Interventions: Antidote or Fad?" *Human Relations,* 1989, *42,* 877–897.

Beer, M., Eisenstat, R. A., and Spector, B. *The Critical Path to Corporate Renewal.* Boston: Harvard Business School Press, 1990a.

Beer, M., Eisenstat, R. A., and Spector, B. "Why Change Programs Don't Produce Change." *Harvard Business Review,* 1990b, *68*(6), 158–166.

Bennis, W. *On Becoming a Leader.* Reading, Mass.: Addison-Wesley, 1989.

Bennis, W., and Nanus, B. *Leaders.* New York: HarperCollins, 1985.

Blasi, J. R. *Employee Ownership.* New York: Ballinger, 1988.

Blinder, A. S. (ed.). *Paying for Productivity: A Look at the Evidence.* Washington, D.C.: Brookings Institution, 1990.

Bloom, D. E., and Trahan, J. T. *Flexible Benefits and Employee Choice.* Elmsford, N.Y.: Pergamon Press, 1986.

Bowen, D. E., Chase, R. B., Cummings, T. G., and Associates. *Service Management Effectiveness: Balancing Strategy, Organization and Human Resources, Operations, and Marketing.* San Francisco: Jossey-Bass, 1990.

Bowen, D. E., and Lawler, E. E. "Facing the Customer: Empowerment or Production Line." *Sloan Management Review,* 1992, *33*(3).

Bowen, D. E., Ledford, G. E., and Nathan, B. "Hiring for the Organization, Not the Job." *Academy of Management Executive,* *5*(4), 1991.

Bower, J. L., and Hout, T. M. "Fast Cycle Capability for Competitive Power." *Harvard Business Review,* 1988, *66*(1), 110–118.

Boyett, J. H., and Conn, H. P. *Workplace 2000.* New York: Dutton, 1991.

Bullock, R. J., and Lawler, E. E. "Gainsharing: A Few Questions and Fewer Answers." *Human Resource Management,* 1984, *23*(1), 23–40.

Burns, J. M. *Leadership.* New York: HarperCollins, 1978.

Business–Higher Education Forum. *America's Competitive Challenge: The Need for a National Response.* Washington, D.C.: Business–Higher Education Forum, 1983.

Campbell, J. P., Dunnette, M. D., Lawler, E. E., and Weick, K. E. *Managerial Behavior, Performance, and Effectiveness.* New York: McGraw-Hill, 1970.

Carlzon, J. *Moments of Truth.* New York: Ballinger, 1987.

Cole, R. E. *Strategies for Learning.* Berkeley, Calif.: University of California Press, 1989.

Colton, J. L., and others. "Employee Participation: Diverse Forms and Different Outcomes." *Academy of Management Review*, 1988, *13*, 8–22.

Commission on the Skills of the American Workforce. *America's Choice: High Skills or Low Wages.* Rochester, N.Y.: National Center on Education and the Economy, 1990.

Conte, M., and Tannenbaum, A. *Employee Ownership.* Ann Arbor, Mich.: Institute for Social Research, 1980.

Copenhaver, L., and Guest, R. H. "Quality of Work Life: The Anatomy of Two Successes." *National Productivity Review*, 1982, *1*(4), 5–12.

Crosby, P. B. *Quality is Free.* New York: McGraw-Hill, 1979.

Cummings, T. G. "Self-Regulating Work Groups: A Socio-Technical Synthesis." *Academy of Management Review*, 1978, *3*, 625–633.

Cummings, T. G., and Molloy, E. J. *Improving Productivity and the Quality of Work Life.* New York: Praeger, 1977.

Davis, S. M., and Davidson, B. *2020 Vision.* New York: Simon & Schuster, 1991.

Davis, S. M., and Lawrence, P. R. *Matrix.* Reading, Mass.: Addison-Wesley, 1977.

Deming, W. E. *Out of the Crisis.* Cambridge, Mass.: MIT Press, 1986.

Denison, D. R. "Bringing Corporate Culture to the Bottom Line." *Organizational Dynamics*, 1984, *12*(4), 4–22.

Denison, D. R. *Corporate Culture and Organizational Effectiveness.* New York: Wiley, 1990.

DePree, M. *Leadership Is an Art.* East Lansing, Mich.: Michigan State University Press, 1987.

Dertouzos, M. L., Lester, R. K., and Solow, R. M. *Made in America: Regaining the Production Edge.* Cambridge, Mass.: MIT Press, 1989.

Dunnette, M. D. *Personnel Selection and Placement.* Belmont, Calif.: Wadsworth, 1966.

Ellig, B. R. "Improving Effectiveness Through an HR Review." *Personnel,* 1989, *66*(6), 57–64.

Ewing, D. E. *Freedom Inside the Organization.* New York: Dutton, 1977.

Ewing, D. E. *Do It My Way or You're Fired.* New York: Wiley, 1983.

Ford, R. N. *Motivation Through the Work Itself.* New York: American Management Association, 1969.

Foulkes, F. K. (ed.). *Executive Compensation.* Boston: Harvard Business School Press, 1991.

Freeman, R. B. *The Overeducated American.* San Diego, Calif.: Academic Press, 1976.

Frost, C. F., Wakeley, J. H., and Ruh, R. A. *The Scanlon Plan for Organization Development: Identity, Participation and Equity.* East Lansing, Mich.: Michigan State University Press, 1974.

Fullerton, H. N. "New Labor Force Projections, Spanning 1928–2000." *Monthly Labor Review,* Nov. 1989, pp. 3–65.

Galbraith, J. R. *Designing Complex Organizations.* Reading, Mass.: Addison-Wesley, 1973.

Galbraith, J. R. *Organization Design.* Reading, Mass.: Addison-Wesley, 1977.

Galbraith, J. R. and Kazanjian, R. K. *Strategy Implementation.* (2nd ed.) St. Paul: West, 1986.

Ghiselli, E. E., and Brown, C. W., *Personnel and Industrial Psychology.* New York: McGraw-Hill, 1955.

Gifford, D. L., and Seltz, C. A. *Fundamentals of Flexible Compensation.* New York: Wiley, 1988.

Goodman, P. *Assessing Organizational Change: The Rushton Quality of Work Experiment.* New York: Wiley-Interscience, 1979.

Graham-Moore, B., and Ross, T. *Productivity Gainsharing.* Englewood Cliffs, N.J.: Prentice-Hall, 1983.

Grayson, C. J., and O'Dell, C. *A Two-Minute Warning.* New York: Free Press, 1988.

Griffin, R. W. "Effects of Work Redesign on Employee Perceptions, Attitudes and Behaviors: A Long-Term Investigation." *Academy of Management Journal*, 1991, *34*, 425–435.

Guest, R. H. "Quality of Worklife — Learning from Tarrytown." *Harvard Business Review*, 1979, *57*(4), 76–87.

Guzzo, R. A., Jette, R. A., and Katzell, R. A. "The Effect of Psychology Based Intervention Programs on Worker Productivity: A Meta-Analysis." *Personnel Psychology*, 1985, *38*, 275–291.

Hackman, J. R. (ed.). *Groups That Work (And Those That Don't): Creating Conditions for Effective Teamwork*. San Francisco: Jossey-Bass, 1989.

Hackman, J. R., and Lawler, E. E. "Employee Reactions to Job Characteristics." *Journal of Applied Psychology*, 1971, *55*, 259–286.

Hackman, J. R., and Oldham, G. R. *Work Redesign*. Reading, Mass.: Addison-Wesley, 1980.

Hackman, J. R., and Walton, R. E. "Leading Groups in Organizations." In P. S. Goodman and Associates, *Designing Effective Work Groups*. San Francisco: Jossey-Bass, 1986.

Hamel, G., and Prahalad, C. K. "Strategic Intent." *Harvard Business Review*, 1989, *67*(3), 63–76.

Hammer, M. "Reengineering Work: Don't Automate, Obliterate." *Harvard Business Review*, 1990, *68*(4), 104–113.

Handy, C. *The Age of Unreason*. Boston: Harvard Business School Press, 1989.

Hanlon, M. D., Nadler, D. A., and Gladstein, D. *Attempting Work Reform*. New York: Wiley-Interscience, 1985.

Herrick, N. Q. *Joint Management and Employee Participation: Labor and Management at the Crossroads*. San Francisco: Jossey-Bass, 1990.

Herzberg, F. *Work and the Nature of Man*. Cleveland, Ohio: World, 1966.

Hoerr, J. "What Should Unions Do?" *Harvard Business Review*, 1991, *69*(3), 30–45.

Institute of Industrial Engineers. *Productivity and Quality Improvement in the 90's*. Norcross, Ga.: 1990.

Jamieson, D., and O'Mara, J. *Managing Workforce 2000.* San Francisco: Jossey-Bass, 1991.

Johnston, R., and Lawrence, P. R. "Beyond Vertical Integration — The Rise of the Value-Adding Partnership." *Harvard Business Review,* 1988, *66*(4), 94–101.

Johnston, W. B. *Work Force 2000.* Indianapolis, Ind.: Hudson Institute, 1987.

Johnston, W. B. "Global Workforce 2000: The New World Labor Market." *Harvard Business Review,* 1991, *69*(2), 115–127.

Juran, J. M. *Juran on Leadership for Quality.* New York: Free Press, 1989.

Kahn, R. L. *Work and Health.* New York: Wiley, 1981.

Kane, J., and Lawler, E. E. "Methods of Peer Assessment." *Psychological Bulletin,* 1978, *85,* 555–586.

Kanter, R. M. *Change Masters: Innovation for Productivity in the American Workplace.* New York: Simon & Schuster, 1985.

Kanter, R. M. "The New Managerial Work." *Harvard Business Review,* 1989a, *67*(6), 85–92.

Kanter, R. M. *When Giants Learn to Dance.* New York: Simon & Schuster, 1989b.

Kirp, D. L. "Uncommon Decency: Pacific Bell Responds to AIDS." *Harvard Business Review,* 1989, *67*(3), 140–151.

Klein, J. A. "A Reexamination of Autonomy in Light of New Manufacturing Practices." *Human Relations,* 1991, *44,* 21–38.

Kotter, J. P. *A Force for Change.* New York: Free Press, 1990.

Kravetz, D. J. *The Human Resources Revolution: Implementing Progressive Management Practices for Bottom-Line Success.* San Francisco: Jossey-Bass, 1988.

Kutscher, R. E. "Projections Summary and Emerging Issues." *Monthly Labor Review,* Nov. 1989, pp. 66–74.

Lawler, E.E. "Job Design and Employee Motivation." *Personnel Psychology,* 1969, *22,* 426–434.

Lawler, E. E. *Pay and Organizational Effectiveness: A Psychological View.* New York: McGraw-Hill, 1971.

Lawler, E. E. *Motivation in Work Organizations.* Pacific Grove, Calif.: Brooks/Cole, 1973.

Lawler, E. E. "The New Plant Revolution." *Organizational Dynamics,* 1978, *6*(3), 2–12.

Lawler, E. E. *Pay and Organization Development.* Reading, Mass.: Addison-Wesley, 1981.

Lawler, E. E. "Strategies for Improving the Quality of Work Life." *American Psychologist,* 1982, *37,* 486–493.

Lawler, E. E. *High-Involvement Management: Participative Strategies for Improving Organizational Performance.* San Francisco: Jossey-Bass, 1986.

Lawler, E. E. "Choosing an Involvement Strategy." *Academy of Management Executive,* 1988a, *2*(3), 197–204.

Lawler, E. E. "Substitute for Hierarchy." *Organizational Dynamics,* 1988b, *17*(1), 4–15.

Lawler, E. E. "The New Plant Revolution Revisited." *Organizational Dynamics,* 1990a, *19*(2), 4–14.

Lawler, E. E. *Strategic Pay: Aligning Organizational Strategies and Pay Systems.* San Francisco: Jossey-Bass, 1990b.

Lawler, E. E. "The New Plant Approach: A Second Generation Approach." *Organizational Dynamics,* 1991, *20*(3), 5–14.

Lawler, E. E., and Ledford, G. E. "Productivity and the Quality of Work Life." *National Productivity Review,* 1982, *1*(1), 23–36.

Lawler, E. E., Ledford, G. E., and Mohrman, S. A. *Employee Involvement in America.* Houston, Tex.: American Productivity and Quality Center, 1989.

Lawler, E. E., Mohrman, S. A., and Ledford, G. E. *Employee Involvement and Total Quality Management.* San Francisco: Jossey-Bass, 1992.

Lawler, E. E., and Mohrman, S. A. "Quality Circles After the Fad." *Harvard Business Review,* 1985, *85*(1), 64–71.

Lawler, E. E., and Mohrman, S. A. "Quality Circles: After the Honeymoon." *Organizational Dynamics,* 1987a, *15*(4), 42–55.

Lawler, E. E., and Mohrman, S. A. "Unions and the New Management." *Academy of Management Executive,* 1987b, *1,* 293–300.

Lawler, E. E., and Mohrman, S. A. "High Involvement Management." *Personnel,* 1989, *66*(4), 26–31.

Lawler, E. E., and Ozley, L. "Winning Union-Management Cooperation on Quality of Work Life Projects." *Management Review,* 1979, *68*(3), 19–24.

Lawrence, P. R., and Lorsch, J. W. *Organization and Environment: Managing Differentiation and Integration.* Homewood, Ill.: Irwin, 1967.

Lazes, P., and Falkenberg, M. "Workgroups in America Today." *Journal for Quality and Participation*, 1991, *14*(3), 58–69.

Leavitt, H. "Applied Organizational Change in Industry." In J. March (ed.), *Handbook of Organizations*. Skokie, Ill.: Rand McNally, 1965.

Ledford, G. E. "Three Case Studies on Skill-Based Pay: An Overview." *Compensation and Benefits Review*, 1991, *23*(2), 11–23.

Ledford, G. E., Lawler, E. E., and Mohrman, S. A. "The Quality Circle and Its Variations." In J. P. Campbell, R. J. Campbell, and Associates, *Productivity in Organizations: New Perspectives from Industrial and Organizational Psychology*. San Francisco: Jossey-Bass, 1988.

Levine, D. L., and Tyson, L. D. "Participation, Productivity and the Firm's Environment." In A. S. Blinder (ed.), *Paying for Productivity: A Look at the Evidence*. Washington D.C.: Brookings Institution, 1990.

Likert, R. *New Patterns of Management*. New York: McGraw-Hill, 1961.

Locke, E. A., and Latham, G. P. *Goal Setting: A Motivational Technique That Works*. Englewood Cliffs, N.J.: Prentice-Hall, 1984.

McCall, M. W., Lombardo, M. M., and Morrison, A. M. *Lessons of Experience*. Lexington, Mass.: Lexington Books, 1988.

MacDuffie, J. P. "The Japanese Auto Transplants: Challenge to Conventional Wisdom." *ILR Report*, 1988, *26*, 12–18.

McGregor, D. *The Human Side of Enterprise*. New York: McGraw-Hill, 1960.

McKelvey, B. *Organizational Systematics: Taxonomy, Evolution, Classification*. Berkeley, Calif.: University of California Press, 1982.

Macy, B. A. "The Bolivar Quality of Work Program: Success or Failure?" In R. Zager and M. Rosow (eds.), *The Innovative Organization: Productivity Programs in Action*. Elmsford, N.Y.: Pergamon Press, 1982.

Macy, B. A., Peterson, M. F., and Norton, L. W. "A Test of Participation Theory in a Work Redesign Field Setting: Degree of Participation and Comparison Site Contrasts." *Human Relations*, 1989, *42*, 1095–1165.

Manz, C. C. "Beyond Self-Managing Work Teams: Toward Self-Leading Teams in the Work Place." In R. W. Woodman and

W. A. Pasmore (eds.), *Research in Organizational Change and Development.* Vol. 4, Greenwich, Conn.: Jai Press, 1990.

Manz, C. C., and Sims, H. P. "Self-Management as a Substitute for Leadership: A Social Learning Theory Perspective." *Academy of Management Review,* 1980, *5*, 361–367.

Maslow, A. H. "A Theory of Human Motivation." *Psychological Review,* 1943, *50*, 370–396.

Miles, R. E., and Snow, C. "Organizations: New Concepts for New Forms." *California Management Review,* 1986, *28*, 62–73.

Mills, D. Q. *Rebirth of the Corporation.* New York: Wiley, 1991.

Mitchell, J. B., Lewin, D., and Lawler, E. E. "Alternative Pay System, Firm Performance and Productivity." In A. S. Blinder (ed.), *Paying for Productivity: A Look at the Evidence.* Washington, D.C.: Brookings Institution, 1990.

Mirvis, P. H., and Lawler, E. E. "Measuring the Financial Impact of Employee Attitudes." *Journal of Applied Psychology,* 1977, *62*(1), 1–8.

Mirvis, P. H., and Lawler, E. E. "Accounting for the Quality of Work Life." *Journal of Occupational Behavior,* 1984, *5*, 197–212.

Mobley, W. H. *Employee Turnover: Causes, Consequences, and Control.* Reading, Mass.: Addison-Wesley, 1982.

Mobley, W. H., Hand, H. H., Meglino, B. M., and Griffeth, R. W. "Review and Conceptual Analysis of the Employee Turnover Process." *Psychological Bulletin,* 1979, *86*, 493–522.

Moch, M. K., and Bartunek, J. M. *Creating Alternative Realities at Work.* New York: HarperCollins, 1990.

Mohrman, A. M., Resnick-West, S. M., and Lawler, E. E. *Designing Performance Appraisal Systems: Aligning Appraisals and Organizational Realities.* San Francisco: Jossey-Bass, 1989.

Mohrman, A. M., and others. *Large-Scale Organizational Change.* San Francisco: Jossey-Bass, 1989.

Mohrman, S. A., and Cummings, T. G. *Self-Designing Organizations.* Reading, Mass.: Addison-Wesley, 1989.

Moore, B. E., and Ross, T. L. *The Scanlon Way to Improved Productivity.* New York: Wiley, 1978.

Mowday, R. T., Porter, L. W., and Steers, R. M. *Employee-Organization Linkages.* San Diego, Calif.: Academic Press, 1982.

Nadler, D. A. *Feedback and Organization Development.* Reading, Mass.: Addison-Wesley, 1977.

Nadler, D. A. "Leadership for Organizational Change." In A. M. Mohrman and others, *Large-Scale Organizational Change.* San Francisco: Jossey-Bass, 1989.

Nadler, D. A., and Tushman, M. *Strategic Organization Design.* Glenview, Ill.: Scott, Foresman, 1988.

Nalbantian, H. *Incentives, Cooperation and Risk Sharing.* Totoway, N.J.: Rowman and Littlefield, 1987.

Nathan, B. R., Ledford, G. E., Bowen, D. E., and Cummings, T. G. *Personality Measures as a Selection Tool for High-Involvement Organizations.* Paper presented at the Academy of Management Annual Meeting, Washington, D.C., 1989.

Nurick, A. J. *Participation in Organizational Change.* New York: Praeger, 1985.

O'Dell, C. *Gainsharing: Involvement, Incentives and Productivity.* New York: American Management Association, 1981.

O'Dell, C. *People, Performance and Pay.* Houston, Tex.: American Productivity Center, 1987.

Orsburn, J. D., Moran, L., Musselwhite, E., and Zenger, J. H. *Self-Directed Work Teams.* Homewood, Ill.: Business One Irwin, 1990.

O'Toole, J. *Vanguard Management.* New York: Doubleday, 1985.

Ouchi, W. *Theory Z.* Reading, Mass.: Addison-Wesley, 1981.

Parker, M., and Slaughter, J. *Choosing Sides: Unions and the Team Concept.* Boston: South End Press, 1988.

Pava, C.H.P. *Managing New Office Technology.* New York: Free Press, 1983.

Peters, T. J. "Symbols, Patterns and Settings: An Optimistic Case for Getting Things Done." *Organizational Dynamics,* 1978.

Peters, T. J., and Waterman, R. H. *In Search of Excellence.* New York: HarperCollins, 1982.

Petersen, D. E., and Hillkirk, J. *A Better Idea: Redefining the Way Americans Work.* Boston: Houghton Mifflin, 1991.

Porter, M. E. *Competitive Advantage.* New York: Free Press, 1985.

Porter, M. E., *The Competitive Advantage of Nations.* New York: Free Press, 1990.

Prahalad, C. K., and Hamel, G. "Core Competence of the Corporation." *Harvard Business Review*, 1990, *68*(3), 79–91.

Premack, S. C., and Wanous, J. P. "A Meta-Analysis of Realistic Job Preview Experiments." *Journal of Applied Psychology*, 1985, *70*, 706–719.

Reich, R. B. *The Work of Nations.* New York: Knopf, 1991.

Rock, M. *Handbook of Wage and Salary Administration.* (2nd ed.) New York: McGraw-Hill, 1984.

Rock, M., and Berger, L. A. *The Compensation Handbook.* New York: McGraw-Hill, 1991.

Rosen, C., Klein, K., and Young, K. *Employee Ownership in America.* Lexington, Mass.: Heath, 1986.

Rosen, C., and Young, K. *Understanding Employee Ownership.* Ithica, N.Y.: ILR Press, 1991.

Rosow, J. M., and Zager, R. *New Roles For Managers.* Scarsdale, N.Y.: Work in America Institute, 1990.

Rosow, J. M., Zager, R., Casner-Lotto, J., and Associates. *Training — The Competitive Edge: Introducing New Technology into the Workplace.* San Francisco: Jossey-Bass, 1988.

Rynes, S. L., and Barber, A. E. "Applicant Attraction Strategies: An Organizational Perspective." *Academy of Management Review*, 1990, *14*, 286–310.

Sashkin, M. "Participative Management Is an Ethical Imperative." *Organizational Dynamics*, 1984, *12*(4), 5–23.

Savage, C. M. *Fifth Generation Management.* Bedford, Mass.: Digital, 1990.

Schlesinger, L. A., and Heskett, J. L. "Breaking the Cycle of Failure in Services." *Sloan Management Review*, 1991a, *32*(2), 17–28.

Schlesinger, L. A. and Heskett, J. L. "The Service-Driven Company." *Harvard Business Review*, 1991b, *69*(5), 71–81.

Schneider, B., and Schmitt, N. *Staffing Organizations.* (2nd ed.) Glenview, Ill.: Scott, Foresman, 1986.

Schumacher, E. F. *Small Is Beautiful.* New York: HarperCollins, 1973.

Schuster, J. *Management Compensation in High Technology Companies.* Lexington, Mass.: Lexington Books, 1984.

Schuster, J. R., Zingheim, P. K., and Dertien, M. G. "The Case for Computer-Assisted Market-Based Job Evaluation." *Compensation and Benefits Review*, 1990 *22*(3), 44–54.

Seashore, S. E. "Quality of Working Life Perspective." In A. Van de Ven and W. F. Joyce (eds.), *Perspectives on Organization Design and Behavior.* New York: Wiley-Interscience, 1981.

Seashore, S. E., Lawler, E. E., Mirvis, P., and Cammann, C. *Assessing Organizational Change.* New York: Wiley, 1983.

Secretary's Commission on Achieving Necessary Skills. *What Work Requires of Schools.* Washington, D.C.: U.S. Department of Labor, 1991.

Servan-Schreiber, J. J. *The American Challenge.* New York: Athaneum, 1968.

Simmons, J., and Mares, W. *Working Together.* New York: Knopf, 1983.

Slater, P., and Bennis, W. G. "Democracy is Inevitable." *Harvard Business Review*, 1964, *42*(2), 51–59.

Stalk, G., and Hout, T. M. *Competing Against Time.* New York: Free Press, 1990.

Stayer, R. "How I Learned to Let My Workers Lead." *Harvard Business Review*, 1990, *68*(6), 66–83.

Sundstrom, E., DeMeuse, K. P., and Futell, D. "Work Teams." *American Psychologist*, 1990, *45*(2), 120–133.

Susman, G. I. *Autonomy at Work.* New York: Praeger, 1976.

Taylor, F. W. *The Principles of Scientific Management.* New York: HarperCollins, 1911.

Taylor, F. W. *Shop Management.* New York: HarperCollins, 1915.

Taylor, W. "The Logic of Global Business: An Interview with ABB's Percy Barnevik." *Harvard Business Review*, 1991, *69*(2), 91–105.

Thompson, J. D. *Organizations in Action.* New York: McGraw-Hill, 1967.

Tichy, N. M. *Managing Strategic Change.* New York: Wiley, 1983.

Tichy, N. M., and Charan, R. "Speed, Simplicity, Self-Confidence: An Interview with Jack Welch." *Harvard Business Review*, 1989, *67*(5), 112–120.

Tichy, N. M., and Devanna, M. A. *The Transformational Leader.* New York: Wiley, 1986.

Ulrich, D., and Lake, D. *Organizational Capability.* New York: Wiley, 1990.

U.S. Department of Health, Education, and Welfare. *Work in America: Report of a Special Task Force to the Secretary of Health, Education, and Welfare.* Cambridge, Mass.: MIT Press, 1973.

U.S. General Accounting Office. *Productivity Sharing Programs: Can They Contribute to Productivity Improvement?* Washington, D.C.: General Accounting Office, 1981.

U.S. General Accounting Office. *Management Practices: U.S. Companies Improve Performance Through Quality Efforts.* Washington, D.C.: General Accounting Office, 1991.

Von Glinow, M. A., and Mohrman, S. A. *Managing Complexity in High Technology Organizations.* New York: Oxford University Press, 1989.

Vroom, V. H., and Jago, A. G. *The New Leadership: Managing Participation in Organizations.* Englewood Cliffs, N.J.: Prentice-Hall, 1988.

Vroom, V. H., and Yetton, P. W. *Leadership and Decision-Making.* Pittsburgh, Pa.: University of Pittsburgh Press, 1973.

Walker, C. R., and Guest, R. H. *The Man on the Assembly Line.* Cambridge, Mass.: Harvard University Press, 1952.

Wall, T. D., Kemp, N. J., Jackson, P. R., and Clegg, C. W. "Outcomes of Autonomous Workgroups: A Long-Term Field Experiment." *Academy of Management Journal,* 1986, *29,* 280–304.

Walton, R. E. "Establishing and Maintaining High-Commitment Work Systems." In J. R. Kimberly, R. H. Miles, and Associates, *The Organizational Life Cycle: Issues in the Creation, Transformation, and Decline of Organizations.* San Francisco: Jossey-Bass, 1980.

Walton, R. E. *Up and Running.* Boston: Harvard Business School Press, 1989.

Walton, R. E., and McKersie, R. B. *A Behavioral Theory of Labor Negotiations.* New York: McGraw-Hill, 1965.

Walton, R. E., and Schlesinger, L. A. "Do Supervisors Thrive in Participative Work Systems?" *Organizational Dynamics,* 1979, *8*(3), 25–38.

Wanous, J. P. *Organizational Entry.* Reading, Mass.: Addison-Wesley, 1980.

Weber, M. *The Theory of Social and Economic Organization.* New York: Free Press, 1947.

Weiner, B. *An Attribution Theory of Motivation and Emotion.* New York: Springer-Verlag, 1986.

Weisbord, M. R. *Productive Workplaces: Organizing and Managing for Dignity, Meaning, and Community.* San Francisco: Jossey-Bass, 1987.

Weitzman, M. L. *The Share Economy.* Cambridge, Mass.: Harvard, 1984.

Wellins, R., Byham, W., and Wilson, J. *Empowered Teams: Creating Self-Directed Work Groups That Improve Quality, Productivity, and Participation.* San Francisco: Jossey-Bass, 1991.

Wellins, R. S., and others. *Self-Directed Work Teams.* Pittsburgh, Pa.: Development Dimensions, 1990.

Whyte, W. F. (ed.). *Money and Motivation: An Analysis of Incentives in Industry.* New York: HarperCollins, 1955.

Wiggenhorn, W. "Motorola U: When Training Becomes an Education." *Harvard Business Review,* 1990, *68*(4), 71–83.

Womack, J. P., Jones, D. T., and Roos, D. *The Machine That Changed the World.* New York: Macmillan, 1990.

Woodward, J. *Industrial Organization: Theory and Practice.* Oxford, England: Oxford University Press, 1965.

Work in America Institute. *Employment Security in a Free Economy.* Elmsford, N.Y.: Pergamon Press, 1984.

Zuboff, S. *In the Age of the Smart Machine.* New York: Basic Books, 1988.

Index